Run Gently Out There

Trials, trails, and tribulations of running ultramarathons

John Morelock

Dedication

This book is dedicated to Kathleen (or, in her public persona, Kathy), she of the utmost patience, courage, and the uncanny ability to know how to keep me going through the distances beyond miles—the days and weeks beyond crossing Spain—the months and years still crossing a marriage—and the seasons we have yet to cross as the journey continues.

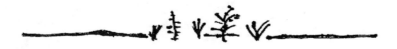

Acknowledgements

I extend my most heartfelt thanks and appreciation for the companionship, advice, and encouragement offered along the way in this apparently endless journey that started before the Internet. In my early days the encounters were always actual people and opened with "Hi, I'm Jill" or some other word that is recognizable as a real name. As time passed the people were still just as real, but the encounters were opened by "Hi, I'm rockypoint_5" or some other e-list, e-mail, or forum alias. Some say our world of ultrarunning suffers from change. I would never agree with the suffering part. The constant presence of a willingness to share, whether in misery or in triumph, our goals, knowledge, and love of running only enhances the change, and the people along the way remain the true gifts.

I am indebted to and owe special thanks to John Medinger for giving me my column in *UltraRunning* and Tia Bodington for being so tolerant with what would be called my eccentricities, if I were rich and successful, in editing. Some of the stories printed herein were originally part of the *Run Gently Out There* column in *UltraRunning* magazine.

In a world where anonymous sources of help are but a click away, Tia's daughter, Sarah Rosen, expanded my Texas connection by spending many hours researching names and nicknames, places and misspelled places, and providing thoughtful insight on how I could make incoherent scatterings of words into complete sentences—a somewhat strange process to me. Sarah's time and many comments were very valuable in reaching a final stage.

Tracey Anderson, Dot Helm, and David Lygre are three people who took a lot of time out of their busy lives to read and offer that rare gift—honesty in review. Their generosity in helping me is deeply appreciated.

Sometimes spirit-lifters came in the form of a message regarding a sentence I thought was innocuous at best, but it touched someone, and that someone was kind enough to tell me—Lisa Butler, Gordon Cherr, Adam Fitzgerald, Lulu Weschler, Juli Aistars, Deborah Bezanis, and more.

A Texas-sized thank you to Lynn Ballard, David and Paula Billings, Char (and Fred) Thompson, Mike Langille, Mike Potter, Bill Rumbaugh, and the rest of the North Texas Trail Runners gang that gave me a home-group to run with when I was far from home.

A sampling of dinosaurs: Dan Baglione, Lary Webster, John Bandur, Stanley Nakashima (barely old enough to qualify), Pete Stringer, Rob Volkenand, Phil Vaughan, Kent Holder, Clem LaCava, Phil Hicks—all reminders that a lot of what we do is timeless. Gels, arm panties, minimalist, maximalist, paisley, or beige, in the end, runners run and strangers become friends to run with as years pass.

And the unknowns that have been part of this unending conversation: CelesteW, The Geetah, ed-bill, trailrunnerjeff, burton, Redbird, trail_animal, Slowdown, shiznitz, AKTrail, fivels, cgerber, Scrapster, Agile, AT-Runner, RunsWithWolves, MadisonMandy, Mmichael, Queen of Nothing, barbinator, preachindablues, mnkiwi, Prairie Runner, spreT, Xtreme Taper, and so many others that I hope to meet so I can turn them into real people before my final page is turned.

Preface

I have no coaching credentials whatsoever, which may or may not matter since this is not a how-to book. The stories, thoughts, and opinions I offer here are based on what I have done (or wish I had done). Some of those experiences led to failures as I roamed from one trial or trail and experiment to another, trying to find what my mind believed to be the correct way to proceed. Failure is sometimes subjective. A time of 7:24:18 for a 50-mile ultramarathon would be considered a successful run by some. It was a failure to me. My intention had been to run in the 6:00–6:15 time range. The lessons I learned came from the process leading up to the ultramarathon, the success or failure of the attempt, and the postrun analysis.

This is not a cookbook, not an offering of recipes for success. Neither of the ultras I won was entered with winning in mind. They weren't even entered with racing in mind: I had only running in mind. The racing came as the day unfolded, not as part of some grand plan made months beforehand. Training is subjective to the extent that it must be something your mind accepts and believes in. This tends to make training for ultramarathons highly individualized.

I have tried to be careful and write about the generalities of training or any of the other quantifiable aspects of running. There is no guarantee that my diet of five pounds of baked Yukon Gold potatoes one Friday will transfer to you and guarantee a competitive performance at the 100-kilometer distance. In this case the lesson for me was about the diversity in the nutrition-riddle solutions. Potatoes for one run, cream of mushroom soup for another. In the end, nutrition requirements, too, are merely generalizations that each person must develop into the rules for their own running. Those of us with cast iron stomachs have a slight advantage over the more fickle gourmets.

The successful completion of an ultramarathon requires patience and determination. There are no shortcuts along the way, or none that I am aware of, and I have successfully experimented with, and found, numerous horrible examples for heading out on the trails unprepared, whether mentally, physically, emotionally, or spiritually. Running ultramarathons requires thinking along the way. You will be thinking about where you are, evaluating what you need to do to continue, and then thinking about how to do that. It is just a simple exercise in decision-making that is sometimes a not-so-simple exercise in decision-making.

Most of this book is concerned with one or the other of the two quotes below. Take your pick:

> The people that I have met are not foolish; they are aware of how tired and cold and hungry and frightened and hurting and discouraged and disoriented and how possibly injured they will become. They know they will face great physical, mental, emotional, and possibly spiritual challenges as they make their way to the finish. This is what they are racing against. This is their challenge. This is what I admire.
>
> —Carolyn Erdman, Silverton, Colorado

> Climb the mountains and get their good tidings. The winds will blow their freshness into you, and the storms, their energy. Your cares and tensions will drop away like the leaves of autumn.
>
> —John Muir

I hope you enjoy the book as much as I have enjoyed collecting the words from my runs, your runs, our runs, and the world through which we run.

Run gently out there.

John M.

Introduction

If the subject of ultramarathons or even just running trails comes up, you will likely be asked: How did you get started? Why trails? How do you find them? And so on. As with most questions, I am unable to simply say yes, no, or "At eleven o'clock in the morning on Thursday, August 17, 1985" and be done with it. Yes, no, or some exact-sounding time belong to a world of running far removed from our world of trails and ultramarathons.

I completed my first marathon two weeks before my first official marathon (an official marathon being something you pay to enter, get a much-needed T-shirt from, and so forth). The curse of doubts and my beginner's lack of self-confidence going into that first official marathon found me at my favorite five-mile loop one Sunday morning with the removal of doubt being my reason for being there. I ran five laps around the lake and then added an out-and-back section just to be sure. I was now confident I could run a marathon. The innocence of being a beginner meant I was blissfully unaware of two weeks perhaps not being enough recovery time between my training marathon and that first official paid-a-fee-and-going-to-get-a-T-shirt 26.2-mile escapade.

I ran my first official marathon on February 23, 1985. The next one was April 21, 1985. The third marathon was on May 11, 1985— four marathons in eleven weeks. I was totally unaware of how "wrong" this was because I was not racing any of them, just running. I was also unaware of the preview I was being given into the world of ultras. Blissful ignorance about running seemed to dominate those early months.

The strong tug of nature's magical carpet ride was first felt as I ran that third official marathon, the Avenue of the Giants Marathon. The course was on paved roads in a redwood forest in Northern California. If I ran on the edge of the road, my footsteps were no longer heard—the layers of those thousands of tiny leaves are nature's sound deadeners. If I looked up, the majesty of the size of the trees slowed me down. These are among nature's biggest plants, her largest living organisms. It was my first encounter with a place where I did not run fast for fear of passing too quickly to see what was there. This was the first time the unconscious part of my mind urged me to see what I was passing through.

For several weeks after the "Ave," my running was directionless. It was 1985, and I had been caught in the post-Olympic running and "gotta run a marathon" craze. Avenue of the Giants had gotten me to the point where I felt I had run a marathon on my terms, finally conquering a course comfortably, finally finishing with fatigue and discomfort but not pain. I still had full respect for the distance, but, without knowing it, I had already made friends with the marathon. A certain amount of comfort was found in those three- and four-hour runs on the various pavements of cities and towns in and around the Pacific Northwest, but comfort often calls out for challenge.

In mid-July I saw an entry blank for something outside my world of running, something not on any roads I knew. The Great Olympic Mountain Run, or GOMR, as we would call it, was 16.4 miles of trails and forestry roads on the Olympic Peninsula in the northern part of Olympic National Park and had a limit of 100 runners. Trails? Forests? Run in the mountains? Memories of the redwoods flooded in. I completed the entry blank. That line about a "limit of 100 runners" meant a special trip to the post office to get the entry form in the mail. The waiting started.

My mind kept going to this "trails" thing. Trails? I ran pavement with an occasional trip through a wooded area from one street or road to another, but basically it was always pavement beneath my feet. Trails? Where do I go to learn to run on trails? I did not know it, but I was trying to do what I would later always include as a fundamental tenet of trails or ultras: Try to train on terrain similar to what you will race on—whether you will be running or racing.

I found what would become "my trails" in the Black Hills, just west of Olympia, Washington. The 84,000 acres of the Capitol State Forest, with its seemingly endless miles of trails, became my training ground. The cryptic trail-numbering system slowly made sense, and names like Fuzzy Top and Wedekind and Drooping Fir and Buck Ridge became familiar landmarks, all on the way to Capitol Peak, elevation 2,659 feet. Almost every trailhead I started from seemed to be about 2,500 feet below. The days were filled with solitary trips, running up or running down, in this newly discovered world.

I could climb straight up the mountainsides on the power line clearings or I could slowly work my way around Rock Candy Mountain learning trails, junctions, and forks along each new route. My playground was crisscrossed with old logging roads and long-deserted railroad beds. A hilltop or two was crowned with old-growth timber— Douglas fir and hemlock trees—some more than 300 years in age. They stood as tall, solitary guardians of my solitude.

My trail running was barely two weeks old when one Saturday I got the letter saying I was accepted into the 1985 GOMR, three weeks away. The blessings of ignorance kept me from knowing that three weeks was not enough time. At that time the 16.4 miles from Deer Park to Hurricane Ridge, all on trails, was simply rationalized as being not as long as a marathon, and the elevation was just thought of as *not real high*. Happily lost in my new running environment, I escaped to the forest almost every afternoon or weekend morning as July turned to August.

Saturday morning on the 17th of August, I was totally absorbed in driving up a winding forestry road to Deer Park. My, oh my! Up here in the Pacific Northwest we have what are called "Perry Como Sky" days. This comes from the song line, "The bluest skies you've ever seen are in Seattle." This was a Perry Como Sky with no ground smoke to spoil it anywhere. I was lost in the "ooh" and "ahh" of miles and miles of mountains in almost any direction I looked. "I get to run up here," I kept saying to myself. When I reached the starting area, I parked and went to check in and get my race number.

The woman found my number, looked at the color, and then said to another volunteer, "We need to weigh him." So that's how they do it, I thought. I had checked "Heavyweight" on my entry blank. They had me step on the scales to see that I did weigh over 190 pounds. We all agreed 198 is more than 190, and I was good to go—to go wait in a field of strangers. That was probably my last time waiting alone. I would find out trail runners remember trail runners and hellos to strangers today would be greetings to friends at some other trail miles and maybe months away.

Race management sent us off in packs of twenty at five-minute staggers. As I waited for my pack, I could see where the trail wound through the trees and decided I could just start slow and use the first mile or two to warm up. Right. And an often-heard lie is born. "I'm going out easy today."

Go! The starter had barely yelled go, had barely got the exclamation mark on the end, before off we went in pursuit of the sixty runners strung out in front of us. And that is what we did, we pursued, because the trail was narrow and the hillside was steep and passing anyone was difficult. My tongue started to dry out after half a mile. I had no idea there was any dry air in Washington. There isn't in the lowlands, but we were on a trail at about 5,600 feet elevation. I stuck a piece of hard candy in my mouth. That was the best I could do. The brief mention of it being about eight miles to the halfway-point aid station rolled around in my subconscious. Who knew about hand bottles or fanny packs? Not me.

Then I lost myself in the panoramic views of the North Cascades, the Strait of Juan de Fuca, and the Olympic Mountains. The trails were high on the mountainside and the clear blue sky seemed to magnify everything. Thirst and distance melted away as my mind met the mountain like an old friend. I grabbed a handful of snow just below Maiden Peak and another handful a mile or two farther along the trail. We had been in a long and gentle climb on a wider trail, and I had passed almost everyone in my stage plus maybe a few in the next group as I kept pace with a guy in front of me.

At the halfway point we left the single-track and stopped at the aid station. The rest of the run was on forestry roads. The guy I had been following turned to look at me as we emptied our cups. How old are you? Forty-three, why? I wanted to know if we are running or racing. Oh, well? I was just running, but the running-versus-racing seed was formed. I told him I was not racing. I did not think of the idea that if he was racing and I was simply running, then maybe I had unknowingly found a comfortable place to run at that pace? Maybe the racing would become secondary to the running. These thoughts were too hazily formed to distract from the task at hand.

And off we went running through the Olympic Mountains toward Hurricane Ridge; slow enough so we could talk, fast enough to keep the effort feeling honest; slow enough that we could see what we passed, but fast enough that we could pass one or two stragglers from an earlier group. The colored banners of the finish line at Hurricane Ridge seemed to be in view forever as we rounded one turn after another before finally climbing one last bend.

Like many other runners, after I crossed the finish line, I went over and sat down on the hillside meadow to rest and enjoy a beautiful day. I had just completed my first official trail run. A brief thought about that word "official" intruded, but it would be years before a story evolved. I thought about the blue sky and the trails, the weather, mountains, and wildlife, and the conversations along the way—how totally different from the time-driven tension of road running. My mind tried to recall the calendar section of *Northwest Runner*, visualizing it for trail runs. I could not recall any, but I had not been paying much attention to the runs on trails, had not looked for them. I decided to drive home via Seattle.

In Seattle I went to the Green Lake neighborhood. I parked and went into Super Jock 'n Jill—one of the best-known running stores in the area. I was right. They had a magazine rack full of running magazines. I found the new issue of *Northwest Runner*. It had a section for trail runs. I was just turning away when another magazine cover caught my eye—*UltraRunning*. *UltraRunning*? What kind of magazine is this? What is an ultramarathon?

It has all gone uphill, downhill, or on around the bend from there. I still have that first copy of *UltraRunning* magazine from August of 1985. It is ragged and dog-eared. The margins have many notes and question marks. I am still immersed in a love affair with running trails and ultramarathons; still chasing question marks.

Over the years running became a tapestry woven of friends and strangers, chili dogs and Slim-Fast, the rain forests of Washington and the dryness of Death Valley. As I ran on unnamed roads or trails scattered somewhere in Texas, Utah, Arkansas, North Dakota, Oregon, or Maine, and the forests, deserts, mountains, and valleys scattered across our country slowly became a part of me.

I ran my first 50k in early January of 1986. The decay and slide into the dreadful abyss of running ultramarathons, the elation and wonder of running way up high, wandering through lowland forests, and traversing rivers on foot continues today, some twenty-five years later. I have never become accustomed to being able to run as far as we get to. To write about running far has, in many ways, been the greatest adventure of all.

CHAPTER ONE

90% of ultrarunning is 100% mental.

—Unknown

Nobody is going to finish this damn thing for me, but me.

—Unknown

A Real Ultramarathon

A marathon has a nice, neat, well-accepted definition...26 miles 385 yards or 42.2 kilometers. The characteristics of the route, be it up, down, paved, trail, point to point, loop, out and back—none of those matters as long as the distance is the standard marathon length of 26.2 miles or 42.2 kilometers.

An ultramarathon is not so easily defined. One dictionary uses: "3: beyond what is ordinary, proper, or moderate..." as the definition for the prefix "ultra."

An online source uses: "A cross-country footrace with a distance of 30 miles (48 kilometers) or more." This arbitrary distance of "30 miles" leaves a gap between the marathon and the ultramarathon. Where are we during those 3.8 miles beyond the marathon but less than the 30-mile ultramarathon?

Another online source and one that to me was more reliable or credible was David Blaikie's now defunct Ultramarathon World Web site. He uses the following definition: "An ultramarathon is any running event longer than the standard marathon distance of 42 kilometres, 195 metres (26 miles, 385 yards)." [Note: David's Web site no longer exists. I leave the reference because it had considerable historical significance in many conversations or discussions about ultramarathons.] This is the definition I use.

After these defining terms come the purists (an arbitrary, self-assuming title) who insist an ultramarathon is at least 50 miles (≈80 kilometers).

Whither goest the author—the reader muses.

I just read the phrase "...and I guess if it was a 'real' ultramarathon it would be great. The race I'm doing on Saturday is however *only* 50 kilometers..."

Now I don't know why these words "only 50k" or "not a real ultramarathon" arouse my ire and cause me to lay pen to paper (fingers to keyboard) so much, but they are self-demeaning, self-degrading, self-deprecatory, and several other "selfs" that I don't feel like fooling with at the moment.

Running a marathon is quite a feat, both physically and mentally. Running 50 kilometers is a major physical and mental achievement as well. Because such a small percentage of people on the planet run beyond the marathon, it is arguably a great achievement. At the least, it is kind of sort of great.

Fifty kilometers (31.1 miles) is well beyond the standard—as recognized all the way around the world by the forces for good in the running community at large—marathon distance. It falls into the definition of ultramarathon by all three sources I bothered with in my research (scant, I must admit, but I used them knowing there are others saying the same thing).

Please, please do not put "only" in front of the distance you run. You ran it. It is yours to enjoy, not apologetically mentioned in a hushed voice. I did ten miles Saturday that I was just tickled pink with because of the way I did the uphill stretch—hardest running I have done in several weeks. Do not put words into describing your running that are driven by someone else's ego.

Do not think a 50k is not an ultramarathon. (There are some 50k runs out there that are just as tough as any 50-miler you will ever enter.) If someone insists some longer distance is the first "true," "real," "honest," or whatever ultramarathon, it is their ego talking and they should be ignored.

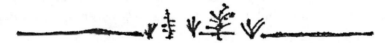

Discomfort, Not Pain

For the newer members of the trail-running, ultramarathon-running, and cello-tuning community who get totally struck down with fear and awe thinking of pain being a necessity and all runs becoming brutal events that are barely survivable, I'll throw these thoughts out.

There are levels of competitive running where the mind and body are asked to do the maximum for which they are trained. This may require entering a realm of discomfort not normally encountered during training runs. Then again, it may not, but that is what "race" day is for, isn't it?

There are levels of running where a person might not have trained quite as much as one should have, but the entry blank was mailed anyway. Mother Nature may have decided to dump 3.72 inches of rain on the course to increase the effort needed that day.

The effort needed to comfortably (whatever that means) compete is negated by weather, fitness, the bad sausage you had on the way to the starting line, and the slow realization that you are in trouble. This realization will come several eternities before the finish line is sighted. The discomfort (mud-sucking factor of 12.47, cramps due to dehydration, mind shot because you went out wayyyyyyyy too fast...) will disappear when you cross the finish line.

Tolerating little aches and injuries because your ego will not allow you to take the time off to recover will cause continual nagging distractions as you run. The little nagging distractions will become major injuries that will come calling at most inopportune times demanding payment in full. And then you will not be able to run for an extended period of time that will feel like an eternity.

If you are trained for the distance and the intended effort level, you can do the event without pain. There may be discomfort, we all experience that, but there will not necessarily be pain. Pain is plans gone wrong, inadequate fitness, aches and injuries ignored, things not thought out—the ego triumphing over good sense.

Endurance running is special. It requires paying attention to the mind, body, and spirit. It requires being honest within yourself. It does not require pain.

Now, about this word "discomfort" and the rationalizing you will do along the way...

The Beauty and Strength of Old Trees

I suppose there is a reason one thought, or story, or memory comes to the surface of our senses at some point in a day's run. A loose correlation of time, weather, effort, wind direction, shifting tides, and the number of chestnut-backed chickadees in the area may shift our thoughts from one story to another. The algorithm for determining what is going to come calling takes up too much space on the scratchpad of my mind and so today, as with other days, the result is all that matters.

This morning finds me listening to the *crunch crunch crunch* of frost breaking as I brush the frozen grasses along the trail. I am running toward the upper bluffs—air just cold enough to wake the senses—fog wisps of breath trailing briefly. I glance at the cloudless, barely blue sky. Today's sky is paler than yesterday's. Each day brings us closer to winter.

My passage interrupts chirpy voices and small, winged shapes flitting here and there in the firs alongside the trail. A passing group of chestnut-backed chickadees looking like Christmas ornaments as they hang upside down looking for food on the underside of branches is the source of the distraction. The summer just past had brought the fun of watching the newest chickadees learning to land upside down on the branch undersides. That is their food niche. Now they are showing me how well they have learned.

I look at the madrone trees, reddish-brown bark glistening, their newly formed berries bringing the bright red of ripeness that attracts cedar waxwings as they pass through, heading south. Each morning winter is about fifteen miles closer on its southerly journey. Each morning there is a different audience of birds as I run. It seems like the snow on the shoulders of the Olympic Mountains is a bit wider, the peaks of the Cascades a little more rounded with another day of snow.

Soon the only dry ground will be under the drooping branches of the cedars. Cedars? Olympic Mountains? What? The old women. Oh. Here comes today's memory. It was late in the summer of 1986...

Kathy (my wife) and I were going to run a twenty-something-mile loop in the southwestern part of the Olympic National Park in Washington State. We drove along the shore of Lake Quinault, deep into old-growth forest. We passed a tree proclaimed to be the "Largest Western Red Cedar in the World," just over 19 feet in diameter and 174 feet tall. The largest in the world? Who would know, we asked each other as we drove to the trailhead.

We parked, pulled on fanny packs, and headed up Three Lakes Trail, our first running leg of the day. We were running under clear skies and the morning coolness was already gone. I rounded a bend in the trail and stopped. Kathy was stopped in front of an Alaska cedar or, as they are sometimes known, Alaska yellow-cedar. Such deep beauty these old trees possess, wind-polished bark, trunks tall and wise, several hundred years in the growing. The sign maker had been here, too. "Largest Yellow Cedar in the United States." Ignoring the presumptuousness of the sign, we paused to look at the very old tree. The two of us could not touch hands trying to reach around it. One hundred and twenty-nine feet tall. We ran on.

Around another corner, up a small hill, past a few slim, new Douglas firs, into a mountain meadow, and then I stopped. It was my turn to pause. Coming toward us were three old women, maybe not as old as the trees around us but certainly octogenarian old, each with a walking stick and a backpack that dwarfed their bent bodies. We stepped off the trail. They stopped and looked at us in our running shoes, shorts, T-shirts, and fanny packs. We looked at them with their hiking boots, long pants, layers of shirts, hats, dark glasses, packs, and walking sticks. My earlier thought of the beauty of the old trees seemed reflected in their eyes, in the color of their hair, the gray bark of the old cedars, in the lines on their faces, the wind-aged and sun-bronzed sculpturing of the old firs.

The nearest woman asked, "How far to the trailhead?" I glanced at my watch, converting our running time to backpacking pace. "An hour, maybe a few minutes more." She nodded and said, with a touch of sadness, "Oh. Well, girls, I guess we're about done." About done? "How long have you been out here?" Their stories poured out. A grandson bringing food up on the Hoh, traipsing along the Bogachiel, five days camping by the glacier...Grandson? Bogachiel? The Hoh? "Stop! Where did you start?" "At Hurricane Ridge, what's the date?" "July twenty-third." She paused, thought, and then replied, "We've been out six weeks."

"Oh" was all I could say. Six weeks? We visualized the days, weeks, and miles and miles and miles they had been wandering in the vastness of the Olympic Peninsula. We thought of our own run, four, maybe five hours. A touch of envy entered our conversation. We parted, returning to our run, but a few steps up the trail a voice came faintly across to us, one of those old voices, "I wish we were young like them, so we could run like they do."

And I, turning my head, said, not too loudly but I hoped loud enough for them to hear, "I hope we are still coming out here when we are their age."

I sit there on the bluff for a while this morning, reliving that day. From where I am sitting, I can look across the Strait of Juan de Fuca. Over to the west lies Hurricane Ridge on the north end of the Olympic Peninsula. Somewhere to the south lies the meadow where we saw the oldest Alaska cedar in North America and some women who inspire. "Old" lost its meaning somewhere along the way. We are still going out there.

There are trails in there, still calling.

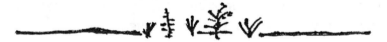

How Do You Explain Ultramarathons?

Can you talk?

I looked over at the probably-never-was-new pickup truck, wondering what was fixing to start.

Yes.

Well, you folks was out here runnin' this morning when I went into town.

Yes.

Well, that was only a little bit after eight.

Yeah.

Well, it's almost three o'clock, and I was wonderin' just what you are doing?

Oh (have to switch from monosyllabic). We are running a road ultramarathon. The people you see with numbers pinned on them are running either a 31-mile race or a 50-mile race, they...

Whoa, dawgies, 50 miles?

Yes. It's a...

Where are you from?

Olympia, Washington (I am running a 50-miler in the Grants Pass, Oregon, area).

You drove down here to run 50 miles?

Yes. It's a...

Did you pay to do this; you said it's a race. You have to pay?

Yes.

Whooeeee.

Fortunately, or maybe not, we reached the intersection (remember, I was running) where I needed to turn right to get to the end of the day. He grinned, said good luck, and we parted ways.

I have never felt there was an adequate explanation for what we do, not that I was able to come up with anyway. Generally, we can't even explain it to ourselves, to our inner self.

To Someone Who Understands...

To someone who understands, no explanation is necessary. To someone who does not understand, no amount of explanation will suffice. I had rolled those few words around in my head for the last several miles, first trying to get them in the right order (while not being sure there was something real to recall), then, while on a trail miles from the nearest Google point, trying to attribute them to someone. I could not; then comes the hardest thing to do with a phrase or tune that has settled into the conscious mind while on a run—I tried to forget it until I got home. *To someone who...*

It had started with "Why are you running?" shouted at me as I was careening down a set of switchbacks surrounded by dense underbrush. I was looking down, concentrating on roots and footing with only minimal glances forward in case there were hikers coming at me. The question broke in on my concentration. I broke stride and looked up to see four alarmed-looking faces, each trying to see up the trail behind me—behind me? Why are...—behind me? I looked at them. The woman, evidently the one whose shout I had heard, repeated, "Why are you running?"

I stopped. I looked at her and her companions, two of them looking at me, the other one still looking up the trail somewhat apprehensively. "I was running because, uh, well, these are the trails I run on." "You mean there is nothing chasing you?" Chasing me? Now I looked up the trail. "No, not that I know of, I was just running because these are the trails that I run." The woman who had first shouted at me resumed the interview by asking, "Aren't you a little old to be running around alone out here?" Miffed that my latest dose of Grecian Formula 44 was obviously a failure, I nodded agreement and ran on down the trail.

Why was I running? To keep my resting pulse in the forties? To justify the largest shoe rack in the neighborhood? To continue to be able to wear the same size Levi's I wore in high school? Because one of these times I am going to do this 10.2-mile (certified, standardized, scrutinized, and stamped) loop without catching a root? It certainly wasn't because I was training for something—the earliest I might show up at a starting line was October up on Orcas Island, maybe. Why was I running? The reasons and incentives to run are many and varied. I once ran home because Kathy had got back to the trailhead first and drove home, leaving me a note on the hikers' registration box, "You can make it before dark if you hurry."

I might be running because I am in the year of my father's death. There are weak hereditary links between why he died and why I might or might not. One doctor assured me the overall health running gives me had long ago negated any inherited physiological defect. His assurances were couched in just enough medical qualifiers to prevent them being facts. As best I can determine the chances of my keeling over and becoming a search and rescue object are so slim that on a normal day's run they don't raise conscious thoughts or cares, and anyway, it would be preferable to watch one last sunset while gasping for breath 'neath a tree that first broke ground before Columbus weighed anchor than to rest not quite comfortably on the cold tiles of a kitchen floor awaiting the sound of an approaching first-aid kit on wheels.

We actually went out one afternoon because Kathy found one of those calorie calculators and calories-burned-per-mile charts then asked what I was fixing for dinner. Enchiladas. With guacamole? Yes. Sour cream? Yes, and black beans and jasmine rice, too, why? After a few minutes of silence, the reply came, "We need to run twelve miles before dinner." Oh, why? You counted what? Oh, hmmm, should I mention the *mantecaditos?* No. No, it is best not to say anything now. Why are you running? Because the almond shortbread cookies (with flaked coconut added), of which I have been known to eat a bowlful with only one glass of milk, are known to beckon at two o'clock in the morning, and I baked 63 of the little rascals just before we left the house.

Mooses! A quick exclamation, a check of the rearview mirror, then hard on the brakes and I pulled off onto the shoulder. We were out of the car and across the road in seconds. Kathy asked where, and I pointed to the left at a small hill we were approaching. We slowed as we got to the skyline, then edged forward to look down at the meadow—noiselessly, we thought, we crept forward. Oh wow! There were two moose calves just below us, next to the creek at the edge of the meadow. One was standing in the water eating grasses along the edge of the creek; the other seemed to be just enjoying the sun. We had been watching for a few minutes when Kathy quietly asked where Mom might be—hmmm, the calves are sort of small looking—Mom? I don't think she would leave them alone. Mom! Apparently Mom did not think we should be watching her calves and (how did she get that close?) had come to ask us to leave. I recalled that a quiet voice will sometimes soothe animals, so I started talking quietly (Kathy later asked why I chose that moment to start reciting *The Charge of the Light Brigade*) as we tried to move backward to get some trees between Mom and us. Mom snorted and charged. We turned and ran for the trees. Someone up above will someday tell me how far we ran (a quarter mile and more fer shure), how far Mom ran (probably only a few steps), which animals bet how much on whom that day just south of Yellowstone, on down by Lewis Lake, and how many variations on why we were running were heard that night in the burrows and caves, meadows and creek sides in the Tetons.

The daydreaming that familiar trails allow was broken by the trilling of the ravens that live about a hundred yards in from the end of the pavement. The trailhead was in sight. I could see a runner coming toward me. As we met she smiled and said, "Beautiful day for running." "Yes," I replied, "yes, it is, and that's a good reason to run," and the thought came back to me, "*To someone who understands...*"

Relaxing So You Can Run

This running thing of ours can last a lifetime, can create memories full of images or just numbers, can fulfill desires or leave us wondering what went wrong or puzzled over how we did—often most troubling are the days of wondering why the training isn't leading to better results. Why isn't it working? How can we tell? Keep a diary, a runner's log?

Yesterday's run took just over two hours and twenty-one minutes, covered approximately thirteen miles, and had, also approximately, three thousand two hundred feet of elevation change. Three ways to record the day's running might be:

1. 2:21:17, 13.2 miles, 3200 rise/fall, 10:42 pace.
2. A bunch of words mentioning birds sighted or heard, plants seen, creeks passed or crossed, trees or lakes that caused us to pause, slugs jumped over, glacial activity, and other useless training information.
3. 2+ hours, 12+ miles, very little flats, hard push on all the ups, tried to relax on the downs, last mile on logging road, good kick to the gate at the end. Good hard run. Weather: warm. Shoes: yes.

I thought back about diary entries over the years—short, long, technical, terse, flowery—and wondered if they were patterned after the intent of the run.

What was the intent of the run? There had been days, even whole seasons, when a route was chosen because it was the hilliest, just as there were days when early spring sent me through the meadows. There was a summer when I added that o'dark-in-the-morning run three times a week because a certain date on the calendar was creating self-doubts that I hoped a few more miles would dispel. If the mind did not believe in the body, would adding three more morning runs help any? Surely a spreadsheet and some graphs would prove my method.

A chart was made. Colors were selected. Patterns established. Blue would show me the *hard* days. Blue weeks would slowly become the dominant color. There was even a week when I found a way to put in a bluer blue—a truly extraordinary week. The watch was worn and times were checked and effort adjusted; numbers were scrawled on a pad of paper as soon as I returned. The colors on the wall and the numbers on the pad were working, but, in spite of my charted statistical consistency...

I was tired. The blues easily outnumbered the yellows. The vanquished easy days of yellow, which allowed stopping at the overlooks, joining friends for casual runs, or just going for a walk if the mind wanted, were missing. There were many numbers recording hours for the day, for guessed-at pace, and even cryptic notes about the route: hilly, really hilly, mostly downs, and so forth, but *nothing about relaxing and enjoying the day on the trails*. All the running was for my body. All the runs were ventures into the woods with strength or speed or endurance the goal.

I got out the box with the old diaries—the chaotic recollections of my chances and falls, proof of strengths or frailties, flashbacks of races and "is he ever going to get here" runs—and looked at some blocks of history. I was looking for what was different from this year. Why was I tired? It was easy to find. My easy days and easy weeks were gone. There had always been one or two days each week when biking, hiking, or walking was just as much a part of training as the push-on-the-ups days.

The Part-Time Runner by Reg Harris was one of my first running books. Harris addresses the need for relaxation—thoughts that have stuck with me more than any other part of his book. The tortures of finding the secret diet vary with each of us, the number of miles might be set in the mind but not in the bones, but relaxation can be taught to anyone. If we can find a way to give the mind a chance to recover, even though miles from the end, we might run better for those remaining miles. For me this extends to needing an easy day each week and an easy week on some regular cycle.

Adjustments to routes (minor task) and intentions (major task) were made. Saturday came, and I received a querulous look when I returned home about two hours after I headed for the trails. It was supposed to be an eight-hour-run day. I'll get the rest tomorrow on the way to the beach, I explained. That may have been the start of my practicing a "weekend total" idea instead of a certain number of hours or miles for the long-run day.

The next morning I scribbled a note about my route and slipped out the door a few minutes before sunrise. I was headed for a combination of trails, dirt roads, logging roads, and byways that would keep me running westerly from Corvallis to the coast. The plan was that Kathy would get up and follow, picking me up about thirty miles out, and we would have a picnic afternoon at the beach. As time passed I became more and more curious about the challenge of how far could I get—could I get to the ruins of the old stone house? The covered bridge? The waterfall with no name known to us?

I had no distances to measure with, only my watch. I was an hour out, then two, then it was "she should be up now" and, finally, "she should be on the road." I filled my bottles at a campground and thought about how relaxed things seemed on this new route with its still-unknown training purpose. It was a morning of quiet running, usually next to a creek or river and with almost no cars to worry about. I started thinking about relaxing. The idea of *concentrating on relaxing* seemed so paradoxical to me. I slowly felt my neck and shoulders lose their tension. I relaxed the death grip on the hand bottles, tightened and loosened the abdominal muscles, did some belly breathing, and this, that, and the other things I could recall about relaxing while on the move.

I did fifty steps of relaxing this one, then fifty steps of relaxing that one, and so forth on down the road. It was going to be like hill sessions, speed work, and all else associated with running: time to learn, time to refine, time to see the results, adjust, reevaluate, continue to run, and learn to believe in the positive effect of relaxing.

It was an hour or so later. I was in the second set of my newly created relaxation series when I heard a muted honk. I glanced to the right and saw a familiar green car pass. Kathy pulled the car

14

over just down the road and stood there waiting. When I finally got close enough to hear, she asked, "Are you going to run all day, or do you want to get in and go to the beach to walk in the sand with me?"

"How Did You Decide Which Ones To Run?"

I thought about the question long enough for Lynn to think I had not heard him. He started to say it again when I rephrased it with, "How did you decide where to take me this morning?" Conversations on trails mean you are talking to the back of someone or talking to the trail out in front of you loudly enough for those behind to hear. If you are running with a stranger, you try to run alongside to make the conversation easier, even though this means running into bushes, trees, or falling over logs while you turn your head to listen.

It was my first run with Lynn Ballard, a friend, though I had never met him other than via e-mail, who lives somewhere way on the other side of the Rockies in a place called Texas. A visit to my daughter had given us the opportunity to meet and the time to share his trails just north of Dallas. We had been running in the crisp air of an October morning when the question came up. His answer was both generous and elegantly simple, "I wanted you to see one of our Texas sunrises from one of my favorite trails." Sounded good to me. But then he repeated his question. "How did you decide which ones to run?"

How did I decide? Decisions about which ultramarathon to run were made somewhat easier by there being so few to choose from in my early years—there were only three in my home state of Washington when I started this running journey in 1985. The only published source of information was a rather thin magazine from somewhere back east that hardly anyone knew about. It was full of black-and-white photos, lists of results with a wide variety of stories about those races, and, perhaps most important to me as a newcomer, a calendar. That calendar was as good as gold for this suddenly avid runner. *UltraRunning* had a calendar that was read a thousand times that fall of 1985—read and highlighted. The question marks and other cryptic notes are still in the margins of that first issue from August 1985. I would read the descriptions and think, "Wow, I'd like to run there."

The first trip to California was because of a picture of an old bridge along a fork of the American River. It was of a design engineers don't engineer anymore, nor builders build anymore, but I had designed a bridge or two in my youth, and surely that bridge would be worth the journey to Placerville, California. I gave no thought to the descent into the canyon, nor of the climb out—only of finding that bridge, then finding the spot where the photographer stood, stopping somewhere on that course and pausing to look around, and then running on to the finish. The builders saved a lot of money by making the bridge short. The bridge is short because it is way down there near the bottom of the canyon, or they put the bridge way down there at the bottom of the canyon so it would not need a long span. The Good Old Country 50k seemed like a good idea right up to the start of the climb out of the canyon. I can still make muscles ache just thinking about that climb for a few minutes.

The Coast Range of Oregon and stories of bears led me to Siletz, and the giant bedroom in the one gym serving the local school led me to Siletz. Pick a gym mat and stake out a claim for the night, then line up at the start, an arbitrary line across a country road, the next morning. The Coast Range has no significant mountain peaks. It said so in the geological guide for the area. Whoever wrote about the bears did not provide any bears, but whoever said there were no mountains there has never run the fifty miles of trails of John Henderson's Coast Hills Ultra.

The scarcity of ultras in the early days led to some compromises as we decided where to go next. The Brookings, Oregon, trail marathon was guaranteed, which may or may not be better than a claim of certification, by the RD to be at least 26.2 miles long. I had never run a marathon that started with six or seven miles along a sandy beach before climbing inland. Who could resist a morning run along the Oregon coast with a promise of food later? I had not seen, and haven't seen since, the promise of a salmon barbecue for all finishers—the beach and the dinner still come up in conversations among a certain small group.

The following weekend—my excuse for consecutive weekends of marathons that last week in May was to get to run in one of the Nisene Marks redwood groves of the Aptos Creek Marathon—was another trail run, but this time beneath the branches of redwoods. No sand this time, but lots of shade from the giants. I don't think there is a better place to run than in an old-growth forest. I have enjoyed the dryness and open spaces of the deserts of the Southwest, the dirt roads of the Ozarks of Arkansas, and the fall colors of trails in Vermont—each holds a beauty of its own, but my heart and soul find comfort beneath the arms of the giants of the coastal forests of the Pacific Northwest that I cannot find elsewhere.

I'm drawn as well to the forests and mountains elsewhere. Bobbie Dixon probably does not know the trip she caused. I had seen a picture of her setting a course record at Le Grizz in 1985. *Le Grizz*—just the name should cause you to wonder about bears, great big shuffling brown, furry bears. It isn't like I wanted to wrestle a bear, not anything like that, but I wanted to go where they live—the Northern Rockies with their bluffs thousands of feet tall, valleys carved by glaciers, and lakes made of water from the glaciers' retreat—and run in a place where nature dwarfs man in a fashion that reminds one of one's place. I am a guest here on this planet, barely tolerated.

The majesty and distant grandeur surrounding Race Director Pat Caffrey's creation just south of Glacier National Park made for a most deceptive day of running. You run through the land, not down into it, not up out of it, just through it without it ever being within reach. He even provided entertainment at the awards ceremony—a mother moose and her calf walked down to the lake, waded in, and swam across without so much as a nod to us. We were just out of Montana driving west when the conversation for the next run started.

Starts at midnight, October 31, Halloween night. What does? A 100k over by Wenatchee. Around, then up and over, Badger Mountain. Midnight? Yes. Why? Why not? Okay. Won't it be cold? Suck it up. Full moon? No, but there should be some meteor showers. Okay—big check mark, a definite yes on my list. It says self-supported, what does that mean? Well, it means someone has to stop every three miles and cater to my every whim and desire. Right? Right. Midnight? Sure, and besides, I'm too old to go trick-or-treating. So, off we went to the Badger Mountain Bean Run 100k. That being the only year they held the 100k, I still hold the course record, set beneath a clear, cold November sky complete with meteor showers and a brown Malibu coupe that stopped every three miles to cater to my whims.

And so it went with the whys and wherefores of trips to here and there as Lynn and I covered the trails along Lake Texoma. Ultramarathon runners have used other reasons, both rational (it's nearby) and not quite rational (because I have never run Leadville), to decide which trail, which road, which state—the world of the Internet has given us runs that start with strangers and end with friends. And *UltraRunning* still publishes that list (progress being what it is, now it has a URL). Patagonia? South Africa? Running circles at Across the Years in Phoenix? Everywhere but North Dakota. I'm still making lists. I'll die making lists. And that's one of the best things about running ultramarathons. The list of dreams is never ending.

The Serious Runner...the First Encounter

It was Sunday. It was also the day after my first 50-miler. I was finally home. The "get up at dawn and drive the 350 miles home" had introduced me to every bit of stiffness and soreness available. I shuffled around the house feeling somewhat stiff and sore from yesterday's running. I was sitting on the porch thinking about what to do next when I finally decided to go to Capitol Lake and do the five-mile loop around the lake as my recovery run/jog/shuffle/walk. It surely couldn't make things any worse.

I drove to the lake and parked and did the usual delaying by trying to decide on clockwise or counterclockwise. There actually are days when the direction makes a difference. When we get a wind coming out of the north you can feel the sting of salt spray on the clockwise loop. On the counterclockwise loop the biggest annoyance is the many headlights in your face. Since it was barely late afternoon and the wind was calm—"calm wind" never sounds right to me. There really wasn't much to worry or care about today; a late March day, first weekend of spring, grass is turning green, birds in the trees—all that sort of stuff. I started off on the five miles around the lake.

Wow? As Gomer Pyle would have said, "Surprise surprise." This wasn't so bad after all. Wow. These legs did fifty miles yesterday, and look at me go today. I made it about a half mile when the first distraction made its presence known. Ducks, small and still-fluffy-with-down baby ducks to be exact, two flocks of them, each escorted by a mother duck. I stopped, watched for a few seconds, and then turned back to the task at hand—five miles around the lake, running.

I made it another several hundred yards when the next flock of ducks put in an appearance. They were my downfall. A dozen or so little yellow fluff balls scurried here and there on the grass next to the lake just a few feet from the sidewalk. Mom had been sitting there watching the kids and me. As I crossed the invisible safe-distance line she quacked, and the fluff balls all headed for the water—each with a muted quacking sound. Duck giggles, squeaks, and noises they surely thought were quacks. I stood there for those few minutes—just watching on an early spring day, warm, legs feeling a lot better than I had hoped—a good time to just enjoy being out and alive.

After a minute or two or three, I turned to start back on my journey around the lake. I noticed a man running toward me and decided to wait until he passed. He was one of the types of runners I am envious of—shirt neatly tucked into shorts, color-coordinated shirt and socks, shoes without a speck of dirt, laces looking like bow ties, symmetrical sweat patterns barely darkening his shirt, no dust swirling up as he ran—he was fresh from, or going to, a photo shoot. As he drew near I waved, pointed at the ducks, smiled, and said something about, "It sure is hard to get started today, isn't it?"

He paused, surveyed my sort of trail-browned socks and mud-stained shoes, dismissed my appearance, and replied in a tone that could freeze children in their tracks, if any were to get near, "It takes dedication to become a serious distance runner."

The human mind, being what it is, can process thousands of bits and pieces of incoming or outgoing information in markedly short periods of time. Only a few hundredths of a second passed as I thought of my fifty-mile run of the day before, the training for it, the physical and mental travails of the months leading up to the successful completion. Those and other thoughts came and went as the "serious" runner continued on his way and I turned back to the ducks and watched them paddle off a ways. The thought that I would probably never become a serious distance runner played in my mind. It still does.

CHAPTER TWO

You move from doing things to show other people you could, to where you do things to look into yourself, into your soul, and see who you are and what you're all about.

—Scott Weber

There are victories of the soul and spirit. Sometimes, even if you lose, you win.

—Elie Wiesel

The words "I am" are potent words; be careful what you hitch them to. The thing you're claiming has a way of reaching back and claiming you.

—A.L. Kitselman

Loops and Pauses at Lake Pondilla

If a long run is going to happen today, it is going to be mechanical, because my mind is rebelling before my feet touch the floor. I
fixed everything the night before, so all I have to do is get up and
head out with only a pause for a quick cup of coffee. The first hint of
an uncooperative mind was when I hit the snooze button at o'dark
thirty in the morning. I stared at the ceiling for a few minutes, trying to track down a phrase that was flitting through my mind—*the
impending rush to doom.*

It seemed like the sort of thought that would wander in and out
of your mind as you hurried to a DNF or didn't hurry out of bed,
avoiding Saturday's long run, mentally justifying a well-earned (yes,
well-earned, absolutely well-earned) DNGOTD (did not get out the
door). Oh me, maybe I'm tired. I'm probably overtraining again.
This would be a good time to quit keeping a diary, because my diary
(corroborated by a multicolored spreadsheet) says I am coming off
a rest phase. (Rested? Really? Doesn't feel like it.) Okay, what is it
then? Who cares? Zap the coffee, grab a bagel, and get out the door.

I cleverly carry my coffee cup with me as I head for the creek
behind the apartments when a voice comes through the morning air,
"Just leave the cup by the big maple stump, and I'll walk out and get
it before I go out." Oh. She is up and almost outbound. Fifty yards
later I set the cup on the stump and head through the blackberry
vines that think this will be the year they cross the trail and close it
for good (not while I have a machete they won't) to the paved bike
path. They have already grown out far enough to brush my hands
as I pass; blossoms are bigger, bees and hummingbirds are busy all
around.

I shuffle, jog, and stumble the mile to the end of the pavement,
and I think I am warmed up enough to pretend to run down Humpty

Dump. That illusion lasts to the first of the bumps. Humpty Dump, or Humpty Dumpty, depending on which sign you read (one of these days I'll change one of them to match the other), is a series of washboards going generally downhill on this particular day. "Catching air" is good if you are on a mountain bike, not so good if you are running and are catching air because of a misstep, again. I apologize to the pileated woodpeckers on the learning tree. They always know which time to fly because I am getting too close or which time to stay because I am about to be entertaining, again.

Since entertainment has entered my mind and, although I have been playing "push on the ups, fly on the downs," it still isn't anything more than a wander-here-and-there run, I turn toward the lake. By now the only waterfowl still there will be residents. All the migrants are gone back to the mountains or the far reaches of the Arctic. Our residents are what some bird books classify as "duck-like birds" (dlbs)—mallards, green-winged teal, buffleheads, mergansers, and a northern pintail or two. Whatever is at the lake today will be well warned of my approach as I noisily descend the last quarter mile of the Pacific Northwest Trail and cross the old wooden bridge.

The lake sits in a kettle created by a retreating glacier from long ago. It is ringed by trees and underbrush, except for the shoreline trail along one side for about a hundred yards. The *click-click-rattle* of a departing belted kingfisher is the last warning of my arrival as I stop to sit on an old fallen cedar to wait and watch the lake come back to life. I'm resting. I've decided my diary is wrong. My arrival has caused a very loud silence. All the chirps, clicks, quacks, squawks, chitters, and whistles have stopped. Nothing moves within fifty yards of me.

A dozen or so mallards barely make ripples as they paddle away from the shore directly across from me. A lone great blue heron, stick-figured and graceful, moves but makes no ripples along the shore by the lily pads off to my right, occasionally reacting to a flit of movement, then pausing to swallow a fish or frog or something I cannot see from here. The kingfisher will be the first to decide I am harmless. That is the system I have discovered. I can see the rust-colored band that tells me it is a female. The heron spears another small fish. The kingfisher dives from the branch, coming out of the water with a tiny silvery fish in her beak—available food outweighs patience this time, or am I something she recognizes as curious but harmless?

I look around the lake and watch the few dozen dlbs slowly re-distribute themselves; then my eyes find the reason for coming to the lake today. A downed log on the far side of the lake has "bumps" on it. Bumps? Large bumps? Aha! The turtles are out. There are five of them. They have, or at least some of them have, made it through the winter. Kathy thinks they are Western pond turtles. We only see them a few times each spring, always on the far side, never close enough to make a positive identification. If they are Western pond turtles, seeing them is a naturalist's treat—they are considered en-dangered by the state of Washington and a species of concern by the federal government.

There won't be any positive identification today, partly because I don't have any binoculars with me but mostly because the turtles are diving off the log as a bald eagle has spotted them and is diving. Its great wings are spread, feathers fully fanned and talons extend-ed, but there is nothing to grab. I sigh, grateful. There is nothing left but ripples and an empty log. The quickness and agility of this great bird leaves me breathless (the turtles did okay, too, diving to safe-ty). Now the eagle has perched on a bare limb, waiting, watching. My mind has fixed on "she" because of the size. Her wings probably span eight feet. The yellow beak and solid white of her head and tail feathers tell me she is at least four years old.

I spend the next hour doing loops on the Pacific Northwest Trail and the lower bluff trail, climbing up and out of the kettle that holds the lake, glancing through the trees at the eagle on the deserted log. On the third time around the mile-and-a-half loop, the eagle is gone, but it is two more laps before a turtle reappears, and it is on the next lap, which I have decided will be the last one, when the four other bumps appear back on the log, probably with heads turned skyward.

I mouth "thank you" softly to the lake and its inhabitants for shaking me out of the doldrums of fatigue then turn up the Pacific Northwest Trail for one last climb to the connector trail that takes me back to the forest trails that lead to the bike path. It wasn't my body, it was my mind that was tired. The pause at the lake took away the day's fixation on being tired by reminding me that we are to *see* while out here—not just pass through.

Ran One, Another Is Only Two Weeks Away...

In response to the often-posed question that goes something like:

- I am running a marathon this weekend, there is a trail 50k two weeks later, is that too soon to run?
- Just noticed a nice road marathon two weeks after a trail ultramarathon I am scheduled to run. If I drop from the 50-mile run to the 50-kilometer event, what can I do to get ready for the road marathon?
- I am crazy, falling-down drunk and want to run a trail 50k two weeks after completing my first 5k, er, 12k, uh, 3.7-mile trail run...

Getting over the mental barrier is the first step. Running a marathon or an ultramarathon two weeks after running a marathon or an ultramarathon is difficult. It is difficult, but it is doable. The first step in successfully meeting the challenge will be to believe you can do it or at least be strongly confident you can succeed. Now, as twenty years ago, it is still commonly thought that two hard-effort marathons a year is the most a runner should do. That view is harbored in minds that think each marathon (or ultramarathon) is an all-out effort, each starting line is approached with a personal best intended, every outing is a race. Nothing else is really running. Nothing else is worthy of mention. These ideas or opinions are factually incorrect. Many runners have done marathons on consecutive weekends, ultramarathons on alternate weekends, and there is the fact that ultrarunners often do training runs that are longer than a marathon, and they do them on consecutive weekends, sometimes consecutive days. The first problem continues to be accepting the challenge of trying it. My first venture into the something sort of long on consecutive weekends was a result of seeing what I thought was a strange quirk in time—calendar time.

March of 1986 was a month with five weekends. I looked at the five weekends and thought that was an odd occurrence. It seemed like an oddity, but it isn't really all that infrequent. I did a more-or-less random check and found two months with five Saturdays or five Sundays, but not both, in four different years. There were three months in each of the four years I checked that had five weekends, and one even had four months with five weekends. Five weekends—could I find a run for each weekend? Schedules were quickly consulted. I got cold feet when I got to the fifth weekend. My first 50-miler was scheduled for the fourth Saturday. I was much too lacking in self-confidence to think I would be running anything that even resembled a long run the weekend following that first 50-miler. As it turned out, I felt better than I had guessed, predicted, or hoped for during those first days—I did an easy five miles the next day. Friday, six days after that first 50-miler, I called the folks putting on that last weekend of March's marathon and asked if they had day-of-race registration. "Yes, we do," came across the telephone lines. I threw stuff in the car and drove over the mountains after work Friday afternoon with a marathon on my mind.

26

For the event or numbers minded, the five weekends of March were:

1. Marathon—3:14:00
2. Marathon—3:58:06 (a long and disjointed conversation)
3. 20k—1:27:10
4. 50-miler—7:35:06
5. Marathon—3:17:44

I never again thought I could not do those things, that sort of running. The fears and anxieties of the starting line have never gone away, but the fact that I did the consecutive weekends of long runs (except for the 20k) was a valuable lesson. That lesson brought forth a well-earned reward. A mental barrier was crossed and banished. I should add a paragraph or two about the fragility of the banishment. None of those March runs were races except for the 50-miler. The marathons were simply long runs. The respect for the distance has never gone away, but self-confidence became a prominent part of the psychological side of the challenge.

Several years later I would try a pair of trail 50k runs two weeks apart. As I said, these were not all-out efforts, but I was pushing most of the time. If I rounded a curve and saw someone just up the trail, I tried to pick up the effort and pass that next carrot being dangled. These were two long runs with aid stations (trail 50k events) that just happened to fit my training calendar.

After the run comes the recovery, or how soon to start and how much can I eat while driving home? The (now long defunct) Greater Oregon Health Service 50 Mile in Grants Pass, Oregon, had one of the best incentives to start recovery properly. There was a double-crust apple pie awaiting each runner at the finish line. It was in your hands before you had gone twenty feet past the finish line banner. I watched one finisher turn his pie into a turnover with just a flick of the wrist—a bare ten minutes later the pie was gone.

Many ultras have food available at the finish line: soup in the McDonald Forest, a burrito up in the Siskiyous, a barbecue sandwich in the LBJ Grasslands. Maybe just beer, salsa, and chips, but it is frequently there, just past the finish line. A mistake many runners make at the finish line area is getting into conversation mode, reliving the run just completed, renewing acquaintances—just standing around enjoying the day. They forget that a key ingredient (recovery food) to feeling good the day after an ultramarathon is often within reach. Recovery starts immediately after finishing. What I did for recovery and "tapering" during the two weeks between two hard-effort 50k trail runs started almost as soon as I crossed the finish line.

I state this emphatically and explicitly because there is a tendency to wait until evening or the trip home or sometime later. As soon as you can after the run is over, start the refueling and rehydrating. I can easily recall the two or three (or several?) ultras with agonizingly long finishing stretches. I am totally envious of the fortunate souls who can run seemingly all day and all night on just water. My thirst in an ultramarathon isn't just a water thirst. My body is asking for calcium, magnesium, potassium, sodium, manganese, and even vitamin B-6 to be mixed in with the liquids. The hours of galloping across the landscape have left me with white lines of salt (in its forms of sodium, sodium chloride, and just plain salt) and the depletion of all those other electrolyte things. Replacing electrolytes is needed to help the body regain chemical balance. The eating is only slightly behind the drinking in importance. Get the electrolytes into the system, get some carbohydrates and protein into the system—then bask in the glory of the afternoon. Take some ibuprofen sort of stuff, *but only if needed—not because you see other runners using it*. Persons venturing into the world of ultramarathons owe it to themselves to read and understand the effects, both good and bad, of the many easily obtained medicines. You will place a lot of stress on your body—learn what you are doing when you add in a few pills.

Electrolyte replacement followed closely by food (with an emphasis on protein—not in huge amounts—then carbohydrates) is the order of events at the end of a day of running. Drink, and then get some salty foods into the system along with the liquids. Oddly enough, or a fortunate benefit of endurance running, is that beer, chips, and salsa are great shortly after a long run. Lest anyone think I am promoting the guzzling of beer or any other alcoholic beverage, any number of brands or flavors of soft drink are just as good— "good" being an entirely subjective sort of word anyway, i.e., you form it in your mind according to your views, especially after several hours of running.

The running guideline for the two weeks in between two 50k trail runs:

Saturday	—50k
Sunday	—easy 3–4, even brisk walking with some jogging is good
Monday	—rest
Tuesday	—easy 3–4, could walk, short bike ride, nothing hard
Wednesday	—6–8, some playing with speed, nothing serious, just pick it up to increase circulation and effort, 50–75 yards at a time, maybe five or ten of them during the run
Thursday	—easy 4–6
Friday	—rest
Saturday	—8–10, moderate effort, not hard, some hilly stuff, just easy, relaxed running
Sunday	—easy 3–5, some playing with speed, no all-out effort, soft routes, if you have them
Monday	—rest
Tuesday	—easy 3–4, just to keep things loose
Wednesday	—easy 3–4, just to keep things turning over

Thursday   —rest and packing and planning and scheming
Friday   —easy walk/jog/shuffle if you had a long
                    drive to the run site, just a couple of miles
                    to recover from the trip and wake the
                    body back up for Saturday morning
Saturday   —time to run, again.

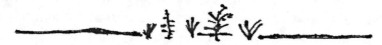

A Rock by Any Other Name

The 15-mile-long Butterfield Trail loop is both in and out of Devil's Den State Park as it loops through the rugged Boston Mountains, a few miles southerly of Fayetteville, Arkansas. An excerpt from an Arkansas state bulletin includes the following:

> An indicator of the roughness of the terrain was the need to hitch a four-mule team to the stage as it traversed the area. Waterman L. Ormsby Jr. of the *New York Herald* described the area in his book *The Butterfield Overland Mail.* Ormsby wrote: "It is impossible that any road could be worse. I might say the road was steep, rugged, jagged, rough, and mountainous, and then wish for more impressive words." Although the Butterfield Hiking Trail does not follow the original stage route, it does come within two miles of it. When hiking the trail, you will get a feeling for what Ormsby wrote.

With that description and the trail comfort we felt from running trails in the Cascade and Olympic Mountains of the Pacific Northwest fairly fresh in our minds, I folded the map and put it away. Okay, let's do this. The fifteen miles would be a nice break from the multiple loops we had been doing around Fayetteville. We put on the two-bottle fanny packs and headed down the trail. By the time we got to this-must-be-about-halfway point, we were wishing for our mountain trails back in Washington. Up, down, up, down, and not a straight piece of trail had we seen. And who on earth designed the rocks—ankle turners about the size of bricks that slide out from under you as you cross and recross creeks. At one point, we took fifteen minutes walking back and forth looking at the wall formed by a 30-foot-high bluff before deciding we were supposed to climb around some car-sized boulders and wiggle our way up where a waterfall would be during a wet spell. At the Holt Ridge Overlook, we sat down and ate a PB&J. Kathy pointed at the plus signs someone had scratched after the distance listed on the signpost nearby. We began to wonder if we were in for a long afternoon. We were. It was. Those fifteen (15++?) miles took us exactly four hours to complete. Back at the trailhead we both agreed that Kathy's role as boat anchor had worked and I would return the following weekend to run the loop solo to salvage our family honor.

The following Saturday, with grim determination and a fanny pack, I set out to run the loop properly. I did not wear a watch. I just ran hard. You don't need a watch to run hard. Several shin scrapes later, with an earned gouge in the right knee, a leg coated with poison ivy welts, and a throbbing knot on my forehead from a low branch on an oak tree, I was back at the trailhead where Kathy sat reading a book. "Time," my raspy voice asked, and she looked up. "Three," she said. "Aha!" "Fifty-six," she finished. Hmmm, was that the best I could do? I had run a 3:10:10 road marathon in these same hills a few months ago: fitness was not the issue. And my boat anchor had stayed in port reading a book. So what happened? Uh, you don't suppose it could be the rocks, do you?

Rocks are for sitting on when you pause for a PB&J miles in from a trailhead. In most areas Gaia scatters appropriately-sized rocks for this energy-replenishing pause. Along the Superior Trail in Minnesota, the rocks run from huge slabs that disappear into the cold waters of Lake Superior to the chair-sized, some round and some not-so-round rocks we sat on eating oranges. The next day we did the run, walk, jog, climb, and shuffle along the Superior Trail—jokingly discussing the sheer torture this route would be by flashlight at o'dark thirty in the morning. The challenge of "100 miles in one day" shifted again.

On the trails of Ricketts Glen State Park in Pennsylvania, Mother Nature left many stair steps, most just the wrong size for running, at least for my big feet. Most were the right size to make you run with arms flailing, clutching at the air to regain balance. The 7.2 miles on the Falls Trail sign was just a teaser. Kathy laughed and said, "It was another plus-plus mileage sign." We "ran" on the slippery rocks alongside the waterfalls. The steepness of the steps demanded we pause if we wanted to look at the many waterfalls. Steep, slippery, and wrong-sized rocks, or right-sized, depending on whether you're a human or a marmot—the randomness of nature remains constant on the trails.

The rocks on the east side of the Mississippi River tend to be slabs or layers tilted this way or that. Great slabs that break into cubical sort of things that roll out from under one foot only to fall on top of the other (never have understood that sequence). These are the smooth-grained rocks that form a bond with leaves in the fall to create a wonderfully smooth, warmly colored photograph that is downright evil to run. Each leaf that falls from a maple, oak, hickory, elm, ash, beech, and all the other deciduous trees contributes to the tension that grips a runner's toes as slippery surfaces are felt for, hidden holes are felt for, sure footing is felt for step after step after step—and the pace slows and slows, and you learn to spell Massanutten like you were born there.

Or you go faster and faster: about seventeen miles into the Siskiyou Out Back 50k, you start the drop from Wrangle Gap to the Siskiyou Gap. As distant views distract, there is a subtle change from a gravel-based trail to the broken rocks where the trail was etched into the solid rock of the mountainside. You are happily unaware that you are now running almost entirely on toe-grabber rocks, the pointy-side-up stuff that grabs at your shoes and—oops, eyes are darting to analyze where to fall, hamstrings are trying to find the surge to get you back to balance, hands are out...balance is, or is not, regained. The huge uplift blocks of the West Coast *allow* us to enjoy long ascents or descents. In the three times I have run down this gorgeous trail, the first time I feel my shoulders relax and think the rocks are no longer grabbing my toes is when I see the aid station through the trees just ahead. As the downhill ends, a long uphill that will not end until next Tuesday beckons. The toe grabbers are behind. The shade of the pines on a sandy stretch waits.

And then there are the rocks that hitch rides. You always hope it is a "real" rock when you finally stop to remove whatever it is that is in your shoe and will not shift around to where you can run without noticing it. We are running a loop on the Frijole and the Smith Spring Trails in the Guadalupe Mountains National Park. The limestone and sandstone layers are easy to see as we run. But where the hard rocks of the New England areas are slow to erode, the sandstone in the Guadalupe Mountains National Park in western Texas isn't. Fine sand and gravel cover most of the trails here, some finding its way into our shoes or, at least, into my shoe. I finally say I need to stop. As always, as I turn my shoe upside down to evict the intruder, I hope a rock of some sort will fall out, not some puny little grain of sand an oyster would use for a pearl starter.

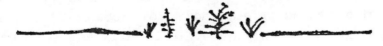

Winter's Gift of Rest

Deadlines create a certain level of pretend in some of my writing. We have just watched a beautiful October sunset over the Olympic

Peninsula. The sun still has almost two months of southerly travel before winter solstice. By the time this column reaches you, some of you will be looking at snow and ice, trying to figure out a way to get in some miles. Others will reach for a jacket or a long-sleeve shirt before heading out the door. And our readers from south of the equator will laugh in the warmth of spring as they read of our plight in our northern winter.

Gloves are now in the pocket of my Windbreaker everyday, just in case I have misjudged the wind direction. I would much rather have a jacket that turns out to be unneeded tied around my waist than suffer the misery of against-the-wind runs. Today, as we shuffled along, we were talking of the upcoming hibernation period, of the drop in intensity of effort on our daily outings, of the invitation to rest that the long nights of winter extend to us. Just as so many of us have a taper regimen for upcoming races, so do some of us have a plan for a yearly refreshing of the mind, body, and spirit—if we can only find time and are willing to rest.

Somewhere along the way, on the trails or roads where we run and train and race, in our sport that knows no seasonal bounds, a time to rest will arrive, acknowledged or not. Even the iron-willed runners, those people whose names you seem to see or read about on every page of results in *UltraRunning* or online or in local newspapers, must pause or else slowly start the inevitable downward spiral caused by physical fatigue and emotional burnout. That pause can come, maybe ought to come, with the season's turning; the opportunity for that pause is a gift of winter.

Pausing to rest seems so foreign to us, but each and every one of us, from the leaders racing down from Hope Pass or across No Hands Bridge to those who wander trails and byways barely beating cutoffs, eating more brownies than gels, naming animals and plants as they extend conversations over hill and dale, can benefit from reduced levels of effort.

Rest has never meant becoming the protectorate of the couch; it only means decreasing the effort level, changing the emphasis from one of continual challenge to one where aching joints and muscles finally get to quit cringing from inner voices talking about an upcoming race or one more fartlek or one last mile in an all-out sprint down the hill.

Believing in rest, its need and its benefits, is not easy for us. The discussions over taper—two weeks or three—are related to our fear that fitness will go flying out the door if we don't go out that same door, shoes laced and intentions serious. My first serious encounter with rest was as the Avenue of the Giants Marathon approached. It was my first year of running, my third marathon—the second having been just three weeks earlier. My legs were dead. My mind was shot. While the latter is not unusual, the former was troublesome. What could be wrong? I thumbed through my then-meager library of running books, finally finding some thoughts on rest.

Whoa! I could rest completely for the next four or five days and still be able to run a marathon? Right, yeah, sure. Aching knees helped with the decision. A mile or two of beach walking on the way to the redwoods and another mile or two amongst the giants was the most I did that week. I don't know if it was the magic of running beneath their limbs and branches or if it was the rest, but the marathon went well that Saturday morning, capping a week with five days of no running. I extended this idea to a week or so of walking, some shuffling, maybe a little jogging, but no running as the following winter passed. I slowly learned (high skull-thickness factor) that rest was okay, was useful, was maybe even important, a tool to be included in the training toolbox. Winter is a good time to look through the toolbox to see which tools are in need of replacement, improvement, or discarding altogether, a good place to put "rest" for use later in the year.

So here we are at the onset of winter. The days are shorter, the air colder, the sky grayer. Everything else is slowing down, and still we ask, no, we demand that our mind's eye see the roots and rocks and twists and turns, we argue with our mind to get out the door, to go faster, to go longer, to remind us to drink as we go along the trail.

Winter fights back with trails covered with leaves to skip through or with frosty mornings turning grassy trailsides into glistening diamonds that find us pausing just for a moment, then for a relaxing day or two or ten. A leisurely Saturday morning spent as a volunteer trail guide exposed a desire in me to learn about berries and bugs and fogs, bushes and trees and tides. A book about astronomy turned night runs into classrooms. Nature's mysteries unfolded with books about tides and berries, trees and birds, and the peoples of long ago.

For some of us it is finding the phrase "active rest" that permits a lessening of intensity. Active rest lets the body enjoy exercise without the jarring and jolting of running. It is not cross-training; cross-training is quite often at just as high a stress level as running. Active rest gives you time to relax, skip stones, or count waves, not count repetitions.

I have long used the migratory patterns of birds to decrease my intensity of training. An active-rest day was a good excuse to go to a wildlife refuge for a walk to see a different kind of ultramarathoner—birds of various sizes that fly hundreds or thousands of miles as the seasons shift.

There is a paradox in these southbound travelers. They are in a hurry to get to southern feeding grounds, but their passage foretells slower days for me, days of rest and rekindling of spirit while I await their return.

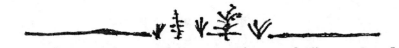

Why Did She Ask, "Is This a Metric Track?" on a Sunday Morning with No Clouds in the Sky?
or
A Short Discussion of Intervals on a Metric Track.

We run 5ks, 8ks, 10ks, 12ks, 15ks, 50ks, and so forth and so on—on the weekends. During the week we revert to the normal American mode and run miles (that is what our diary requires). Sounds innocent enough, doesn't it? But eventually in a person's running, regardless of the level, a tiny voice puts forth a question, "Could I run faster if I did some track work?" A quick reading session of the favorite running bible or perhaps a conversation with a running cohort ensues. A plan is formed. A Saturday or Sunday morning trip to a nearby high school track is scheduled. There, unbeknownst to most of us, a fiendish plot to confuse is unveiled. A lap is 400 meters? This is a metric track? Metric? A moment's thought provides the following:

- Almost everything we read is for quarter-mile, half-mile, or one-mile interval times, e.g., 90-second 440s, 7:30 miles, et cetera.
- Almost all track results you read about refer to 400 meters, 800 meters, this meter, that meter (except for a certain 26-mile, 385-yard event), and several other meters.

You look at the 400-meter track and you look at your 440-yard schedule and try to remember some handy conversion factor. Let's see—640 acres per square mile; no, 3.785 liters per gallon; no, one meter equals 3.2808 feet; no. Wait! Yes. Now using the quick mind all runners are known for, look what happens:

400 meters = 437 yards, 1 foot, 4 inches
800 meters = 874 yards, 2 feet, 8 inches
1600 meters = 1749 yards, 2 feet, 4 inches

or

400 meters is about 2 and a half yards short of a quarter mile,
800 meters is about 5 yards short of a half mile, and
1600 meters is about 10 yards short of a mile.

All of which raises other questions (curious little rascals, aren't we?). At the speed I am running, what adjustments should I make? Several choices are available. If you are doing quarter-mile intervals, every 172 laps, you need to run one more metric lap. Everyone else is running "short" laps, too. Therefore, you will all collapse 63.4990 yards short of a 10k finish line.

Do you do one 65-yard dash at the track each weekend and leave, knowing you, dare I say it, have an edge? Or do you do some more quick mental work and find out that for 440-yard intervals on a 400-meter track, you are missing out on a scant 0.4 seconds at a 75-second lap pace up to a whopping big 0.7 seconds at a 120-second lap pace? After all, it is only a 7-foot, 8-inch difference.

For the 880-yard intervals (15-foot, 4-inch difference), a 2-minute, 40-second pace is 0.9 seconds short of 880 yards, i.e., an 800-meter run of 4 minutes needs to carry on for another 1.4 seconds, at the same pace, to be 880 yards long. Four laps equals 1600 meters, which is 30 feet, 8 inches short of a mile. At 5-minute, 30-second pace, hang on for another 1.9 seconds; at 8-minute pace, struggle along for 2.8 more seconds and you have done the mile.

Confused yet? Ready to give up your interval workout? Well, don't, because, basically, a lap on a 400-meter track is so close to 440 yards that you can forget the difference.

Now, if we were closer to the equator...

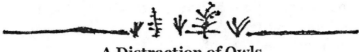

A Distraction of Owls

Hoo! Hu-hu-hu, hoo! Hoo!

Three great horned owls are just up the hill from me. Two males and a female, two quite near, one farther out in the field where the wind is bending the branches of the tall Douglas fir he has chosen for the evening.

Hoo! Hu-hu-hu, hoo! Hoo!

Sometimes we hear them just after sunset as we leave the bluffs and wind our way back to the car. We saw them as ghosts off to the right one evening, great wings as silent as the dusk they flew in making a mockery of our slow passage.

Some rare evenings, just as dusk arrives, as the reds and oranges and yellows are vying to be the last stroke of the sunset's brush; they pause on a tree for us to see—run slows to shuffle and then to walk, then to pause and pointing—sometimes.

But right now, as ten o'clock on this chilly and wind-laden evening draws near, they are just up the hill.

Hoo! Hu-hu-hu, hoo! Hoo!

Comes a deep voice from the upper limbs.

Hoo! Hu-hu-hu, hoo! Hoo!

Replies the lass from farther over in the madrone.

Sorry, I was going to write something about an inspiration to run, but I was sidetracked again.

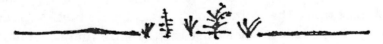

DNF, the Hardest Teacher of All

I have long thought that the two most difficult things to do in an ultramarathon are to:

1. Stop when you are in trouble, stay in the next aid station, eat, drink, sit for a few minutes to recover, and reevaluate before (if) continuing
2. Recognize you are not ready—the dreaded *Did Not Start* (a DNS)

Part of my reason for feeling this way for such a long time is my ability to ignore the obvious, usually simple solution while rationalizing my way into layer upon layer of complex "if this, then that" situations—most of which are not at all feasible.

My first year of running ultras was highlighted by those first months of easy finishes. I ran ten laps at Green Lake and a 3:50ish 50k was completed. An almost delusional ignorance about the physical challenge of running 31 miles allowed me to mistakenly believe that first ultramarathon, the veritable piece of cake, was typical of the effort needed. I was blissfully unaware of how well rested I was, how a certain social isolation actually provided an almost perfect taper. The Mudderfell Six-Hour was run a few weeks later, and I had my first taste of trails and mud and another success. Say now, these things aren't much of a challenge at all, are they? The warm and fuzzy blanket of blissful ignorance continued.

Then came magical March—the March with five weekends—weekends that would see me run that marathon, marathon, 20k, 50-miler, and close with a last marathon. The magic was dimmed by my "failure" at that inaugural 50-miler—a 7:35:10 time that I totally misunderstood. I had gone there sure that I could run fifty miles in about six hours, maybe six and a half if things went bad. The Internet did not exist then. The plethora of "do this and do that" sources that are so common now did not exist then (1986). All my running was alone. Even more unfortunate was the idea that I was alone with my misbegotten sense of how easy the 50k in January had been. I had no one to ask about right or wrong. As I caution newcomers nowadays when offering advice about their first ultramarathon, I can look back on there being no one to tell me how far away from reality I was. Things were just going so easy, so disarmingly easy.

A top-ten finish on a road 75k, another relatively fast 50k down near Placerville, California, and a sub-eight-hour 50-miler on trails only served to reinforce my newly found bulletproof status. I transferred some of the strength from the ultras to the track, covering ten miles in less than 64 minutes—wowzeewowzis—surely I must be good, maybe even bordering on great. Small children waved from windows as I passed. Finally I had a social agenda, and it was full. I was having trouble getting my head through the door. Then, with no fanfare at all, things came tumbling down.

Dum dee dum dee die—late July and the Headwaters 50-miler. Fifty miles of single-track trail alongside the Rogue River of Ohryghun, beeyooootiful—for a while anyway—then it turned to work—then it turned to a struggle. I was being passed by people with no right to pass ME. Ingrates. Run was replaced by shuffle. Finally, "trudge" entered my running vocabulary. It didn't come in quietly, it came in accompanied by cramps, nausea, and strange walking patterns, and my mind, never a model of stability anyway, went south with the current of the river. I dropped at the 46-mile aid station. The almost cryptic diary entry reads:

> Disaster—finally a DNF—dehyd—not enough to eat-mind shot-total breakdown of everything-could not even think clearly enough to figure out what I needed to do to correct things-mental disaster, and that led to a physical breakdown at the last aid station.

Woe is me. I felt like an intruder at the postrace dinner. Our tent was strangely silent that night. As we drove home the next day, the analysis started—did this, didn't do that, hmmm, could have done that, why did we try that (I use "we" so I can blame it on anyone but me—remember, I had not made any mistakes to learn from so far this year). Yes, I should have done more single track leading up, more of this, more of that...after a while as we added, discarded, adjusted, rewrote, revised, re-revised...there didn't seem to be anything that couldn't be fixed (I did find 632 things Kathy did wrong while crewing—that helped).

A few of the items that I felt contributed to the DNF, in no particular order, because other than needing a lesson in humility, no single mistake seemed any more important than another:

- Poor packing—I did not pack the night before. Ended up just throwing things in the car. The little, nagging annoyances start because I can't find things as we go. The start of nothing being quite "right."
- Food—we normally fix a humongous pasta salad to eat on the day before an ultramarathon, especially if it is within one day's driving distance as the HW 50 was. This time we did not. We stopped at this deli and that sandwich place, this grocery store and that convenience mart, arriving at the campsite totally bloated from junk eating.
- Shoes—poor packing comes calling again. My preferred shoes are not in the car—argh? becomes **arrggghhhh!!!!*^!^#@*@!!!**
- Changing shoes—at the river crossing, also a highway crossing, and Kathy was there. She asked if I wanted to change shoes. I looked around—five or six steps in the water, maybe knee-deep, other runners are grabbing shoes to change to, uh, er—sure. Kathy put a pair of shoes in a bag for me to carry across (put wet shoes in bag, throw bag back to her). This seemed innocent enough. I got across, took off shoes and wet socks, put on dry socks, put on shoes, and—the second **arrggghhhh!!!!*^!^#@*@!!!** of the day—my oldest, most beat-up pair of shoes, the work-in-the-yard shoes, are in the bag, sigh and sniff. I pull on the shoes and head on down the

trail. The height of this silliness (not remembered at an opportune time) is that I am from Olympia, Washington. I belonged to the Rain Runners Running Club. We run in the rain, the mud, the ankle-deep wet stuff. We run in it for weeks at a time. I have never changed to dry shoes during a run before! Why now? This thought did not surface until the next day. We were many miles up the highway when Kathy quietly asked why I changed shoes. Uh, well, everyone else (there were four or five of us crossing the river at the same time) was doing it. Sheep syndrome? Big sigh.

- Hurrying—it would be years before I would understand effort was much more important than pace. Raw strength and bullheadedness got me through many miles, more miles than my inexperience with trails warranted. There is a difference between running fast and hurrying. Hurrying is a form of fast but inefficient and wasteful movement. Hurrying is running while tense. Hurrying is good while getting from first base to second base, not so good when you have hours to go. I was several runs away from being comfortable on the trails, several runs away from comfortably racing on the trails. The only thing I was hurrying to was the aid station I would not leave as a runner.

- Eating and drinking—hurrying also meant I did not pay attention to eating and drinking along the trail. I wasn't emptying bottles between aid stations. I barely grabbed a mouthful of food. In retrospect it was as if I wanted to see how soon I could hit fully depleted.

- The rest week that wasn't—the previous week should have been a rest week, this being a trail 50-mile race (not a run but a race) and all that it entailed. Monday (five days before DNF day) I found some stairs that went from a building next to the lake (doesn't matter what lake) up the hillside to a parking lot—steep stairs, but wide steps and not overly worn concrete construction. They had always been there but were suddenly visible because of some brush removal. I went over—no gate, no "get away from here" signs. I walked up them counting the steps, 148, hmmm. I ran back down them, then back up, then down again. All sorts of benefits from this new drill went through my head—strength from going up, agility from doing a quick-step down. I did three more round trips that afternoon and then went on around the lake and back home. The next day I went back to my new, secret hill-work station. I ran up the stairs, did what felt like a quarter-mile recovery jog around the big parking lot, zipped down the stairs, did a recovery loop—do you remember where I mentioned "raw strength and bullheadedness" earlier? I thought about having done five round trips the day before and decided I would try to do ten today, and I did. The sixth trip was uncomfortable. The seventh crossed from comfort to pain. The last three were only done because there was a memory of you-can-do-one-more deeply implanted from many years of football practices. I could not run home. I could barely jog. The 50-miler only four days away did not even cross my mind.

- Unable to stop/regroup/go—the six ultramarathons I had done in the first half of the year had not required anything more analytical than a casual glance at a water bottle, maybe relacing a shoe, grabbing a few cookies, a handful of this or that as I paused at an aid station—nothing needing thought. As I ran alongside the river I was not aware of the down-hill path all the demons were riding and never thought they would take me along. I doubt I was aware of how poorly I was doing. I was still probably in the upper fourth of the field but did not know it. I had run alone most of the time. There was no one along to evaluate me. In the time since the last aid station, I had paused because of cramps in my calves, noticed my arms were incredibly heavy, and I actually ran into a tree because I did not turn soon enough. That should have told me something. It did not. When I pulled into the aid station, if I had known to stop, eat and drink, wait a few minutes, eat and drink some more, wait a few minutes, and evaluate, I probably could have regrouped and left, maybe not in the best of spirits but most certainly several levels above death march. But I did not know to stop, be honest with myself, pause to regroup—instead I found one last mistake to make. I would...

- Externalizing the negative—when I stopped at that last aid station, the two volunteers smiled. Good. One then looked at me and asked, "Are you okay?" Oops. Grabbing at the straw, I quickly said, "No. No, I am not." I then sat down in one of the chairs. There was one last emotional convulsion as the last demons abandoned ship and the mental defeat joined the physical. All the stuff that had been held under a tight control surfaced. Fingers cramped from carrying a bottle. I started to turn to accept a cup from one of the volunteers and my neck locked. I looked down at my legs as both quadriceps locked. Hmmm, I can't turn my head, can't get up, sure glad I don't need to pee. (I didn't need to pee because I was seriously dehydrated.) Later, as we analyzed all the little things along the trail, one of the "don't ever do this again" items now understood was "Do not ever say aloud anything negative while still on the course." You can slow from run to jog to shuffle to trudge, but you can keep going without saying for all to hear, "No, I am not okay." Once you say that, you are at the bottom, and if you don't know about stop/regroup/go, you are done for the day.

There were other things that helped ensure the defeat, but they might not have become visible if the primary ones I have listed had not happened. It was about 300 miles home. It was 300 miles of "what if" or "maybe this" or "could you have" and so forth. The analysis of a DNF requires a person to be honest with oneself if there is any intention of continuing the journey to becoming an ultramarathoner.

The "healing" was helped considerably on Monday when I was doing an easy recovery run around the lake in Olympia. The woman I was running with asked if I ever had any problems with my running. She knew of no bad stories from me, only that another trip out of town meant another T-shirt or trophy. Immediately sensing a source of sympathy and attention, I replied, "Karen, I just DNFed. I dropped at the 46-mile point of the Headwaters 50."

Pause. Pause to turn around and notice Karen had stopped and was sort of laughing. Karen, not being aware of the need for sympathy, empathy, and any other available 'pathies, laughed and said, "John, there are so very few people that even try what you do, let alone run 40-something miles before stopping."

Oh.

Strange, someone with no knowledge of ultras uttered the words that put the total defeat in perspective, and things got better. Even in our defeats we have tried to do things most would shy away from, we have looked behind all three doors, faced whatever was there, known and unknown, and continued to try. As we tasted the bitterness of defeat that comes with trying, we got to know ourselves a little bit better. It may not seem like much of a reward at the time you sit down, not to get back up, but it is—and we will try again.

As time passed, the number of DNFs increased. At the time of my writing this, the chronological list and a brief why is:

- Headwaters 50-miler, trail, July 1986—above
- A Winter Run 50k, paved 5k laps, January 1987—dropped at 24.8 miles. My wife had knee surgery just a few days before. She assured me all was well and I should get myself on up

the road to Green Lake. I went and was having a good run (on schedule for a 3:45ish effort). John Bandur and I were running and talking. He was getting ready for his Grand Slam year—only one person had done that. I was just sort of rambling along during the eighth lap when someone asked about Kathy. I said she was at home on the couch, recent knee surgery, and so forth. I paused at the aid station at the end of the lap, thought about her being home alone, told the RD I was done for the day, and went home—no regrets.

- SOB 50k, trail, July 2000—dropped at 26.1 miles. A day with a not-so-well-behaved sweep. Kathy and I were training to run the Leadville Trail 100 *together.* We had taken the early start and were quite happy with how the run was going when the sweep caught up with us. Instead of the usual banter about running, she almost immediately started making comments about hurrying along, need to get on down the trail, need to get...uh, faster? When we got to the aid station, Kathy said let's drop. What? She had become hyperconscious of the sweep wanting us to move along, never liking to inconvenience anyone, and now she just wanted off the trail and "out of everyone's way." We were well within the 8-hour cutoff.

- Leadville Trail 100, August 2000—dropped at May Queen outbound (13.5 miles). We were attempting to run the LT100 together. The training had been done and had built the confidence as much as was possible. On the trip from Corvallis, Oregon, to Leadville, Colorado, we talked of the one thing that would stop us. Mud. Kathy's artificial hip does not like the pulling action of muddy trails. There is only one place where the trail can get muddy enough to be a problem, the "Boulevard." We ignored those thoughts until the thunder boomed and woke us at about one o'clock in the morning, three hours before the start of the run. Rain. Torrentially hard rain. A couple of hours later we slowly got dressed and walked to the start under a mostly starry sky. It is just over a mile to the "Boulevard"—the wide ore-truck haul road was a mess. We wandered from one side to the other and back again trying to find footing that did not pull at our shoes. The 13.5 miles to May Queen required the fastest pace of all the LT100 sections. The last straw was the glow-stick vandalism. Someone had moved some of the glow sticks, and we overshot the power-line climb to the trail around Turquoise Lake. Each straw added its grains of sand to the hourglass of cutoff time. Somewhere past Tabor boat ramp the hourglass tipped over. Dan Baglione was both kind and gracious when he snipped off the bracelets at the May Queen parking lot.

- Cascade Crest Classic 100 (CCC100), trail, August 2002— dropped at Blowout aid station (18 miles). What, were I possessed of any good sense at all, should have been a Did Not Start, the worst of all possible worlds, the dreaded, to be avoided at all costs DNS. There I stood at the starting line for the Cascade Crest Classic 100 Mile Endurance Run on a warm August morning in 2002. I looked down at my ankles. For the first time in many years, both of them were taped.

I twisted, rolled, sprained, or some other uselessly descriptive word my left ankle in early March. I dutifully did strengthening exercises and started taping the ankle before heading out each day. The imbalance of running with one injured ankle quit being a problem a few weeks later when I did whatever I did to the left ankle to my right ankle. Now I could limp symmetrically. I did what rehab I could fit into the running schedule that a 100-miler demands. Those injuries began a period of decline, a fight for fitness.

The next phase of decline came in mid-May when I caught a root with my right foot. The stylistic grace of a carefully choreographed Broadway musical was strangely absent as I pushed hard trying to accelerate and regain balance to avoid a face-plant. The acute pain from an ice pick being inserted into my right hamstring told me I might have won the balance war, but I had sacrificed a muscle tear in so doing. It was four miles of limping home on a day gone sour.

I taped the ankles and wrapped the right thigh. I used every ointment known to man and, as time passed, one known to horses, too, DMSO. There are jokes about horseback riders taking better care of their horses during endurance events than we do of ourselves. They are, for the most part, true. My right hamstring kept a nice red hue as I applied DMSO before each run. The five-day run week gave my leg two days, Monday and Friday, to recover. As May turned to June I felt better. I needed to feel better as I was pacing at Western States 100 Mile Endurance Run. I needed to not only feel better, I needed to believe I was better. The belief part, fragile in the best of times, was a challenge.

Pacing is a patience thing, a mental-alertness-for-the-other-person thing. It would not need speed, relatively speaking. At Western that year, we were crewing and pacing. I had picked Linda Samet up at Foresthill. We had run all through the night. We were across Highway 49 and doing okay...when I caught a root with my right toe. I have to give credit to Linda for not looking around to see why I yelled. Right after the "ummnnph" came, I yelled, "Run!" I like to think it was my inner-pacer self coming to life and protecting my runner from injury (me falling over her). With ninety-five or so miles on her legs, she sprinted the needed few steps to let me have room to regain my balance, all done with no footprints on her back. She asked if I was okay, and I said yes. I was okay, but only because I was somewhat accustomed to having an ice pick stuck in my legs at some point or another.

The hamstring had been reaggravated. I was going to need to buy more DMSO.

A few weeks later at the Siskiyou Out Back 50k (SOB50k), what was intended to be an easy long run with aid stations fell apart. It was one of those "best-laid plans of mice and men" things. In the early morning sun as the entrants assembled, I noticed a lot of beards. Generally, that is not a bad thing, but most of the beards were gray, or gray with white. The place was full of old guys. I had been fifth overall here in 1999; surely three years wouldn't make that much difference, would it? The easy run turned into a toe-slightly-on-the-gas-pedal all the way through. It was not a top-ten-overall thing, but I did lead the old guys to the finish line. It was a sweet victory and did not become bittersweet until we were halfway home. We had stopped at a rest area, and as I swung around to get out of the car after sitting for a couple of hours, I felt the twinge. Ratz? But this time, the ice pick was kept in its scabbard. The twinge was just a twinge, nothing more, and somewhere the sun was shining bright. I held that thought all the way home.

August finally arrived. We drove to the CCC100 area on Thursday, looking forward to a day or two just relaxing in a campground. Friday afternoon we drove up to French Cabin, the one part of the course we had not seen. It was a beautiful place, one of our rewards for running trails. It also was a place full of the world's biggest horseflies (from a dictionary: "the female of which is a bloodsucker and inflicts painful bites on horses and other mammals."). It was the "other mammals" part that would be of interest. Within thirty minutes my right arm was about the same size as my right leg and I could no longer bend it at the elbow. This was disturbing. We stopped at a waterfall and I held my arm under the cold water. That helped. I took some Benadryl or whatever we had in the first-aid bag. The swelling in the left arm was barely noticeable. The right arm was getting a lot better. We drove back to the campground. By late evening the swelling in both arms was noticeable but not ugly or anything serious looking.

The next morning I taped both ankles, swabbed the right hamstring with DMSO, and took some more Benadryl. I was good to go, ya know, like wow—let's go run...okay, not quite brimming with confidence, maybe not tanned, fit, and ready, but a one out of three success rate would get a big-bucks contract in baseball, right? And besides, I am an ultrarunner. Right? It's all going to come together a few miles down the course, right?

I would drop at Blowout, about eighteen miles in. If the volunteer experience the DNF turned into had not been so enjoyable, it would have simply been another failure. My wish that I had recognized that a DNS would have been the correct thing to do was overshadowed by how well the weekend went after I DNFed. Some good came of starting on a bad day, but, standing there at the starting line I had no idea we would stay as badly needed volunteers.

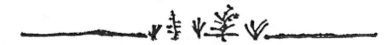

Knowing Before Learning

When I started running trails and ultramarathons, I knew no one else who ran beyond the marathon and certainly no one else who ran trails. I would run for hours on the trails of Capitol Forest seeing only horseback riders, the occasional dirt-bike rider, and, the rarity of those days, a mountain biker or two. I could run in the blind ignorance of not understanding effort, hills, or hydration. I just ran up the hills until muscles locked or I tripped over my tongue as I gasped for breath on the five-mile climb to Wedekind or up the backside of Rock Candy Mountain—another climb that went on forever with no soda-water fountain awaiting.

In those first months and miles and miles on the trails and in the forest I called home, I did not meet another runner. The variety of surfaces—a paved road here and there crossing from one highway to another, the hard gravel roads the log trucks roared up and down, leaving me coughing in their rooster tails of dust, and the maze of horse trails—all served to build something I didn't know I needed: a base. The things I didn't know led to some interesting last few miles of some runs. Left to myself I would occasionally learn from my mistakes on their first occurrences. More often than not, I would bunch several things together and correct the wrong ones, leaving myself open to struggling down a hillside trail back to the car, once more wondering what went wrong.

As time passed and conversations took place in Placerville and Wartrace, Wenatchee and Aptos, or alongside the Rogue and Deschutes rivers, my ignorance was slowly replaced with bits and pieces of conversations snatched from the miles in a forest or along a road many miles removed from the evergreen forests of Washington. The sharing of information and knowledge about how to get on down the trail, how to put in the miles needed to have good runs, and how to enjoy endurance running was a gift from the many runners I met (that gift, I am happy to report these many years later, continues to be an intrinsic part of the ultrarunning community). The leaps and bounds of my journey often brought forth an old sentence, old both in time and in my memory but still appropriate, about how much I have enjoyed the experience and knowledge of others to help me along the way, "We are like dwarfs standing [or sitting] upon the shoulders of giants, and so able to see more and see farther than the ancients," (Bernard of Chartres, circa 1130).

Those early years of ignorance (and sharing information) came back to me today in the first mile or so of the run. As I was just about to leave the trailhead, someone was getting out of his pickup and hollered over, "Do you know these trails?" "Yes," I replied. "Do you mind if I run with you? I've never been here before and I have never run on trails." Well, he looked harmless and it was a beautiful fall day, why not? "Sure, c'mon along," I smiled and replied, thinking about how different it would be to run with someone.

I looked at him—obviously new shoes (when did I last have a pair of shoes that clean looking?), fit and cheerful looking, great big GPS thingie on his wrist, cocker spaniel eagerness in his eyes—why had I said yes? We started down the trail. For the first mile the Kettles Trail, the spine of our local trail system, is a one-lane gravel road with lesser trails branching off along the way. He was kind enough to not scuffle his feet as he altered pace to run with me instead of a few feet in front (and constantly pulling away). He lasted about a quarter mile before the questions started.

Do you always have a bottle with you? Are my trail shoes good enough for these trails? How many miles a day do you run? Is a backpack better than a vest? What is the longest run you've ever done? Do you run every day? How fast should I run?

I answered in my standard there-are-no-yes/no-answers format, rambling on about the whys and wherefores of the answers. He was from Alabama. As I tried to shape some of the answers for the heat and humidity of running in the South compared to our above-60°-is-hot environment, his questions that interrupted my answers showed he was listening with more than just passing curiosity. Would the trails be different in the South? Sure. Why? The running conversation switched to geology and geography. The geology lecture was interrupted by a large flock of passing birds—I muttered something about southbound travelers from way far north of us and this being the time of year phenology becomes as much a part of my running as what I wear, important enough to sometimes affect the decision of routes. Phenology? Yes, the science of nature's changes with the seasons. I enjoy knowing what is changing or who is passing through as the season turns. He sort of scrunched up his nose at this nonrunning intrusion and returned to questions about running on trails, wanting to know why my pace varied so much. As we worked our way up Cedar Grove, I rambled on about pace versus effort and he interrupted with how long would he have to run before he knew which effort level was equal to what pace? A week? Two weeks? Later this afternoon?

As each answer led to new questions, the whole conversation took on a recursive quality that I feared would make the end of the run a blur of confusion. I was thinking about that—one ear open for his next question—and asked him how much longer he wanted to run. He responded, appropriately enough, with, "How long should I run?" Aha? Something I know something about. "You run as long as you want to; want to, not need to." "Won't I need to run a certain amount if I am training for one of these ultramarathons?" Uh-oh. It is his first trail run, and already ultras have crept into the conversation. My answer? No, not a certain amount because...because... hmm...because some of this stuff is to be discovered along the way, not learned as if from a book, especially not a speed-reading book. It is the learning that is important at the end of the day, not the reading. The learning takes time and cannot be hurried by adding miles to a day's run as if that will accelerate the building of your foundation for running—not if you want the running to last through the years.

Another saying, one which I will never memorize in its original form, came to mind, "non cupidus cognoscendi quae rara miraque sunt" (*The Golden Ass*, Book Two, by Apuleius) which roughly translates to "too great a desire to know..."

He wanted to know before he learned, but learning takes time.

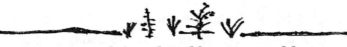

Fitness Reclaimed, Self-Image Problems

I had wanted to run without thinking of the dancing hippos in *Fantasia* just once before the leaves started falling and covering the trails. The hope was born of one good week where some sort of relaxation was there; some long-forgotten sense of lightness seemed to beckon. Then, for some reason I decided to abandon the trails and use a block of my highly structured training for speed work.

Why this thought of change made sense I do not know, but the next day I headed for the track with a fully visualized recall of an article by the late George A. Sheehan wherein he described the need to run a track workout so hard that collapsing on the infield grass at the end of each lap was the goal. He wanted to get to the end of each lap with nothing left. I did the first several laps with a good effort, picking it up through those last few yards, but they did not end with the jelly-legged collapse that I could recall. "*Push*," whispered an inner voice. I am. "*Push harder,*" it repeated.

Okay, I'd start at the head of the straight. I could push around the second curve better than finishing on the straight. Okay. Go. Oh boy, here we go. One last lap. Keep the back straight. Look ahead. No rocks or roots to worry about—relax and run; don't flail, move the arms smoothly. Actually it went smoother than I thought it would. It wasn't until midway through the last turn that I could feel— what was it we used to say? Ah yes, about halfway through the last turn the bear climbed on, but it was supposed to, and that was good. I could even glance at where I had put the water bottle to mark the end of all-out-assault number one. Three-quarters around and the bear, thinking the additional weight was not enough, raked its claws across my calves—no friendly park bear this one, this one wanted to inflict pain. Suck it up, sweetie, you're in the relay-exchange zone— the end is near. Tell the bear to find its own way home. My left foot brushed the inside rail, balance went away in those last three steps, and all the grand and glorious memories of sliding across the grass of the end zone came back—except I was not wearing a football uniform. I collected grass burns for half the width of the end zone, finally stopped sliding, then stopped wheezing, and noticed how wonderfully blue the sky was. I'll just lay here I thought. It seemed like something a person should do, just lay there on the grass for a while, especially since I had somehow stopped close enough to my water bottle to reach it. It was, if you will, a reward for my effort. *I'll just lay here.*

"Are you okay?" I heard the words, but since I was alone at the track I did not even raise my head to see who was talking. "Hey! Mister! Are you okay? Mom!" Hmmm, the voice seemed closer, sounded concerned. Was he talking to me? I raised my head and looked in the direction of the voice. A small boy and his mother were about ten yards away, looking at me. Uh-oh. I sat up. "Are you okay?" Yes. "What are you doing?" I was seeing how fast I could run laps. "Why?" Why indeed? It's a long story. I convinced them I was okay, and they continued on to the playground. I gathered up my stuff, got on my bicycle, and pedaled home, telling myself they meant well and there was nothing to be concerned with—trouble is I am barely getting comfortable with running or thinking of myself as a runner again. My mind's eye again offers an uncomfortable view— a view through a very fragile pane of glass from far outside.

The next day I was back at the trailhead, once again seeking the solitude of the trails. At the trailhead I saw someone I had not seen since before we went to North Dakota. He said he thought he had seen me out running a few days earlier. I barely heard his next few words. The idea that someone saw me on the trails and thought what I was doing was running meant I must be making some prog-ress. The mind's eye can bring us both grief and joy. The memory of how effortless running was conflicts with the actuality of how dif-ficult it is. These little stumbling blocks can cause the journey from lost fitness back to even the lowest foundations to bring forth moments of embarrassment and the blankness of despair—rebuilding is hard work, not fun at all when plans fall apart so easily.

The original plan was to regain fitness, enter some turn-of-the-season ultra, and enjoy the company of old friends before winter. The plan fell apart after reality came calling in the form of a difficult 18 (*paltry* said the old voice) miles of trails. I found easy excuses—the rocks were wet from the morning's fog (should have waited until the dryness of afternoon), the amount of ups and downs was too much, too soon (I had laughed about the loop having *only* 3700 feet of change), I should have stayed on the forestry roads instead of the trails (just because I fell and bloodied a knee doesn't mean I need the easiness of smoother surfaces), the list of should haves, would haves, and could haves seemed remarkably like the topics of the trip home after a DNF.

DNFs restrict the mind to the anger and despair of negatives and bring the three Rs into play—revenge, retribution, or redemption. I sat there eating a sandwich, pondering revenge. How soon could I run this route again? I took a sip of chocolate milk. How can I extract revenge from those hillsides? I finished the sandwich. Do I take retribution on the same route? If I could leave the dancing hippos behind—my mind's eye sees what my memory wants it to see.

As I finished cleaning the blood and dirt off the scraped knee I could hear the sound of footsteps and running on the trail. Two people slowed as they came into view. The woman had a bloodied knee. The man's shirt and arms were dirty from a roll or two down the trail. They looked at me. She laughed, pointed at her knee, then at mine. "We have a matched pair, don't we? It was ugly out there today, wasn't it?" Yes. Yes, it was. Maybe I hadn't done so poorly. The three Rs were banished, the mind's eye blinked and memories clouded over, the plan resurfaced.

Development

This is something I wrote in response to the beauty of a ground-clearing, tree-removing, road-building development of stick-frame housing on the northerly side of 29th Street NW in Corvallis, Oregon—on the hillside just below Chip Ross City Park, a hillside I had run up many a time.

Some of the trails are going away:

I knew it was coming. They had put up the "Public Hearing" signs.

This afternoon as I start the walk/jog/shuffle through the field
that leads to the trail
that leads to the hill
that leads to the forest—
Ratz!
A barrier has been put up.
It is part of the erosion control, the "'scuse us while we dig up everything," make-believe erosion-control system.
The long-awaited subdivision is coming.
I have been spoiled by the nearness, both emotionally and physically, of the trails and the forests.

The subdivision is coming, and some of the trails are going away.
It was a place of steep ups and downs,
boggy spots and muddy springs,
thorns and poison oak,
frogs, rabbits, squirrels,
and one hawk that used to scare me half to death with its "screeeeee"
as the sun cracked the nearby hillside during my morning runs.

It's just a couple of hundred acres that will soon be crosshatched
with pavement and houses.
It will drain better.
The houses will all be code compliant and properly inspected,
the plants and lawns will all be nicely watered and manicured,
but
they are ugly,
and
some of the trails are going away.

Buggy Tracks and Trails

Thursday morning is when some of the local mothers meet and take
their offspring of various sizes and shapes, all carefully stuffed into
a buggy of some sort, for a walk on some of the trails in the Kettles/
Fort Ebey area. The fewest moms with buggies I have seen was two
or three. The most was about a dozen—which seems like about a
hundred and seventy-four if you are passing them.

Seeing them getting ready to leave the trailhead, I am reminded
of watching Ward Bond, one hand raised, somewhat impatiently getting ready to say, "Wagons ho...". The equipment varies with the
seasons and the buggy. The first time I saw the gathering I just
noticed them in the parking lot, not close enough to see enough to
generate curiosity. It was a short-run morning; work would beckon
at (Wow! An adult bald eagle just landed on the porch rail. One
large pane of glass and about fifteen feet separate us. How do I
ask it to turn around so it is looking at me instead of out at Penn
Cove?) noon, and as I was on the last mile back out to the trailhead,
I started passing them.

As with any group doing something that requires equipment,
there were all sorts and sizes, colors and shapes of buggies. The

"amateurs" had the hard-to-push buggies with narrow, solid-core, six-inch wheels—what I would have thought of as a stroller. There were a few with larger air-filled tires and even fewer of the three-wheelers—the buggies designed for runners. I ran along, weaving from one side to the other of the single-lane gravel road that serves as the trail for the last mile, exchanging hellos and smiles on that warm, sunny morning.

Being somewhat a creature of habit, I saw them again the following Thursday; this time they were a short way down the trail as I started passing them. As I was passing the leaders, one of the trio pushing the three-wheelers suddenly said, "Ask him." I slowed. What? Do you run here often? Yes. Do you know these trails? Yes. Where can we get a map that shows which trails we can take the buggies on?

Do you have one of the Kettles/Fort Ebey trail maps? Yes, but the trails vary so much. We need to turn back frequently. Oh. I pulled my fanny pack around to the front, unzipped the pouch, and took out a highlighter. Okay—the reason I have a (eagle just flew away, good, really hard to do this typing stuff with it perched on the rail like that) highlighter in my fanny pack is because these 28 miles of trails are in the park I work in part of the time. I frequently need to give directions and have learned that it is almost impossible to tell someone how to get somewhere. There are too many junctions, twists, and turns along the way. It is easier to mark up a map. So, it turned out to be something I put in the pouch.

I thought a bit on this trail and that, finally marked out three or four trails that were a bit wider, not quite as hilly, and still got to the bluff in a place or two, and continued off on my run. I was on a longer run that day and did not see the buggy pushers again, noting an empty parking lot as I headed for home. My schedule changed, and that was the last I saw of the buggy people for a few weeks until one afternoon...

A mile or so in, just a little way after the single-lane gravel road narrows to a wide dirt trail, I met a young woman, not one I recalled from the Thursday morning regulars, pushing one of those three-wheel buggies. The professional-grade type, big wheels, brakes, and a carefully bundled someone somewhere inside all those blankets—three, maybe four tiny fingers was all I saw. I was on a downhill section of trail when our meeting took place, and I stepped aside so she wouldn't have to break her climbing rhythm.

I noticed the brace on one knee, the slight limp, even the difference in musculature of her legs. I also noticed the bright smile and eyes and her hello. I helloed back, watching her push the buggy on over the rise and around the turn. The thought of how seldom I see mom and buggy even this short distance off the gravel passed through my mind—like most thoughts, it fled. I wandered here and there, checking for new buds in one kettle, looking for harlequins from one spot on the bluff, heading up—hmmm, tracks? Buggy tracks. Daniel Boone I am not, but I can spot buggy tracks. Her?

How long had I been seeing those tracks? I backtracked to the last junction. They came from Grancy's, turned up Cedar Grove. I returned to running, sort of; part of my mind was elsewhere again—she pushed that thing through here? I only glanced at the tracks. There was no place she could go, just on up and up and around, unless she turned back, but even I could see there was only one set of tracks.

I passed the Old Men of Cedar Grove. They were as silent as always about who had passed. There was not even a raven to help me that day. I stopped at bluff's edge to check for whales, saw none; noted that one group of rhodies is already turning its darker green for spring. Spring? It was still winter! Yes, but we were on the "warm" side of the island, and there were all these little spots of botanical anomalies. Tracks were still there. Whoever was hidden in the blankets was getting rocked and rolled and bounced along the way. Cedar Grove is not very wide. Would they turn right to Kettle's Trail and become the strangers I saw an hour or so ago?

Yup. Wow. I am always proud to get through Cedar Hollow and Cedar Grove without falling, without more than one pause to suck air on one of our few hills—my mind started playing with going through there with that buggy in front of me. Could I run here while pushing...?

Nope, not even on a dare.

Wow?

Wow!

Keep Going Out There

I used to wait for darkness so the prying eyes behind windows could not see me shuffling along—knowing full well that if I turned my head quickly enough I could see the curtains moving as fingers let go, the curtain hiding another watcher snickering at me from behind a window.

As ever-baggier clothes became popular, I found clothes big enough to hide me, almost big enough to let me go outside in the daylight, certainly big enough I could go out at dusk.

I found a bike path separated from the highway by a row of bushes. I could use it to get to and from the trails, almost hidden as I worked my way back to the "me" that was a runner from the "me" that was not.

I knew which trails I could not run without stopping, without being beaten down again, but I slowly found ones I could continue forward on, slowing only slightly but still working my way along at good effort. I knew if I went left, left, right, left, straight, and then left I had a route that I could run without stopping for almost an hour. An hour, what a victory that day was. Now I could look at the hilly part of the park.

It took months, months of fighting the memory of long-gone nimble feet and flying legs to find my space out there again. It seemed like a lifetime passed looking for the will to run before the desire to go out overrode the fear of looking like I did not belong, was not a "real" runner, and had no "right" to be out there. But time passed and the trails became just as much mine as his or hers or theirs.

Don't ever think everyone out there has always been fit and fast and slim and faced no battles getting there.

Just keep going out there.

Believe in yourself and keep going out there.

Always keep going out there.

Running or Racing—a Comparative Analysis

Runners...	Racers...
stop to look at the trees as they pass by.	ricochet off trees as they zoom across the landscape.
worry about their flash-light batteries lasting.	get to the finish line before dark.
enjoy the aid stations.	sometimes pass through before the aid stations are set up.
take naps in tents at aid stations.	take naps as they wait at the finish line.
watch flowers open-ing in the morning sun.	pass through in the pre-dawn darkness.
worry about cutoff times.	worry about course or age-group records.
write next-of-kin informa-tion on their wristbands.	write split times on their wristbands.

Runners...	Racers...
wonder if there will be any beer at the aid stations.	wonder what kind of electrolyte-replacement drinks will be at the aid stations
get a hamburger as they pass through towns.	slap down one more bit of tofu-enriched yoghurt, whey, and scampi granola.
talk to local farmers as they pass by.	scare chickens, cows, and small children.
are relieved to hear someone approaching from behind.	feel the pressure of someone approaching from behind.
seldom get lost as they follow those hundreds of sets of footprints	worry about course markings (color, context, intent, malcontent, bent...).
admire the view as they amble on across the landscape.	are vaguely aware of something off to the right—or was it left?
know the names of the "sweep" at 17 different events in 8 counties and 3 states.	drop if more than 17 minutes behind predicted time for the day.
say, "Thank you. Yes, I do believe I'll have another brownie," just before being pushed out of the aid station.	smile and say, "Thank you," over their shoulders as they head for home.
have been seen grabbing trees, cactus, and other runners to keep from careening off the course on a switchback.	make it look so easy, seldom stirring up dust or even disturbing the llamas.
have out-of-body experiences as the day goes by and the finish line recedes in the afternoon sun.	have been heard to wonder admiringly about how the rest of us cope with being out there so long.
sometimes curse day-of-race registration.	follow a plan conceived months ago.
have long, involved conversations with others as they pass or get passed.	surface long enough for a smile and an often monosyllabic response. '
have teddy bears, dragons, and other karma caretakers of the foray jangling from their fanny packs, CamelBaks...	have a hand bottle.

Runners...	Racers...
have been seen in cotton T-shirts.	have all that super-neato logo stuff.
slay inner dragons on good days.	slay inner dragons on good days.
compete in their time, in their style, on their terms...	compete in their time, in their style, on their terms...
Sweet?	Sweet?
Sweet!	*Sweet!*

Some Odds and Ends on Maintaining Confidence and Good Spirits along the Trail
or
The Usual Getting-to-the-Finish-Line Drivel

Believe in yourself—nothing else will get you to the finish line.

Decide before you start what will stop you—if that doesn't happen, you continue to run.

Are you racing or running? Do you have a specific time goal (sub-24-hour, big buckle, age group) or simply running to finish? Don't let the initial goal be etched in stone. Something may go wrong out there—adjustments will need to be made as the day unfolds. Evaluate, adjust, and keep going.

Run your plan. Stay within your realm. Don't feel bad if someone passes you. Don't chortle with glee if you pass someone. Keep a sense of what you are about. Keep pressing on, maybe it will be one of those good days when you pick it up and then keep on picking it up.

Have faith in walking. Walk when you need to or when you want to (hopefully not often), but walk with purpose...no trudging...no survival shuffle...keep a good mind-set and walk with a purpose. Smile and enjoy what you are passing through.

Be sure your crew (if you have one—a crew is not a necessity) understands that you might go through a transition from nice person to "not so nice" person. Have a talk with them about the need to kick your butt back out on the course. Sympathy may exist, but not to the extent of shortchanging the runner.

Problems? Is it a problem or just an inconvenience? Decide which. Find a solution for the problem. Block out the inconvenience; it will pass.

Food: Stick with the safest food there is at the aid stations. If necessary, use as much of your own stuff as you can. Don't be inflexible about things not being perfect. Be flexible and adapt to the day as you go.

Equipment: If some equipment change comes into your head, ask yourself is it a need or a want? If it is a need, solve it at the next crew or drop-bag point. If it is a want and can't be fixed fairly easily, drop the thought—keep running.

Throwing up, vomiting, and coughing the cookies: It may happen even if it has never happened before. It is not fatal. It is an inconvenience. You will probably need more water between the point it happens and the next aid station (vomiting can be dehydrating). Drink more. Get some form of electrolyte-replacement stuff. Stay at the next aid station long enough to drink and eat more. Your body is now low on fuel and water. You must pay attention to eating more. You can restore the liquids fairly quickly, but you must eat every chance you get. Oh yeah, try not to throw up on anyone.

Don't stop. Keep moving. Somewhere along the way, emotional low points will come; don't stop for them. Continued movement will bring you back around. Don't sit in those chairs at the aid stations unless you really need to. Think about how far you have come.

Encourage other runners. Smiles and laughter will help others. Helping others will help you.

Smile and joke with the aid station folks. Say thank you to the volunteers. They will help you all through the day and night and... be good to them. They are a great source of energy—those people who donate all that time to get us through our little escapades on the trails.

Do not externalize negatives. No comments like, "Hot out here, ain't it?" or "This is a long hill, eh?" Just believe in the person that signed the entry blank. Remember all that training, all those folks you ran with throughout the winter, spring, and summer that got you so strong.

Properly Distorted Race Reporting

A few summers ago my wife and I participated in the first Staircase to Dosewallips Trail Run, a 38-mile crossing of part of the Olympic Mountains on the Olympic Peninsula in the state of Washington.

My version goes something like this: It was one of those grand and glorious days when everything went right. I was first (overall), set the course record, and beat my wife soundly. She, on the other hand, came in dead last—even needing assistance at the Hamma Hamma river crossing.

Her version: John and I ran the Staircase to Dosewallips run last Saturday. I finished second overall. He came in next to last.

What actually happened: What we did was we woke up early one morning, checked the sky for rain clouds, noticed none, jumped in the already-packed car, drove to the trailhead, and ran the Staircase to Dosewallips trails. Just over First Divide the Hamma Hamma River emerges from the snowfields. It was early in the season and the river was high. We stood looking at the icy waters. The water was too deep for Kathy to cross safely. It was twelve miles back to the car, and our daughter had probably already moved it to the Dosewallips end of our run. I gave Kathy a piggyback ride across the waist-deep (on me) river.

We paused to eat our PB&Js beneath a blue Pacific Northwest sky. We ran on with nary a sound to be heard but our footsteps and breathing. We crossed Second Divide on a southern exposure just below the snow line, skirted Mount Constance, and followed the Dosewallips River trail on down the valley.

A ranger stood talking to Kim, one of our daughters, as we rounded the last bend late that afternoon and got to the trailhead. They turned to look at us. Kim smiled. The ranger shook his head, muttered something about "ill-equipped" and "I surely do wish you folks wouldn't do that," then smiled and asked how long it took.

Another training run was done.

Fixed-Time Running—Reflections on Time Events

Did you get me? Yes. Okay. One lap finishes, another begins. The brief moment of wondering if the lap counter saw me or the person next to me but not me vanished as her eyes met mine. My eyes went back to the table full of foods, positioned just past the three-sided tent holding the people with the clipboards. My mind went on to the next lap—almost; first I looked at the cups of warm soup, mindful of the dropping temperatures and rising wind. The next lap would wait for my soup stop. There was plenty of time. I was doing a 24-hour time run with about 18 hours to go.

Time runs are an often-overlooked member of the ultramarathon family. They are held more commonly on smooth, well-groomed, and flat surfaces—highly suited to covering as many miles as desired in some given period of time. However, for the trail purist, there are time runs in Wyoming, Virginia, British Columbia, Mississippi, Washington, and just about anywhere else you care to search for them. During the depths of winter there used to be time events at a variety of indoor facilities—six-lap tracks, eight-lappers, and whatever would fit in some armory in a forgotten part of town.

Time runs, time events, track runs, checkpoint runs—no matter what they get called—are great variations for the runner who has not participated in one. The racing is still there, or not there, depending on the intent of the day. Many events record splits as the various standard distances are reached so the anally-retentive-inclined can have the requisite basketful of numbers at day's end (you know, marathons, 50ks, 50 miles, 100ks, etc.). Time runs can be dress rehearsals for many other runs—can I change shoes? How long will it take to change shoes? How long to pause and eat a can of chili? Which shirt, bra, socks, shoes, shorts, and so forth feel good, better, or best after a few hours out there? A time run provides a ready-made test bed for you.

For many of us, however, the real gift of time runs is, surprise, time. As trail running became more popular, many trail ultras became crowded. Entry limits were needed to prevent overuse and abuse of the trails. Time limits came next as the time asked of aid station volunteers became excessive (everyone who does an ultra should do at least one stint on the other side of the table—it is as much a part of ultras as is the running). As the clock ticks down towards the often proscribed cut-off mark, the relative speed needed to complete the cherished trail runs increases. But time, probably the most critical resource in all our journeys, is simply there to use as you want during a time run.

At the Pacific Rim One Day, a one-mile-loop course gave me a perfect way to practice (test?) the "walk two, run one" idea. At Watershed Park 12 Hour, the 5.375-mile loop gave me a chance to see if I could run with some sort of even effort, knowing I could carefully review the spreadsheet that would arrive attached to the results e-mail a few days later. There was also a side bet since Kathy was running—when would I catch her? Could I run four to her three, five to her four, 57 to her...uh-oh, five to her six? During the Banana Belt 12-hour, I started finding constellations as darkness fell and the night sky became my constant companion for each lap—no one said the mind had to stay between the lines of a lane on the track. Locked in the comfort of an obstacle-free running surface, my eyes went up with each trip down the straightaways.

During a stop at the aid station, I watched another person come in and look at his watch and heard him tell his crew (a woman with a really thick book in her hand), "Ten minutes," and then he plopped down in a waiting chair. After he left I asked her about the ten minutes. She said he was practicing getting back out and running after various times in the chair. I asked if she would finish the book before he finished the run, and we got to talking about how she had to restrict her reading to books that did not require full attention so she would remember that the dinging on her watch was telling her it was time to get ready for his return (there's that other-side-of-the-table thing again. Do you have any idea what your crew goes through to support you?).

I left the aid station with a cup of soup in hand and a hundred yards in which to drink it before getting to the thoughtfully placed trash bag, fifty yards after that to transition from eating pace to running pace, and then another lap would envelop me. Hey, John, how's it going? Hi, Linda, how ya doing? And a conversation that had paused when I switched from running to walking several laps earlier began again as our varying paces and plans overlapped. Through the day and evening talks of many subjects started, paused, or continued, only to recede as another iteration of fuzzy logic changed its definitions of fast, slow, and what fits this lap.

What fits? The wind had shifted and the rain was cold now; bits of ice were felt on my face as the forecasted freezing rain arrived. I was wearing two shirts, a wind vest, and a light rain jacket. What would fit over them? At least I did not have to wonder if I had more clothes with me. At time runs you usually have easy access to the car, footlocker, or large pile of stuff on a tarp that you brought with you. You can even climb in your own tent set up at the side of the course. I had lots of stuff—pack-rat mentality she calls it—and at the next passing I found another jacket, a hooded one with "XL" on the tab. The sleet followed as the cold set in. The runners, who had become so familiar all during the day, morphed into multihued Pillsbury representatives, unfamiliar strangers shuffling around the course.

Shuffling, jogging, walking, running, and almost any other form of forward ambulation will be seen at a time event. These aren't the pedestrian events of huge popularity in the late 19th century where the participants were a small group of professional athletes. These are events that welcome all. Go to a time event and you might run with a world-class endurance athlete on one lap and with a small child on the next. You will likely meet people from within our borders and without, but more importantly, you will be surrounded by others being treated to the gift of running for as long as they want or for as far as they want, all while in the company of friends or strangers.

And somewhere, not quite in the background, is a race director who has once again managed to get a park director or high school administrator or some other public entity to agree to the event. As bureaucracies increase in complexity, so too have the race director's tasks and efforts increased—it's that other-side-of-the-table thing again—a special thank you is owed to all race directors for giving us a place for our time.

Types of Finishes

We started talking about the mind-set, intentions, and preparations for an ultra and what they might lead to as the day unfolds—six hours later we had some generalities worked out and were back home. Here's our list:

1. Pushing hard all the way
2. Pushing moderately all the way
3. Finishing with increased effort in the latter part
4. Finishing feeling good
5. Just finishing, no time goal
6. Doing the survival shuffle
7. Ending with a death march

Pushing hard all the way: Whether you go out hard and die early or go out hard and hang on, this is quite likely the most difficult way to run. It requires the highest level of confidence and belief in your training. None of this means you are necessarily trying to win the race. There are people at every starting line fully aware they will not win that day. They might not even be in the chase for an age-group award. However, some of those people have trained with just as much dedication, determination, and discipline as the elite athletes with the goal of "beating the course" as their impetus. They will have tweaked food, drink, training miles, and mental preparation in the hope of reaching a level of fitness that will get them to the finish line in less time than ever before. They probably know more about the course than most other entrants. They know when they can drop the second bottle, vest, or hydration system and make it to the end on a single hand bottle. A tree alongside the course might be the secret marker where whatever energy is left will be called forth for the last surge against the sand in the glass. This is racing with no time for running. The goal for the day might be a secret, known only to the inner self—too fragile to say out loud.

Pushing moderately all the way: I was "sitting on sevens" and happily going along the course. It was a road marathon in the flatness of the Skagit Valley near Mount Vernon, Washington. I had my watch on. As each mile sign was reached I glanced at the watch. Oops, the metronome had gone awry. I had been running at 7:00 per mile, plus or minus a couple of seconds. The last mile was 7:08. What happened? I wasn't running hard enough to need to give the effort total attention, but the flatness of the course should have kept me in the four-second window. Puzzled, I looked back, knowing there were no hidden hills out here. Kathy was pedaling along nearby and asked what I was looking for, and I explained the pace change. She immediately said, "You moved over into the loose stuff on the shoulder." I looked down. I had been running on the fog line, the painted line along the edge of the driving line that is, from the runner's point of view, the separator between gravel-free pavement and gravel-coated pavement. The fog line is sure footing. I had moved over to the gravel, where each step slipped a tiny bit, not enough to notice until the next glance at the watch took place. I adjusted by moving about eighteen inches to the right. My steps were suddenly quieter. I had "lost" about eight seconds. Now I needed to be calm in regaining the lost time. I was not running at an all-out level. I was on a controlled pace, pushing all the time but with quite a bit left if I wanted to call on it. It was a carefully controlled hard-effort training run. I was running sevens with the intent of being comfortable running seven thirties for a fifty-miler. The fifty-miler would require full attention to every mile with no wandering. Today my mind was allowed to wander and I could talk to Kathy as the course took us here and there in the valley. I just needed a moderate amount of physical and mental effort to achieve what was intended—a long tempo run with aid stations. Some people use fifty-milers in this same way as preparation for a hundred-miler. Some realize you cannot race every event and show up, run at a controlled effort, and have an enjoyable day running without the stress of all-out racing.

Finish with increased effort in the latter part: In a vague sort of way, these people can objectively evaluate their progress along the route. They know they are a bit short of endurance fitness but are confident they can get through by starting conservatively and staying aware of how they are doing. Some walking might be needed. Hills that were viewed with more caution than usual in the early miles are perhaps run farther up in the latter stages as they realize things are going pretty good and they don't feel nearly as tired as they usually do. As the day, and miles, passes, it might be that confidence builds and they start looking ahead for another shirt to track down. Somewhere in those last miles, tension leaves and a newly found strength comes in as they come to believe in themselves, their fitness levels, and what they can do out there. This scenario is not reserved for new runners. You just never know which day will turn magical as the last few miles get shorter and shorter.

Finish feeling good: Enough running has been done, so the runner can tell a good run from a bad run. Comfortable tiredness being different from the cumulative effects of fatigue is understood, even cherished, while sitting on the front porch having beaten the darkness as the sun sets. Eating and drinking are thought out, but a lot of tolerance for variety exists. They are not restricted to a certain brand or a certain flavor. These are the runners who sort of glide into an aid station, nibble here and there, have smiles for everyone, eat, refill the bottles, say thank you, and disappear. They are part of a never-ending background conversation on a course somewhere. They are comfortable on road, trail, or track and have more T-shirts than most clothing stores.

Just finish, no time goal: As ultramarathons have become more popular (sort of reminiscent of the marathon craze of the eighties, when seemingly everyone needed to complete a marathon just to qualify for Monday-morning water-cooler conversation), the guise under which many first timers stand at the starting line, inadequately trained physically and with little, or no, knowledge of hydration and nutrition, is "Oh, I'm not interested in time. I just want to finish before they close the course."

These runners are the source of many of the "How soon can I..." or "What is the shortest long run I can do and still do..." questions. They believe, not think but believe, that there are shortcuts to endurance fitness and that nutrition is secondary. A gel or two here, a sip of water there, and anyone can run an ultramarathon. After all, I'm not racing; therefore, I don't need the high-effort stuff, do I? They will argue against training to run the entire distance, whether on a flat course or not. For newcomers, they already know more than most veterans.

Doing the survival shuffle: As the day passed I found I could no longer run. I could do something above walk—jog or shuffle, yes, but there was no more running to be done that day. On one occasion a later visit to an emergency room would reveal an insect bite, thought to be a spider, just above the ankle. The ER person ventured that the bite certainly could have caused the respiratory problems of the day before.

There was the six miles of downhill that left me with quads turned to jelly, tender to the touch and no longer willing to respond to my command to run. I learned that day that hill work did not always mean "run the ups." As I got closer to the finish line, I considered walking down the hills backward. In the last couple of miles, I did do just that. A strange look and the "Are you okay?" from one runner was topped by a commiserating smile and a voice that told an understanding story and assured me I could fix the problem with just a few downhill sessions.

Living in the Pacific Northwest on the coastal side of the Cascade Mountains means I don't run in heat very often. I sometimes still have two shirts on as the calendar goes from April to May. All a person can do when they encounter unexpected (untrained for) heat is slow down, reduce the effort, and get through as best they can. One April found me in California for a 50-miler. I had made the trip to race, not run, but, in my usual blundering way of ignoring a major issue, had not considered the temperature. More specifically I did not think of the noonday sun driving the temperature above eighty degrees. The second half of the run took an hour and forty minutes longer than the first half. Dunking my head in horse troughs alongside the trail became one of the means to get me to the next aid station.

Ended with a death march: I remember, barely or with reluctance, one 50k that I had no business entering. Training had not gone well. Whether viewed with quality in mind or "how many weeks" in mind, training had not gone well. Friday night the rains came in—gentle showers followed by a deluge followed by a repeat through the night. Somewhere around o'dark in the morning, I gave a last thought to how muddy it would be and hid under the pillow. Saturday morning arrived with one last rational thought flitting emptily around in my head, something about it not being too late to volunteer. The RD would let me roll the entry over to next year if I volunteered. Silly me. Real runners don't do the DNS stuff. I started getting dressed to run. About six hours after Clem had sent us off into the woods, I returned, muddy, cramping, and in poor spirits. There was no solace in having avoided the DNS and the DNF.

Kathy took one look at me and quietly walked alongside as we headed for the car. It was not a day to linger and socialize at the finish line. It was time to tuck tail and go home. She finally asked, "Survival or death?" I had to laugh at the memory of an old jingle I had come up with on an earlier bad day, "We're doing the survival shuffle, down at milepost 43, but it'll soon be a death march. Oh Lord, have mercy on me." Yes, it was a death march. All the points of discomfort had been replaced by pain. If I had sat down, I would not have been able to get up without help.

I have avoided a death march or two by honestly evaluating my fitness level and running within it. They were days of carefully monitoring how I felt, how much effort I was expending, and making adjustments. They were what could be, if it could be done, called the opposite of a death march. In a death march there is a refusal to acknowledge capabilities, or would that be lack of capabilities—like a day when I showed up at the first aid station as part of the lead pack of eight runners. It sounds innocent enough until you find out I had been down for five days with the flu and there would be no reserves to call on in a few hours. Actually, it wasn't a few hours. It was about two hours of running, followed by almost five hours of walking—blindly ignoring several people, who suggested I sit for a few minutes, eat and drink, and evaluate before continuing. The people whose advice I was ignoring were all veteran runners, all people who knew me and knew the size of the hole I was digging for myself. It was a death march, and there would be no good memories at the end of the day.

A death march is to be savored as one rationalization after another enables the avoidance of a DNF. The runner seldom sees a death march as an undue burden on the volunteers or race management. After all, the volunteers and race management are here to serve. Aren't they? They are here to suffer my self-abuse and snarls. I have no responsibility to show up ready to run rather than barely survive. Do I?

CHAPTER THREE

You guys just shuffle from concession stand to concession stand!

—Helge Zimmet, said to
Karen Claire at Way Too Cool

BTW, I still think the WS trail is one of the most beautiful places that I have vomited.

—Mary Gorski, e-mail,
1999 WS attemptee and 2001 finisher

You can't die from a stomachache. The worst that can happen is that you'll throw up. Then you can eat some more and start running again.

—Jack Bristol

I Cannot Find What I Wrote Last Whenever I Last Wrote about Food While Out There

In the "Before Energy Bars" (BEB) years (no gels, no PowerBars, no giant electrolyte pills, no S!Caps, no...), I developed my own way of eating during a run—baked potatoes. I prefer Yukon Gold, cut into bite-size chunks, salted, and put in a plastic bag. I usually put the bag in my shorts pocket so I would remember to nibble. I eventually got a cloth bag that hung on the CamelBak belt and held a bag of potato chunks and whatever salt things I was using. That was the standard during-the-run fuel. On longer runs (whatever that means) we would have a plain HERSHEY's bar or 3 Musketeers in the fanny pack. That might become several somethings instead of one something if we were planning to be out for the day instead of just five or six hours.

We would run for about three hours with nothing but drinks. In those early years my drink of choice was defizzed Dr Pepper (sometimes mixed with Gatorade—that is all there was to try in the mid-eighties). It worked for me, so I left it alone. Kathy preferred defizzed Coca-Cola.

For runs beyond three hours, we usually knew how far beyond in terms of total time of the run, e.g., 4–6 hours, 6–8 hours, or "we're going to be out here all day" type of things, we would take the following:

- 4–6 hours—just potatoes, maybe a chunk or two of HERSHEY's bar
- 6–8 hours—potatoes, chunks of candy bars, maybe half a PB&J or BLT (yes, bacon, lettuce, and tomato—eat the BLT first if you have both)

- Longer—two or three sandwich halves, maybe an orange, and some hard candies

Over the years, the choices evolved to all the stuff that is out there today. Fight over what flavor is best and so forth. There are so many brands and flavors that each label needs to be studied in the hope that your preferred energy supplement or something similar will be at the aid stations on the day you go to earn another T-shirt. I tried them and then reverted to the simpler foods of our early years.

Our big experimenting was with soups (pretending access to the car was like aid station stops). I would run a trail loop, stop at the car to eat the sample of the day, run another loop, and repeat. I found ramen-type noodles stayed down. They are probably horrible from a nutritionist's point of view, but a few hours into an ultra they are easy to eat, have lots of electrolyte sorts of properties, have a few calories, and the warm food often just plain tastes good.

I found that a can of soup (the standard size [smallish] can of soup), unheated, just opened and drank straight from the can worked well. The kind of soup is sort of important. I liked chicken gumbo. It is very difficult to drink cream of mushroom soup straight from the can. One can of typical soup (not the low-salt varieties) has lots of the electrolyte stuff and some needed calories. Please note that I am not using numbers. You need 300–400 calories per hour just to keep the calorie deficit from going crazy. The first part of the experiment is simply finding what will stay down as you continue to run. After that you can start playing with the number of calories in a particular food (fuel).

We tried some of the creamy cuppasoups sort of things. They were all good. The problem was having the soup at an "eatable" temperature at the time the runner arrived—too hot often means no food, because the runner will not take the time to wait, while too cold means some soups just don't taste good. This was experimented with during training runs where we knew how long it would take me to run those familiar training routes...timing went to heck at Leadville, Le Grizz, and a few others. I was seldom early, often late.

We experimented with the sandwiches and found the PB&Js or BLTs (who knew which would be preferred on a given day) to be better if wrapped (foil) in halves. On runs long enough to need sandwiches, I almost always had the CamelBak, so storage was not an issue.

Tuna sandwiches did not work at all—mush, ugly cat-food-like mush.

My diet the day before a scheduled run or on the way to one was slowly developed through experimentation. I had found a recipe I liked for whole wheat plus honey plus a few other things (fruits, wheat germ...) rolls that I would bake a couple dozen of and add to my regular diet. I was nibbling on them all day long. I did not eat regular meals, just a lot of big snacks during the forty-eight hours preceding an ultra.

We might also make a big (16- or 24-ounce package of pasta) pasta salad, not too spicy, just olive oil, black olives, green peas (raw), finely chopped carrots, boiled eggs, and an onion or two. I would start on that the day before, maybe even Thursday evening plus the day before, i.e., Thursday evening and all-day Friday for a Saturday event. I kept eating on the trip to wherever, eating as we sat around the campsite the afternoon before. I greatly preferred lots of nibbling over big meals.

The record setter was eating five pounds of baked Yukon Gold (yes, just as there is a preference between baked and boiled, true connoisseurs have potato-type preferences) potatoes and about eighteen of my rolls Thursday evening, Friday during the day (finished the last potato about eight o'clock Friday evening—race started at midnight). Other than Leadville, that was the best I have ever fueled for a run (it was a 100k).

We were almost vegetarians when we were running hard (an ultramarathon or marathon-length run about every third weekend).

We mixed in some salmon or chicken, but mostly veggies. The cumulative effects of dehydration were kept at a minimum by keeping lots of juices around the house (and drinking them).

If you haven't figured it out already, one of the more difficult challenges to being successful at completing ultramarathons is solving the eating and drinking riddle. When writing about the two it is almost automatic to include electrolyte replacement. I see the trio, eating, drinking, and electrolyte replacement, as inseparable. I have no credentials to validate my opinions of electrolyte replacement and, for the most part, I simply did what many others did—experimented until I found what worked for me. I am just as much an expert at eating at aid stations as anyone else might purport to be. If I can reach it, I might eat it.

There are some generalities that can be made about eating and drinking for ultras.

- A 50k is just a couple of cups of something to drink and a few handfuls of potato chips and a slice or two of orange or two or three gels beyond the marathon. You can almost fake it. You don't really need to know much about nutrition or hydration—blind luck will get you through, sometimes—there is always the weather and stuff to get in the way of ignoring good practices.
- A 50-miler will require the runner to take in a significant amount of calories while on the course. What you eat between miles 20 and 35 will have a tremendous effect on how you perform between miles 40 and 50. Most runners can no longer get by on just water.
- At the 100k you have entered the realm of serious calorie- and liquids-replacement needs. Everyone on the course needs to know what they are doing in regards to staying fueled and hydrated. They can vary from plans as the weather

forces adjustments, but the variations have been thought out and experimented with over the preceding months.

- At 100 miles you are not simply extending the 100k needs. Where the 100k will forgive a lapse here and there, the 100-miler demands strict attention to food and hydration. The long-run experiments of eating and drinking during training might not apply as the runner passes the 24-hour point. The physiological stresses encountered need to be understood by the runner, aid station personnel, and crew (and pacers, if used). Finding what food and drink works at the 100-mile distance can take two or three years.

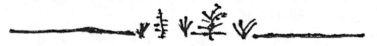

My Search for the Elusive Chili Dog

Apple pies, ice cream parlors, all-you-can-eat buffets, and more—these are among the more rational reasons for running ultramarathons.

My first excursion into the benefits of the wonderful ultramarathon world of high-calorie-expenditure runs was on the way home from the Mudderfell Six-Hour, a muddy funfest in Portland, Oregon, put on by Patty and Warren Finke. An hour or so up the road, my stomach demanded I stop, so I pulled off at the next exit ramp and pulled into the generic breakfast place. I ordered breakfast. Hmm, that feels good. As I was finishing, the waitress asked if there would be anything else. I paused and then said, "Yes, bring me another one of these." She looked and then said, "Do you mean another breakfast?" "Yes."

* * *

Just after I crossed the finish line at the 50-miler in Grants Pass, Oregon, someone handed me a still-warm double-crust apple pie. I watched as one runner and then another ate their pie while relaxing after the run. One runner in particular earned my respect and admiration. He took the pie tin, gave it a practiced twist, and, presto, he had the pie, now a turnover, in his hand (these were homemade pies, not from some factory store). We always saved ours for the trip home the next day. The pies would be placed on the floor of the front seat by the heater vent. An hour or so later, we had warm apple pie to eat as we drove north.

* * *

Speed has its rewards, and ice cream is one of them. In recognition of the magnitude of my victory (age group) at a 50k near Placerville, California, I was presented with a $25.00 gift certificate to an ice cream parlor. This was a few years ago, and $25.00 was a lot of ice cream. How was I going to do this gift certificate justice? Prayers and happenstance have a way of providing answers as each day passes. As I pulled into the parking lot of the ice cream parlor, I noticed four smallish boys talking *as they shared one ice cream cone.* Hmmm. I got out of the car, looked at the menu on the side of the building, and noted that I could get a "Biggest and best genuine malt in town" for $2.99. Hmmm. "Kids," I said, "you want an ice cream?" The unspoken answer was big smiles all around from the little people. I went inside, ordered my malt, handed the clerk the gift certificate, pointed at the foursome, and told her the rest was for them—more smiles.

* * *

Page nine of the May 1986 issue of *UltraRunning* magazine shows a picture from my first 50-mile run, The Greater Oregon Health Service 50 Mile Ultra Championship, ably directed by Rene Casteran and held in Grants Pass, Oregon, on March 22, 1986. The picture shows three laughing faces but only the top of the well-stocked aid station table. The caption reads:

> *"Everyone seems to be having fun: John Morelock stops to cheer up the crew at an aid station..."*

The smiles and laughter were in response to my having looked over the wide and generous variety of foods at the aid station and, this being my first exposure to a full-service (food stuffs) table, commented, "What, no chili dogs?"

* * *

It was the morning after the 49er Double Marathon down in the Marin Headlands. We had driven north far enough along US 101 the previous afternoon to be able to get to the Samoa Cookhouse near Eureka, California, for breakfast that morning. It is a simple place patterned after the old logging-camp cookhouses of years gone by. The menu reads:

- Breakfast, served family style, can include eggs, French toast, pancakes, sausages, biscuits & gravy, hash browns, coffee and orange juice.

There is but one price and one marketing ploy; that ploy is what brought us there for breakfast the day after completing our tour of the hills just up the coast from the Golden Gate. The ploy: all you can eat for that one price. We keep a list of places like that. They have never asked me to leave, but there was a comment made about how a relatively thin person could eat as much as I did.

* * *

I noted in a write-up for the Rain Runners', the running club I was a member of in Olympia, Washington, newsletter describing an aid station stop during the Coast Hills 50 Mile that took place in the "hills" around Siletz, Oregon:

> *"...There are no chili dogs at the 24-mile aid station. I settle for a banana, defizzed RC, and a promise of chili dogs next year."*

* * *

At the Headwaters Run, 50 miles of trails alongside the Rogue River near Crater Lake in Oregon, Rob "Old Goat" Volkenand of Bend, Oregon, surprised everyone with the great meal he prepared on the 76 camp stoves he had assembled like a symphony orchestra for a philharmonic assemblage yet to gather here in the woods. There was corn of several kinds, beans of many colors, rice, both white and brown, and even a mix of potatoes, *but nowhere could I find a chili dog.* Rob, surely in cahoots with the folks at Siletz, smiled and promised, "Next year, John, next year."

* * *

At an aid station at the American River 50, a small boy who stood behind a table, beaming with excitement and wanting only to help, asked me what I wanted. I scanned the many plates and bowls, bottles and jugs—a smorgasbord of grand proportion filled the tent—and finally turned to him. "A chili dog?" The small face froze in horror. He turned to a nearby woman. "Mom! Mom, he wants a chili dog. We don't have any chili dogs, do we, Mom? Mom?" Mom glowered at me. I apologized, took some cookies, topped off the bottles, and continued on toward Auburn.

* * *

Joe and Joyce Prusaitis provide entertainment for the masses with their "there are no hills in Texas" Bandera 25, 50, and 100k runs. I was there in January of 2007 as a volunteer while a friend (Lynn Ballard of the North Texas Trail Runners) was running. Under the watchful eye of Sammy Voltaggio, breakfast, lunch, and dinner—pasta, rice and beans, Texas-style smoked brisket, sandwiches, macaroni and cheese, breads, and soups—came forth from the kitchen in the trailer. "One starting time fits all" means the kitchen will open in time for breakfast before the start and will be open until the last finisher gets home. As the night passed on, the temperature dropped and the combination of snow and freezing rain gave new meaning to being in the "soup line."

* * *

Sunday, May 24, 1987, Brookings, Oregon, Brookings Marathon, the usual odd assortment of somewhat-healthy-looking people gathered in a parking lot next to the beach. Phil Hicks, the RD, explained which trash can we were to stand next to so as to assure ourselves of the correctness of the course's distance. We were told it is definitely a marathon, possibly closer to thirty miles, and nobody will come looking for you until well after dark. It is all trails except the last half mile, when we would come down into town from the hills. Off we went along the beach we were to follow northerly for a "few miles" until we got to some creek, which everyone assumed someone else would know when we got there.

And so we ran until we got to the creek. Then Rob and I headed off up the hill across US 101 and on up and up into the hills, pausing at the VW van long enough to refill our bottles while listening to the mantra of the stranger at the van, "right at the power line, right at the power line, right at..." Some three-tenths of forever later, having emptied our bottles while following the power line and still looking for some sort of trail marker—Phil (the RD, remember him?) had promised the turns would be marked—Rob paused at a road crossing the power line trail looking down at a white arrow on the ground. Was it the work of Phil or an artifact? It was new looking and pointed to the downhill side of things—that would be nice. Rob went a few steps toward the hill's edge, looked over, then pointed down at what looked to be another VW van, a second van, and several persons. We left the not-quite-a-trail beneath the power line and started down the dirt road. A half mile of ball-bearing gravel and three switchbacks later, we were close enough to see the two vans and several women clad in dresses and aprons as you might see in a quaint little bakery or tea shop...somewhere? There were two tables with white lace tablecloths, teapots and pitchers, bowls of strawberries, cream, and biscuits (and off to one end were some chips and regular stuff)—wha...what was going on? Someone pointed at the barely legible hand-scrawled sign, "High Tea aid station."

I paused to take it all in, finally asking, "So, where's the chili dog?"

Giggles, smiles, and laughter broke out as all heads turned toward Marsha. She had turned so her back was partly to me and had bent to get something from beneath the table. When she turned to face me she was holding a large paper plate and the biggest, ugliest chili dog I had ever seen. It covered the entire plate; the melted cheese was sprinkled with onions and peppers. Chili oozed lavalike out from the edges of the cheese topping. It was a chili dog done royal. Marsha's arms were trembling from holding the plate. A place was cleared on the table. The entire High Tea aid station staff, Old

Goat, Frank, and a stranger to be named later all looked at me, waiting. Hmmm.

"Could you wrap that to go?" was the best I could do.

"No, John."

...smiles and snickers in the background...

"Oh. Hmm, uh." Never thought anyone would actually have a chili dog.

"John, would you like us to bring it to the finish line when we are through here?"

"Yes, that would work. I can eat it after the run."

Rob, Frank, and I turned back to the gravel road and ran on toward the finish line down at Phil and Marsha's house somewhere below us in Brookings.

The rest of the story, part one: (explained to me by Marsha Hicks and Gail Volkenand as we sat around waiting for the postrace salmon dinner. The postrace dinner is one of the great things about "low-key" runs because of the small number of entrants. Basically it was just a gathering of friends and a fun run.)

Early that morning when the kind ladies of the aid station were putting together the last of the supplies for the High Tea aid station, something was missing, and they needed to stop at a convenience store. While waiting to pay for things, some kind soul noticed the chili dogs and same now-not-so-kind soul remembered me and the always-asked-for chili dog. Several other now-downright-devilish souls asked for one chili dog—insisting on double onions, cheese, and apparently anything else that was in the condiments arena. Thus was the world's largest chili dog built and paid for and placed in a VW van for delivery to an aid station somewhere just east of Brookings, Oregon.

The rest of the story, part two: As the afternoon passed, finishers sat at scattered tables and chairs in Phil and Marsha's backyard talking and glancing up as another runner came in. Finally someone came in and said one runner was missing, not to be found, had not showed up at High Tea. A change in mood and tone swept over the formerly relaxed and laughing gathering. Phil and another runner or two who were familiar with the trails and roads of the area were now talking of where to start looking. "How soon do we go out?" was among the first questions that needed answering.

Just as that discussion was ending and we were starting to shuffle to cars so we could drive back up to start looking, the VW van and High Tea entourage came down the street and pulled into the driveway.

"The chili dog saved the day" was the first thing we heard.

Our lost, stolen, or strayed runner had finally showed up at High Tea. He had done the often-selected bonus-miles option by following the power line a bit farther south than most of us. He finally turned back, found the earlier overlooked arrow, and went down the hill to High Tea, the last aid station. It was said he drank what was left (the tea had really been defizzed soda), ate the strawberries, looked at the empty plates, and then noticed my chili dog.

"Whose is that?"

"John's."

"Where is he?"

"At the finish."

"Can I have it?"

"Why not?"

And so it was on a sunny afternoon in May in the hills just east of Brookings on the Oregon coast that my long-awaited chili dog was bought, taken to an aid station, delivered, declined, and, as the afternoon waned, used to revive an anonymous runner from his death march. When he arrived at Phil's he looked around and said, "Which one of you is John?" I held up a hand and said, "Me."

"Good chili dog, thank you." And the story finally ended.

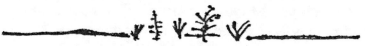

Thanksgiving Morning, Very Early
(Simple Pleasures, or Is It Treasures?)

The frost glistened 'neath the fading moon. I looked at the clock, not quite three a.m., too early—I turned away from the window and returned to bed.

A couple of hours later, I gave up and headed into the kitchen to start the chopping, cutting, and slicing. Puttering in the kitchen with the light of false dawn allowing me to see just enough so I don't have to turn on a light seems such a simple thing. One pan is quietly filled with water and set on the stove. The bowls are placed here and there, not randomly at all.

The sounds from the chopping board are muted in my half-lit room; garlic is peeled by hand, potatoes are sliced instead of chopped, the beans are snapped, not cut. I raise my head and see the hillside's solid white coat of frost, soon to be gone. What the moon had reflected on the sun will now drive away with its first rays of light on another Thanksgiving morning.

No one else is stirring yet. I finish peppers and onions, set out a bowl of okra and corn, add bay leaf and basil, red and black pepper to the big pan, and turn the heat to low.

The first part is done.

In the quiet of the half lit kitchen, the smells have started to reclaim the house; the sun is only a few minutes the other side of the ridge; my running shoes are only a few steps away in the hall by the door.

I'll be right back.

Happy Thanksgiving to all.

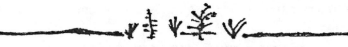

Nature's Self-Service Aid Stations
(Stephen and the Berries)

One summer while we were living in Corvallis, Oregon (that's Ohryghun to those of you on the far right of the U.S. land mass), Perry, one of our sons, was visiting us from Tucson, Arizona. Perry had brought Stephen, a very bright young man whom we will get to know better, with him. This was Stephen's first visit to the Pacific Northwest in general and Corvallis in particular. The combination of Stephen's good-natured ignorance of the area, some late rains that were timed perfectly for berry ripening, and our walks on the trails of the Willamette Valley and the McDonald Forest was to become a particularly ripe source of enjoyment and one of my favorite stories.

There are berries of some sort along almost every trail throughout this land. We have pulled the offered snacks from bushes or vines in many states and, since we were in about the same latitude, we saw familiar plants in many parts of Spain as we walked *el Camino de Santiago*. Some, the *rubus* species, come in several recognizable forms. We know them as raspberries (red and blackcap), thimbleberries, salmonberries, dewberries of many kinds, a few berries with no prefixes, and our (local) blackberries—the Pacific, Cutleaf, and Himalayan. Of the three blackberries, only the Pacific is native to North America. The Pacific and Cutleaf are evergreens, sometimes bare of fruit but never turning into the leafless tangle of arching stems with prickles (what I, until reading about the plants, thought were stickers or thorns) like the Himalayan blackberry. The stems grow upward and then bend back to earth, partly so the tips can root and enable a single plant to spread and become the humongous briar patch we see alongside trails. The berries come from the flowers that form on the ends of the many branch tips. There are male and female plants—which explains the mystery of why there are some berry patches with no berries—and only the female plants have berries.

On the second day of their visit, Kathy and I were getting ready to go for a walk/jog/run/shuffle—never sure what we will do—and asked Perry and Stephen if they wanted to go with us. Where? I pointed at the hillside that was our access to the McDonald Research Forest, Oregon State University's several thousand acres of woods that hold "our" trails. How far? Oh, I don't know, three or four miles, just a walk to get out for a while—howzat?

And so it was that the four of us wandered up a trail with no name that leads to Chip Ross City Park. We paused at a bench in the shade of one of the old maple trees while the two city kids caught their breath. Pointing at Dan's Trail, I mentioned it was downhill from here, and off we went—weird how the idea that downhill going out means uphill coming back never was mentioned. On we went through the switchbacks and down to the meadows alongside Jackson Creek, then turning onto Lower Horse Trail to go across and up the hillside. As we climbed, Kathy and I were both looking with interest at the blackberry thicket next to the trail. For the past week or two, we had been sampling from various thickets we passed, mostly making a "Ewww, that is sour" comment and waiting for a day or two of rain for the final ripening. It had been a couple of days since we last climbed Lower Horse, and there had been some rain, so...I reached over and pulled on a very dark, fat-looking berry. Sweeeeeeet! They were ripe. We continued up the hillside trail, staying within reach of the berry thicket. I was about ten berries up the hill (using a one-berry-every-second-step picking method) when it happened.

"What are you doing?" boomed across the hillside—okay, it wasn't alarmingly loud but certainly not conversationally quiet, and it was out of place—several rabbits had turned tail and fled. I looked around for the source of the now-echoing-off-the-hillside question.

It was Stephen. He was a few steps below and was looking at us with a starkly puzzled expression.

"What are you doing?"

Kathy and I looked at each other. What were we doing? Nothing—in our minds. That was what I thought, nothing. Stephen pointed at my hand and asked, "What are you eating?" Oh. These? Yes. Blackberries. Blackberries? Yes, sorry, I didn't even think of this as doing something.

I explained about the wild blackberries, Himalayan blackberries in this case. "Ripe blackberries," I said as I pulled another and plopped it in my mouth. I pointed at the plant and told Stephen to pull one—quickly explaining the "pull test." If the berry requires a solid pull, leave it. If it is ripe, it will literally fall off into your hand. He reached over, way more hesitantly than was necessary—'they won't spring at you; just gently pull the berry off,' I told him. He did. And then, with the movements of someone demonstrating how to not crack eggs, he put it in his mouth... and...and several very shallow breaths later he chewed ever so slowly. Okay, that is dramatized somewhat. But I ate six more berries while waiting and Kathy ate four more as we kept looking at Stephen. The time elapsed from pulling the berry off to the appearance of a wide smile of satisfaction was less than 27 seconds. It only seemed to take forever.

The perceived time for him to pull a second berry and put it in his mouth was blurred by how quickly he reached for the third, fourth...

"C'mon, Stephen," we yelled from the far side of the meadow, "there are berries all along the trails where we are going." We wandered around, up Horse, over to Dimple, down Dan's, finally arriving back at the trail up the side of Chip Ross. Kathy and I ran part of the time, then would turn and run back to Perry and Stephen. As we returned from one trip ahead, Kathy pointed at Stephen and started laughing. There were purplish stains on the front of Stephen's T-shirt, a big purplish ring around his mouth, and an almost euphoric look on his face. What had we done?

Breakfast with Oscar

Breakfast? Sure. Where? We were somewhere east of the Bighorn Canyon National Recreation Area and had spent the previous day running trails perhaps known only to the wild horses and bighorn sheep of the canyon lands, after which we had spent the night on the high plateau near Medicine Wheel, a sacred site for Native Americans. As we drove easterly along U.S. 14, I was paying more attention to the geology signs along the roadside than to my growling stomach. Instead of the more common elevation signs seen along some highways, in this part of Wyoming the signs showed which geologic age we were driving through. The change in philosophical environment from yesterday's Medicine Wheel and its Native American mysticism and almost mythic seduction to today's scientific realm of geologic ages was causing our conversation to take jumps several millennia apart.

Okay, the conversation was about eating; back to breakfast. A rustling of unfolding the Wyoming map, a review by Kathy, and the announcement that Dayton was the first town we'd come to. Okay, breakfast in Dayton. And that turned the conversation from rock strata and Native American sacred places to breakfasts we have had along our ultrarunning journeys.

Leadville, Colorado, is a sleepy little town way high up in the Rockies. The whole "sleepy" bit goes out the window, though, as almost every eating place in town opens at three o'dark in the morning on a certain Saturday in August each year. Strangely garbed, almost awake people (runners) are accompanied by strangely garbed, way too cheerful people (crew), all checking out the eateries. Many have been up most of the night staring at the ceiling and waiting. Breakfast fuels the morning but also fills the remaining time.

As much as I liked our stay in Leadville, it was the Monday-morning departure breakfast that was special. There were no private tables, no strangers anymore. "Mind if we join you?" was heard time and time again. Some ate two breakfasts before an attempt was made to walk to the door—the beginning of a long trip home accompanied by a reluctance to leave this place of triumph. Stan Jensen, three-fourths of the way through his summer of The Last Great Race, grabbed the just-vacated chair. A soft voice with a Tennessee accent I recalled from somewhere in the night stopped to offer a hand of introduction as race numbers and midnight shadows become people. Monday morning is full of breakfasts of hello and good-bye.

Siletz, Oregon, is now a ghost town on the ultra circuit. But back in the eighties, breakfast before the Coast Hills 50 Mile trail run was a major event for the only café in a town with less than a thousand people. It was also my introduction to eating breakfast for an ultra. I had ordered toast and coffee, mostly just to pass time. The place was packed. Then I started noticing other runners eating really big breakfasts—eggs and pancakes, waffles and bacon, toast and sausage, even oatmeal was on the tables waiting to be devoured. Were these really my fellow runners? How could they run after such a breakfast? The following year I ordered bacon, eggs, toast, and hash browns with no hesitancy.

"7:00–9:30 A.M.—Breakfast at the firehouse for runners and crew," says a line in the Cascade Crest Classic 100 Mile information novel. Firehouse? Yup, sure enough there is a firehouse full of smiling volunteers serving breakfast when most ultras would have you out running for hours already? The CCC100 doesn't start until ten o'clock in the morning, thus giving everyone the privilege of running through the night—and of having a great social hour while *relaxing* over breakfast. Food and conversation take your mind off *things.* Some folks stand outside, slowly turning as they pop blueberry muffins in their mouths, taking in the grandeur of the Pacific Northwest.

A few understand they are in the middle of the bowl they will climb out of, run around, and drop back into at the end—they turn a bit slower as they look at the challenge the North Cascades offers.

Crater Lake Rim Runs always meant going home on the "back-side" of the Cascades so we could stop at an all-you-can-eat break-fast buffet in Bend, Oregon. The second year, our breakfast stop brought forth the *well-earned* but hesitantly asked "Do you always eat this much?" question. I thought of one more plausible-sounding story of running from bears, ate one more serving, said thank you, and it was back on the road again.

And then there was breakfast with Oscar. Road trips mean camp-ing for us, and we tend to be up and traveling early each morning, stopping for breakfast an hour or two down the road. This particular morning found us passing through another barely-a-town on the Pacific Coast. A small, hand-painted sign, nailed crookedly to a tree, said Café, and the arrow pointed to the rear of a large house. We pulled off and drove around back to find a three-stall parking lot and a back door. A sign on the back door said Enter. We entered.

Six stools, all occupied by quiet conversations that paused to see who was coming in, lined the counter that filled one side of the room. Five tables were squeezed into the rest of the room. We did our best "stranger here" smiles and said good morning. The room suddenly filled with smiles and good mornings and returns to con-versations. We sat down at the one vacant table. We said yes to the offer of coffee and a menu.

As we read the menu the door opened, and an old guy stood there looking at all the full stools and occupied tables. He looked at us and quietly asked if we would share our table. "Certainly," and he sat down. "I'm Oscar," he said and offered his hand.

Are you from here? Yes, except for the war, I've been here 76 years. We listened to Oscar tell of 76 years, a farm on the outskirts of town, his visit to a war-torn Europe for the war, his daily writing of letters home to Mary Helen, the woman he loved and was married to for 57 years, and the return to the farm that was home, never to leave again. Hands, strong from the many years of farming, moved gently in accordance with his stories. The lines in his face showed that the memories of the years gone by were still fresh and strong. A promising career as a pitcher was forgotten as he became a soldier. He remembered Salerno in Italy, then Normandy, Bastogne, the occupation, and finally orders to go home. He had ridden the train from New York to San Francisco. He recalled breakfast in the Rockies on the City of San Francisco streamliner. He paused, looking at our shirts quizzically. Do those mean you ran 50 miles? Yes, but...Fifty miles? My goodness, how on earth do you do that? It was a long breakfast that morning, that breakfast with Oscar.

Food Fairs and Fare at Ultramarathons

- Burritos at the SOB 50k down in the Siskiyous
- Smoked brisket and soup from scratch from Joe P. and his Bandera cohorts
- Bacon? Bacon at dawn at French Cabin at Cascade Crest
- Vegetable soup and all that homemade bread courtesy of Jan LaCava at the McDonald Forest in Corvallis, Oregon
- The Dam Aid Station at Rocky Raccoon, the North Texas Trail Runners putting on a show of feeding and caring for strangers in a strange land
- McKenzie River Trail Run—all that food in the big room
- Strolling Jim, chicken (cooked)
- Leadville, Fish Hatchery, brownies, potato soup
- Barbecue at Le Grizz—and a moose in the background
- Brookings Trail Marathon, barbecued salmon
- Siletz, strawberries and cream

- 49er Double Marathon, beer and chips and the San Francisco Bay
- Syllamo and the almost potluck table
- Grasslands barbecue sandwiches at the finish, NTTR again— there is something about Texas and hospitality
- Homemade chili at the Finke's in Portland after Mudderfell

Anyone ever thought of creating a recipe book from the aid stations whose fare they have sampled along the way?

CHAPTER FOUR

No matter how well you know the course, no matter how well you may have done in a given race in the past, you never know for certain what lies ahead on the day you stand at the starting line waiting to test yourself once again. If you did know, it would not be a test, and there would be no reason for being there.

—Dan Baglione

The Frailty of Confidence

Frailty (an incomplete list): amiable weakness, bad habit, change-ableness, collapse, decrepitude, deficiency, ethereality, feeble-mindedness, fragility, imperfection, indecisiveness, infirmity of will, shortcoming, something missing, susceptibility, tenuity, unsubstantiality, valetudinarianism, vulnerability, wispiness

I had been on a six-week roller coaster and wanted off. I didn't really care if I got off in a dip or at one of the many apexes being offered. I was at the point of wanting a few days of something I could call consistent, even if it had walk, trudge, or shuffle in it. I simply wanted it to be the same for all of recent memory, my recent memory.

It started with the decision to enter something. I didn't care what, sort of preferring something close to the island yet something far enough out in time that I could get ready to run it, not just show up and survive. That thought led to me wondering about my current fitness level—what was my baseline fitness? I had a few four- to five-hour runs in the past few months, but none were hard efforts, just simple runs in the woods. The closest I came to measuring anything, if I had a watch on, would be the loop on Cedar Grove.

Cedar Grove and the Cedar Hollow connector is a mile and a quarter with one climb of about 250 feet in about a quarter mile of trail, then three-quarters of twisting and turning, gradually falling to the last quarter mile, where there is a drop of about 150 feet back to the start. An easy loop takes about sixteen minutes at thirteen minutes to a mile pace. A comfortable push and I could get around it in fifteen minutes—twelve minutes to the mile and I can feel good about how well I am running.

That is what I had done. I had run fast enough to feel good. I felt good about how I was running just after I did three laps on Cedar Grove. The numbers were 14:06, 13:52, and 13:41. I had gone under elevens on that last lap. The yay-for-me was barely audible as the three-laps-doesn't-prove-anything chorus started. Ratz.

I turned toward the trailhead. It seemed like the positive reinforcement should have lasted longer. I got to the last quarter mile, hit the "split" button at the quarter-mile tree, and pushed up the hill to the gate. That last quarter mile (wheeled twice and witnessed by one raven and two squirrels) is wide and smooth, fully runnable, free of rocks and roots, drops about twenty feet in the first half and rises about thirty feet in the last half, and has served as a measuring stick for some semblance of fitness for several years.

In years gone by Kathy would prod me with "100 seconds to-day?" as we got to the tree. One hundred seconds: six minutes and forty seconds to the mile is what that represents if I could hold it. What it really represents is the belief that a seven-minute mile is still there. With memories of one thing and then another, I glanced at the tree, stabbed the button on the watch, and started for the end of the trail. The trick here is to be in control. If the effort will cause me to fall to my knees, then I ran too hard. I want to run hard enough to test but easy enough to know (believe) I could back off a few seconds and hold that effort for a mile. The 100-second quarter pointed at a comfortable seven-minute mile. That was in years gone by. Today was a quarter mile to the end of the trail at a controlled effort with part of the mind detached enough to wonder about the pace. I don't time things often enough to judge pace. I can judge effort on the trails, which, sadly, has little to do with judging pace on the trails. It is the smooth stuff that confuses me these days.

A couple of weeks ago, I did a 7:55 first mile followed by a 7:52 second mile on a paved road leading to a trail. That felt good but mostly merely led to the question of how long can I run at just below that eight-minute pace? That was part of the fluff, flora, and fauna that went through my mind as the quarter mile to the gate was being crossed. There was some reward in being able to climb to the gate without the feeling of an oncoming death. About thirty yards out I tugged at my shirtsleeve so I could see the watch face. At the double poles that mark the end of the trail, I glanced down: 1:47. Hmm, a 7:08 projection that immediately starts a raucous squabble amongst the voices that govern my training. *I'll bet you can't hold that for four laps.* Excuses being what they are, readily available, I said to myself, "If school was not in session, I would go down and run a mile on the track." Yes, I thought to myself, if school was not in session I could do that.

A few days ago I got out the trail maps with the squiggly lines. I looked at the legend to see how far apart the squiggles were. It said "Contour Interval: 20 feet." I found a trail that followed a contour and then abruptly turned and started crossing the squiggles, headed for the top. I carefully wrote down: 204, rt on 207, on 207, on 207, lt on 21, on 21, and so forth until I had a spaghettilike course that went back and forth, winding around the top of one mountain before dropping off to wiggle its way up the next mountain to the west. It would not be the hours and hours of running in the forests I did in the past, but it would be a good test course in this early part of winter. Up and down and all around it went. Fourteen miles with about 3800 feet of rocks, roots, and ups and downs snaking through the two hills would be my test for the week. The mind-set was decided on; there would be no walking unless I tripped over my tongue. I needed to see if I could concentrate for however long my sheet of squiggles needed. I guessed at three hours.

Kathy pointed out if I would finish one trail to the left I would have a nice seven-tenths of a mile on an almost straight and almost downhill forestry road to finish on. Maybe I could do a burst-of-speed thing to bring the day to a proper close. Sure, why not. I will either be totally demoralized by then or...

Thursday morning's wintry drizzle coated me with hesitancy. Shorts? If I wear shorts I will have to run or I will freeze. Okay, maybe not freeze, but I will need to keep moving. Kathy pulled over by the gate, smiled, and said something about going to get a latté. She also said, "Get out." I got out. My "shorts and needing to run or freeze" was the morning's blunt truth of greeting. I was shivering as I started running up the trail, knowing I had a half a mile of following a contour line and then the climb up the first roller coaster would start.

It's hard to curse the course when you did the design. That was only true for the first thirty minutes. After that I had several conversations about "why this" or "why that" and couldn't I just believe in what I had been doing? I had done a good job. I could stay above trudge most of the time. My attention stayed on run, not shuffle or jog, and even rock-free stretches of only a few steps meant I quickened my pace. The one longish climb, 1.6 miles and 1120 feet of climb, was the only concession to walk breaks. Actually, it was a walk section with a few run breaks. It, too, was completed, and it held the reward of being the point where I could look at my watch for the first time. I did not know the miles to here. I felt it was about two-thirds of the way through the course I had designed. I knew the ugly part of the long climbs was behind me, but the truly ugly part was the next half mile or so of downhill. I smiled at how good I felt and then peeked at the watch—2:03. Or 2:03! Or 2:03? I looked at the numbers and realized they meant absolutely nothing to me. I did not know how far I had run. My cryptic notes only told me to turn left or right or go straight ahead. I felt good but did not really have a sense of if I had been running hard or not. I did note that I had emptied one bottle and was a few sips into the second.

As I started down the first of the many drizzle-slickened rocks, I wished I had not looked at the watch. The route was seldom run-nable, certainly not open-stride runnable. It was rocky and rooty, and I kept telling myself it was a hard course to run, seldom get-ting fifteen yards of it's-okay-to-raise-your-eyes-from-the-trail trail. I scrambled on down. I did a repeat loop because I forgot to go right at the fork. I almost decided I had gone the wrong way completely when the long-sought gate finally came into view. I seldom ran this trail in the down direction, using it mainly for uphill training, and had to pause more than was really needed at some of the junctions. Oh well, I ran and enjoyed how good I felt as I neared the bottom of that leg.

Two more junctions and I was at the road crossing where Kathy had pushed me out the door. A half-formed memory of it being 2.4 miles from here to the gate where the car was crossed my mind. The trail seemed to be a mix of crushed gravel for the faint of heart, roots for the twinkly-toed, and a series of annoying little hills. A hallucination was chased for a few minutes, and then she either disappeared or never was. The trail passed by several backyards, each with a No Trespassing—Stay on Trail sign. I looked at the houses that back on the woods that are never visited by the children that are inside staring at a study in animation on a wall they think is real. The next street crossing is a real memory point. It is 0.56 miles to the junction with the gravel forestry road. The car is seven-tenths of a mile farther. The voice I have been ignoring comes crashing into consciousness. Push!

All the fears of not being able to run at a sustained high effort were gone. The next dip was crossed. I could see the road through the trees. I quickly gauged how wide a turn would be needed at the speed I was traveling and risked dislocating a shoulder as I grabbed at a tree to slow myself and spun out onto the road. I regained balance, completed the turn, and hit "Split" on the watch. The fun was over for the morning. There was seven-tenths of a mile of truth in front of me. Seven-tenths times...what? Nine? Seven times nine is sixty-three. Six point three is six with three-tenths left over. Three-tenths of a minute is eighteen seconds...nines is 6:18. A brief discussion followed about a nine-minute pace being really running while on a slightly downhill forestry road in the drizzle of an early winter's day. Okay, how about eights? Silly boy, but do go ahead on. Seven times eight is fifty-six. Five minutes plus six-tenths of a minute, uh, remember I am doing this while running...eights is 5:36. Compromise number one will be six minutes to the gate. If I am anywhere below nines as a run ender in January, things are good, reallll good.

The total time was a few minutes off of three hours. The last seven-tenths of a mile was ran at just over an eight-minute pace. There were no cramps, no face-plants, and a lot of it felt like running. I looked up into the drizzle and thought about the run. I thought it was a good run for this early in the year on that course in this weather; then, just as the demons of doubt started to say something about it only being three hours long, I changed my mind.

I decided it was a good run, period. And I told them to shut up.

Running Within the Words

I was sitting in a meeting, admiring the grain of the wood from a tree felled long ago just to decorate a corporate meeting room. The meeting was to convince a very reluctant manager that a thorough documentation program was needed. I was trying to explain that the document was nothing; the documentation was everything. It is the examination of processes, noting the things done or not done, evaluating the wants and needs as the process is optimized, that create the history that will be of critical importance in the future. It is like a ticket to somewhere being nothing but a piece of paper, but the trip is left in our heart and mind and, on some rare occasions, our souls.

What others might call a trip or a journey, we runners call train-ing—the time spent in preparation for reaching a finish line—and some dutifully write down each day's activity in a diary, a log, or a journal. Some of us note the temperature, shoes worn, distance, time, elevation loss or gain, amount and type of liquids consumed, the route, and who knows what all else. Cryptic symbols are stan-dardized for our pages, emoticons and strange punctuation marks are added to give life and meaning to a day of mechanical plodding, and the end of the week is adjusted depending on whether *the day of accord, the day you go to the starting line,* is a Saturday or a Sunday.

Over the years, the pages in my running diary have slowly filled, sometimes with so much detail (*17.23 miles, 13:10.6 pace, 3120 as-cent, 1830 descent, 88 ounces...*) that an accountant would think I was keeping history for an IRS audit. Sometimes just a note suffices (*17+, hot, hilly*) and I am done. I can look back and find days when I even recorded the amount of time I was stopped—the day's pauses and diversions—wanting a *true* representation of pace, even though on race day no one was going to subtract my pauses, move me up in the standings, or point out how sloth-like had been my passing.

I find entries showing how hard it was to decide on a route in early spring. There are meadows bursting with color to run through again, waterfalls full of snow-fed energy, and even trails to avoid because of poison oak, nettles, bears, and the like. Where and what to do now is often influenced by where and what I did back whenever. Each day's passage is recorded in my diary, becoming both almanac and biography, a clarifier of my running life.

A single line from the Aptos Creek Marathon—"I could never run fast here"—brought back the memories of curves rounded and giant trees bringing me to a stop. After the Le Grizz 50-miler, I failed totally at describing the vertical majesty of the Northern Rockies but thought I caught the mother moose and calf pretty well. Le Grizz was followed by several blank pages. I wondered what caused the cessation of writing. Weariness? Traveling home? Pensive thoughts? Celebration? Do others experience this? A goal was reached, the reward reaped, and now blank pages take up space as I slip down from the peak of euphoria, the run over. I'm resting, recovering. Training waits, but not yet.

My first DNF caused a proliferation of squiggles and lines and words that would not form sentences and more anguish than I knew existed in this simple world of running. How could I drop 46 miles into a 50-miler? Why wasn't I wearing gloves, why didn't I drink earlier, how come I changed shoes—I never change shoes—why did I today? Oh, shut up. Dummy. Tweazlebrain. Maybe I should have walked earlier. Was it really hot? I didn't know it would snow. Ratz. The string of completions and runs with no problems was over; reality had come calling. Two pages of whys, woes, and self-pity were recorded, folded, and inserted between the appropriate pages. Over time they served their purpose—reminding me to drink, to eat, to train, or to just pay more attention.

I can find the ten weeks where I tracked calories and fats and leans and starches and moon phases and ate well and felt better and then bought a bag of fried bacon rinds. I know breakfast helped. It says so, "Two hours in, no energy drop—breakfast? Yep." The failed discipline of eating properly is more often noted by the inclusion of the words *tired, blah, couldn't push today*, and all their loosely connected friends. The entry on October 31, 1986, drew attention over the years as I would read it again and again, just to be sure of my memory: "Since dawn I have eaten five pounds of baked Yukon Gold potatoes and fourteen of my homemade multigrain rolls. I have never eaten this much as a fueling idea..." I won that day. Eating does help. And I can still find the day of the chili dog, too, waiting for me on a white linen tablecloth at mile 23 in Brookings, Oregon.

A spring day in the Coast Range mountains of Oregon is condensed to a few lines: "Threw my jacket to Kathy as I passed the car at 14 miles" followed by a blurring of the words about snow, sleet, rain, freezing rain, wind, and then strangely ending with mutterings about blue sky and puffy white clouds.

An August day somewhere southeast of Tonopah, Nevada, was responsible for an entry that always causes me to pause: "118 degrees, sweat is not seen nor felt, two bottles for six miles and I'm done for."

A random flipping of pages finds glimpses of confidence in newfound skills: "Fastest time on the four miles down the 417 trail to the gate." Other pages record the seasons' changes—visits to waterfalls dry a month ago, notes about a tree full of hummingbirds or the changing color of the glistening oil of poison oak. A day of interrupted solitude was duly recorded by "four and a half hours, McCulloch loop, saw Clem about two hours in—quiet today." Night runs were pages with question marks—what made what noise? Whose tracks are those? What was that? Some things are best left unlearned, unrecorded.

The pages become a conscience, prodding us to do things that worked but also reminding us of days of failure. Well, not failure, but of days that I called mechanical, days barely above trudging through the woods, days when three words were all that told of that time on the trails, "I got out." Fortunately, those entries were often followed by some seemingly silly little challenge, something to make up for the off day, the down day. Bailing out on Thursday was followed by something I had never done before: 22 miles a day, Friday, Saturday, and Sunday—three days in a row. The doldrums had been banished, trudging was replaced by running, and the trails beckoned again with blank pages yet to be filled.

Patience and That's a Lot to Learn?

I have raced (whether or not my competitors knew it or ran differently because of it) sprints, hurdles, and one lappers on the track and trail or road events from five kilometers up to and including 100 kilometers.

I have run on roads or trails, with no thoughts of competition, distances from five kilometers up to and including 100 miles.

Somewhere earlier in this book I espoused and expounded this idea of mine that there is a difference between running and racing. To the reader's great delight, I am not going to revisit that difference. I only brought it up because of the two lead paragraphs. I did race. I did run. I did both at a wide variety of distances. The common track distances that I never ran competitively (raced) were the half mile (800 meters for the youth audience) and the mile in its many disguises (1500 meters and 1600 meters). In a caught-in-the-wrong-age category are the 400-meter intermediate hurdles—an event I think I would have fallen in love with if it had been available when I was still eligible to run track in college—but that has nothing to do with this chapter. Oh well.

There is a thread through both the racing and the running that is integral to the successful completion of a run or race. Actually, there are quite a few things in common with running or racing, but being patient with the distance is a critical issue. Patience remains one of the most difficult parts of running ultramarathons. Rest is right up there with patience. Rest is vastly underrated in the world of ultra-marathons. Rest is seldom believed in and easily replaced by more miles if you do not believe in your training.

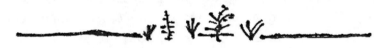

Training, Yes, No, Maybe?

When thinking about training for that first ultramarathon, runners often elicit vague references as to the how part. The first question, however, is not "how" but "what is the goal?" From that will come the how.

Do you want to finish (without the numbers indicating ranking):

a) comfortably, or
b) feeling good and running at the end, or
c) racing, or
d) starting to wonder about the pain of it all, or
e) just doing the survival shuffle, or
f) finishing in the throes of a death march?

Running ultramarathons requires thinking, more so than any other type of running. In the preceding sentence I had originally written "...*perhaps* more so than any other type of running." As I worked on the remainder of this page and section, I kept looking at that sentence, at the *perhaps*. Slowly I came to see the first sentence in this paragraph as one of the few truisms of running ultramarathons. There is no *perhaps* about it. We get time to think about what we are doing. We get more time to think about what we are doing than entrants in any other type of running events simply because we are out there longer.

> *Running ultramarathons requires thinking, more so than any other type of running.*

The unending quest for the correct training program haunts us, each and all. The single question that rattles around in a person's head while in pursuit of a goal event might be "Am I training correctly to improve my time at the Fumblyfoot 50k?" It is almost as unanswerable as the often-repeated questions about the best shoe, best hydration system, best stuff at an aid station, and so forth and so on down the what-is-best line. As with all person-driven processes, there is a certain amount of subjectivity, which removes the definitive *bestness* we all pursue.

If you are running your first ultramarathon, doubts will be a major part of training. By the time you stand at your first starting line, there will have been at least one time in the dark of the night that you found yourself clinging to the ceiling by your fingernails, and, if any are left, your toenails, wondering did I train well? This is the dark side of ultramarathon running—the doubts about doing all we needed to do and is what I am doing the best way?

Newcomers to ultramarathons and trails usually come from a road-running background where they have almost unlimited resources for training. They have Web sites and books, videos and seminars, and a multitude of magazines that frame training down to specific time goals for the full gamut of standard distances, e.g., if you want to run a 3:20 marathon, follow page 229 through 254; if you want to run a 45-minute 10k, turn to chapter 17; and so forth and so on. These cookbook solutions lead to the idea that there is a single correct way to train for any distance.

This is one of the great fallacies about ultras, that, like standard training for road events, there is a simple, guaranteed "two weeks to a fast 50-mile ultramarathon" secret. There is not. Time comes into play, and not just racing time. Time spent running will be the prime determinant in the early years. The preeminent requirement for fast (whatever that may mean) or, more important, comfortably finished ultras is a base—miles and miles of running to get you ready to run a long ways, perhaps quickly. Simply put—you must put in the "time."

The increase in popularity of ultramarathons has brought in more than its share of participants who are impatient, a group unprepared for the complexities of running ultras. After all, an ultramarathon is run at such a slow pace, anyone can do it, right? These newcomers have little patience or interest in putting in the time and the miles of training first. Learning about proper hydration often only comes after the death march from a dehydration encounter. Rest is seldom understood, and the psychological game is simply ignored.

As newcomers to trails and ultras venture off the road or beyond the marathon, they are immediately confronted with the lack of recipes, no more cookbooks to thumb through, and only a few Web sites with scattered bits and pieces of what might be wisdom. There is the frequent generalization of 50k training being almost identical to marathon training. Even that offering is tempered with the always-appropriate advice to get out and run trails as much as you can.

How I train or trained might have very little to do with what works for you (you might not believe in anything I do). At a time when I was training for a sub-seven-hour 50-miler on 55–65-mile weeks, my wife was doing 100–120-mile weeks training for her first road 50-miler. As I went from one method to another, all sorts of chaos played in my head as I did this, that, and t'other to my body. It seemed no one could get me to believe in the new program. Belief in a training program comes from within, not from any pile of words typed by someone hidden in a basement miles away. And each finish line brings triumph that is often quickly followed by doubt and curiosity.

Shortly after finishing a 100k I was rolling the numbers over in my head—9:13:22, hmmm, I have 14 hours, 46 minutes, and 38 seconds left to complete the 37.86 miles that would allow me to say "one hundred miles in one day." Why, that can't be near as difficult as people make it out to be. Can it?

Yes. Yes, it can because of things still to learn while training, things like:

- The riddle of miles needed and what your body (and mind) can tolerate over the prolonged training period
- Finding the magical fuel (one friend of mine took four tries before he found what worked to get him beyond 70 miles)
- Learning which electrolyte stuff to use (powder, pill, liquid, little salt packets stolen from Burger King?) and how many, how often
- The shoes, the shoes, the shoes (tell me you don't have a pair of shoes that feels so good...for about an hour and then they are too tight, or a pair that you pick out because the trail you are going to run is covered with pointy-side-up rocks)
- Clothes that were okay for two or three hours become sandpaper after eight hours
- Elevation (finding out you cannot [physiologically] run above 6,000 feet or 3,000 feet or some other number that you had not known existed
- And, in a concession to all those who run with sound, finding the music that doesn't cause you to rip the 'buds out of your ears and toss it all to the side of the trail

After that incomplete list of things that you should find out in training comes the part you might not be able to train for—the course difficulties:

- The weirdo geology of the U.S.—which types of rocks (what trails are made of) will destroy your body and soul, i.e., running in Huntsville, Texas, is not the same as running in Corvallis, Oregon, which is not the same as running in Quoddy Head State Park in Maine, which is not the same as...
- Mind-frazzling, simple thoughts can go away, and there you are at a trail junction unable to decide on right or left even though there is a ribbon tied to the tree, beckoning
- How come the stuff I did for the last one did not work for this one (what do you do when a DNF follows on the heels of success?)
- And other stuff, the most dreaded of which is not related to the course, the time of year, or anything logical. The evilest of evils, the Did Not Start (DNS)

Confidence, Staying Positive, Kicking Porcupines (Coming to Terms with the Leadville Trail 100)

A sentence in an e-mail from someone as yet unknown to me had caught my eye, *"I get a point in your writing that it seems to be a lot about trusting your training, and having confidence to just keep moving."*

Yup. The one bit of cheating I did for Leadville was going there first to see if I could run at higher elevations. All the confidence in the world will not help if you have a physiological barrier. Some people simply cannot run at higher elevations. And so I signed up for the training weekend. Training weekend was great. It was a great confidence builder. As I entered the last week of training before Leadville, I looked back at the sixteen weeks I considered the core. I had maintained the stress, rest, and recovery cycle. I had maintained my basic five-run-days-a-week thing. I had mixed a bit of biking in with the running, and, of major importance, I had rested or mixed other things in to keep my feeble little mind enjoying the journey I was on. I grew totally fed up with checking to see that I had done everything on the list of things to do. I looked at the training log and the three or four "special" weekends and was able to say, "I am physically ready. It will just be up to my head to get me through." Being the basket case that I am, that is not always the easy part.

If you have practiced eating, worked on the run/shuffle/walk (run the downs, shuffle the flats, walk the ups), and become really narrow-minded about moving on, there will be no bonk. Speed is not an overall issue—an 18-minute pace will get you through, but you want to cushion it every chance you get. Keep the mind set on something above walk when you are on flats. When you need to walk, walk with a purpose, remember good posture and no trudging. The farther in you get, the bigger the smile, the lighter the heart—feed off the aid station people—they are bright lights in the night, always helping. Okay, almost always, but they do mean well and are there for you.

Bonking is not something you will do. It is not in your mind. It is not in the contingencies. If it happens, it is to be a total surprise. You go there to finish—to get back to the red carpet (yes, there is one) at 6th and Harrison. You may have setbacks as the day unravels (or reveals itself) for you. You will get tired, but you get to eat, see llamas up toward Hope Pass, get a Popsicle at Winfield, and enjoy the company of a lot of wonderful people on the way back to town.

I think night running is one of the most important parts of the training for the hundreds. Except for those privileged few that run under 20 hours, most of us will be out there from sunset to the second sunrise (along Turquoise Lake—I hope, I hope. Oh, how I hope).

It is good to be comfortable with living in the beam of light and running confidently

All, or almost all, ultras can be completed without crew, period. The use of a pacer is a very touchy subject amongst a lot of runners. I don't know why. If it is legal and you have someone who wants to and you think it would help you, by all means do so. (I had a great time pacing a friend, Linda Samet, at her first trip to Western States—an honor, a lot of fun, and a tremendous responsibility.)

A pacer can help. A pacer could hinder. Almost all trail hundreds have a pool of pacers willing to help. The runner has to worry about personality matches. You are going to change out there as the night passes, may be a little grouchy at times and may be a bit doubtful of anything you hear or see, may be, might be...

If it is legal and you want a pacer—go ahead. That should be the end of any concern about it being okay. It is your run. Keep it yours.

Will it help? You still have to cover the distance. You still need to eat, drink, go to the bathroom, stay awake, and keep going. You have to do that. The pacer may be good company—I had fun with Linda—but you still have to cover the ground with your own two feet. She is the same age as my daughter, and that probably had something to do with our relationship during the night. It is an interesting experience, but it is each runner's decision.

The crucial parts of Leadville were getting back over to Hagerman Pass Road (the stretch between Fish Hatchery, up the power line, over Sugar Loaf Pass, and down the other side to May Queen)...85+ miles done, between midnight and two o'dark in the morning. Kathy was with me for three or four miles on some of the easy downs from Halfmoon, then she had gone back to move the car. She could not go up the hills with me. You will need to think about your pacer's capabilities, but you can't let it be an emotional burden on you.

Everything must be directed by you and for you; simply getting you on down the trail is the goal. Everything must point at that goal.

If your pacer trips on a rock, root, armadillo, whatever and cannot continue, you must be able to leave him (or her) there and continue on (medical emergencies are, of course, excluded).

Leadville, as do most hundred-milers, handles drop bags very well. Someone a few hundred yards out from the aid station radios ahead and they have your bag located for you. They have big aid stations. The only problem one is getting to May Queen on the way out—that is the only one with a sort of serious time margin. Get moving and keep moving. Once you clear May Queen and head for Fish Hatchery, you get a little bit of time cushion, but nothing big, not a you-may-dawdle-now sort of thing. You can use just the aid stations and your drop bags at Leadville and have no reason to worry—at least not about the logistical end of things. Snicker, snicker, hee hee...

What, me worry? Yes. Yeth. Yup. I have been known to take small, meaningless issues and turn them into monstrously big negative obstacles—more than once (see the 536 pages regarding DNFs).

One of the most difficult things to do in an ultra—when you are tired, cramping, and so forth—is to stop at an aid station. Stop to eat an extra amount. Stop to drink an extra amount. Stop and then stay there long enough for it to get into you system. You can recharge the system enough to make up for all the time "lost" by pausing to regroup. This is an etched-in-stone rule, one of the few, and it is one of the hardest things there is to do while out there. Your mind rebels against stopping for those few "extra" minutes. The whole of your heart and soul will be against pausing, but those "lost" minutes will be made up by the renewed physical energy, which renews the emotional energy.

If someone says, "Hot out here, eh?" just nod; don't open your mouth unless you can counter with, "Yeah, but doesn't the breeze feel good?" I thought about the Leadville Trail 100 and the return to Hope Pass from Winfield. Up toward the top, the climb was getting hard, breathing was a raspy rattle in my throat, and my legs were sore when that special cooling wind sometimes called "angel's breath" came across the mountainside. The groans of ecstasy were loud up high in the Rockies. Ignore the hard, the steep, the heat—it is going to be there, you just have to pass on through. You simply have to cope—continue to cope.

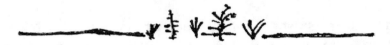

We Have Run...

Have you ever won one of these ultra things you talk about?

Yes. We won a...

Interrupting

We?

Oh. Well yes, we—there are a few ultras I never think of as having done alone. The failures have always been mine and mine alone, but there are some successes that are just as much because of the crew as they are because of my running abilities.

Having someone holding up a dry shirt as you get to an aid station, as if your mind was read several miles back, is pure trail magic. Seeing someone with a crunchy, instead of creamy, bite to eat, again matching your mind, lets you relax just a bit and saves one more ounce of energy for running. That saved energy, mental or physical, became a precious commodity as the miles were covered. Kathy has the knack of knowing what I am doing and how the various voices in my head might be tugging, poking, and prodding to find the weak spot that would shut me down for the day. She is then able to prevent it. I was able to continue to run instead of wandering off into the woods never to be seen again or something like that.

What the crew does depends on whether you are running or racing. And that depends on what you are doing. You might start off a runner and end up a racer or start off a racer and end up a runner. Your crew should be able to analyze the difference (See chart below).

Find a Way to Continue

I had a 50-miler where things went wrong about 15 miles in. I couldn't breathe well when running. I kept moseying along, jogging the flats, but I just couldn't run; something was wrong. I was not in pain. I recognized that I could still go forward. I jogged along, walked along, got passed by people most of the afternoon, but kept feeling okay, just couldn't run. I had fun with the aid station people and kept going on, finally finishing. A trip to an ER later would find a bee sting, a mosquito sting, a fly bite, some kind of sting of some sort that could have been the breathing problem I had—the big thing was that I figured out what I could do, not what I could not do, decided whether it was pain or discomfort, and then continued.

Look for a positive-feedback side of things. As you get farther in, things get better—I was doing a 100k once, running conservatively early, and as we passed the 80k mark I commented I was feeling pretty good. A small person suggested I start chasing and quit just running. As I passed people I felt better, felt stronger, pushed harder—that was a good day, a good win.

You can almost always talk yourself into trying to get to one more aid station. As the day and night wears on you will probably pause and run with other runners, you will lean on each other, support each other, and help each other through the journey. That's why we run, isn't it?

Something to Build On

Warmth. A day of running with less than three layers has arrived. The sting of the wind is not felt today. Spring, in its many forms—*leap, hop, bound*—brings the time of year when we begin to realize the dreams born in winter, the hopes and possibilities that come with each step, thoughts of training that will bring personal success when running and racing.

Warmth and contrast are hidden in the numbers that describe where I live and run these days. I live at latitude 48.2134° north, longitude 122.7084° west—not very revealing information for most readers. I can see into the Olympic Peninsula to the southwest. There are glaciers in there; winter's snow covers ice a thousand years old. The Cascades are in sight to the east; their massive shoulders, too, are cold and covered with snow. I run on the bare dirt of trails almost at the water's edge on an island of moderate climate. I run in early spring while looking into distant winter.

Spring returns to each of us, traveling northerly, covering about 70 miles—a degree of latitude—every four days. To complicate the weather we run in, spring can be slowed by elevation. Each one-hundred-foot increase in elevation delays spring by a day. This fickleness of spring is, perhaps, hinted at by its being a feminine noun in Spanish—*la primavera*. The three other seasons are masculine, seldom leading to rash behavior. Spring brings us longer days, lures us out with greening grasses, plays with our senses—showing blossoms coming from buds for some, retreating snow for others.

For the first time in what seems like forever, I do not have gloves on as I leave the car. Like the groundhog, I have been used as a seasonal indicator; "Must be spring, John doesn't have gloves on." The whole process of running seems slightly off-center without all those winter layers. There is a sense of freedom on those first spring days of running while wearing just shoes, shorts, and shirt. An easy stride emerges without the long pants, memory slowly finds muscles unencumbered by long sleeves—the first runs of spring are magical. Our days become split between training and running, between watching and seeing, eyes watching the trail, mind seeing the daily changes, races in the summer we're running for now.

I love the changes of early spring, life's emergence from the many weeks of drabness and cold. The flowers of the Pacific rhododendron, "rhodies" to the locals, spray the trails with thousands of pink, red, and white powder puffs scattered throughout the forest. The buzz and hum, *whirr* and *rrrnnrr* of countless insects rise as I pass by. Unlike my quick passage, they have a million and more buds and blossoms and blooms to visit before winter comes again. I think about all these changes as I run on, and then the spring sunlight of the open forest is replaced by deep shadows holding on to winter as I enter one of the groves of old-growth Western red cedar. The Old Men of Cedar Grove are back here. I haven't visited them in a while.

There are a dozen or so Western red cedar up here. These very old trees are so special to me. Surely they were here before 1792, when Puget Sound was *discovered* by Captain George Vancouver. One of the trees reminds me of the bristlecone pines of Great Basin National Park. Age shows in the bark, in the fire scars, in the wind-polished bare spots. Hundreds of years of wind have pushed at it, but still it stands. I have passed that tree many times—wondering about its death, wondering if it would fall in the next wind. More than once I have come this way after a night filled with wind, just to check, just to see if *my* aged giant with its eight-foot-thick trunk still stands. Today I pause in its shadow for a drink. In tilting my head back to drink, my eyes lock onto three branches way far up on that grayed and deeply grooved trunk, branches with the green needles of life. Three branches, green and alive. Spring has climbed the old tree as well. Life continues in the grove.

I barely glance at the rest of them. If any others had fallen, my way would be blocked and a great stream of sunlight would shine through the hole in the forest roof. It does not. I run on as the dimly lit silence closes in. Back here the cedars and firs have slowly carpeted the forest floor with layer upon layer of leaves. The softness of this carpet and the dense thicket of snowberries and Nootka rosebushes creates a sense of isolation on the twisting single track I follow out through thickets of salal and tall Oregon grape—all coming back to life with innumerable shades and variations of young green.

Warmth again—out of the shadows of the trail and onto one of the two stretches of pavement in the area. It is one mile to the white gate that keeps the cars out. One mile? Warm. Run! Run hard! It's spring! Run as fast as winter's legs will go. I run. My suddenly ragged breathing strives to become rhythmical, tries to get in time with the footfalls—almost succeeding. The map kiosk at Kettles trailhead is on my left. I am halfway; a push up the hill and Grancy's Run is crossed. A quarter mile to go; my tongue has developed bristles and burrs and tastes of decayed cantaloupe rinds. My arms and hands have turned to stone. Can I really do this? The first pangs of surrender from the hamstrings arrive as I pass Spencer's Ridge. I look up at the *slight* rise leading to the gate. If I can just keep from tripping over my tongue, victory is mine.

The horizontal white bar of the gate comes into view as I top the rise. Sixty yards and it is mine. Spring's early challenges should be ignored. I pant to myself, thinking briefly that this intense exertion could wait for another day. Forty yards. Thirty yards to go, and a twinge from my right calf vies for attention. Twenty yards. Ha! I can fall across from here. Ten more yards, five yards, and victory is mine. Yes! I lean on the gatepost for a moment or two, gasping and panting and wondering why I have done this. Then the warmth of the sun is felt again, and as I turn to run back toward the car, the joy of inner victory on this warm day in early spring seeps in—the why is answered—there is something to build on.

A Tale of Two Fifties
or
Don't Change Things That Aren't Broken
or
Just Needs Some Minor Tweaking
or
Phooey, Ratz, Shuckey Darn...

They were only a year apart. The distance was the same fifty miles on the same course in similar conditions on a beautiful fall day just south of Glacier National Park in Montana.

The first resulted in a master's course record, adoring fans and huge crowds waving and cheering, a long-awaited endorsement contract, an appearance on national television, and an inner feeling of elation, the second only perfunctory congratulations for having completed the run and a deeply personal feeling of disappointment. Both were intended to be races; the second was successful as a run, not a race.

What had happened? The first resulted in laughs and giggles as we drove home. There was nothing negative to detract from the giddiness of success. The second caused analysis to start before we even found a place to pitch the tent that evening. too worn out to go more than an hour's drive from Hungry Horse. The analysis-centered conversation was similar to the type after a "Did Not Finish"—the dreaded DNF. What was being analyzed was my departure from a successful training program (6:31:43 50-mile time) to try a new training program that resulted in a relative failure (7:24:18 50-mile time on the same course).

How do you know if what you are doing is right (as if there is a right or wrong in training—there are only guidelines, and each person is left to find out the width of the line)?

It isn't that the training I was doing was wrong. There was no right or wrong at that time (25 years later there still is not a right or wrong). I had nothing to compare to or with at the time. I had done okay that first year (finishing, finishing feeling good, having fun running, finishing in the top ten, the one DNF had been rectified—redemption gained with a 3:06:03 marathon and the 6:31:43 50-miler). What was there to feel wrong about? It isn't so much a wrong as it is doubt about needing to change. In my case it was an ignorance thing. I did not know if there were changes needed. There was no guarantee of improvement, so there were doubts all along the way.

Why change?

I was new to running ultramarathons. Running ultras was more the result of an ever-growing love affair with running than a venture into some sort of challenge. A run on some trails in the Olympic Mountains of my home state of Washington had created an instant, though never felt before, deep connection to endurance running and running trails or, at least, dirt roads a long ways from town. A happenstance encounter with my first issue of *UltraRunning* magazine had introduced me to organized endurance running.

Enthusiasm, some level of latent talent, and blind luck carried me through that first year. The almost fast 50-miler was followed by a very satisfying 100k that concluded the season on the first day of November—there were far fewer ultramarathons in the Pacific Northwest at that time. I was happy to be in maintenance mode for running while I wondered if I had been training in any way that could be called optimal. I used a "running versus racing" idea to keep my mind in the game; not every Saturday morning starting line was a race. Kathy and I ran together sometimes. I went to some events just to have a training run with aid stations. The common theme through the last couple of months of that first year and the first three or four months of the next year was asking the veteran ultra-runners how they trained.

I learned that most had way more structure to their training than I did. I learned that maybe I did not need to run as often as I did (the foreteller of "rest is good"?) and that, maybe the most important single point, running slower could be beneficial. I learned enough to give serious thought to a need to change my training. I vaguely remember one conversation late in the evening about discipline. Perhaps it is the vagueness of memory that is the message. I did not attach a lot of weight to discipline. I certainly did not think of the psychological energy adherence to a well-planned training schedule would demand (that realization would come later, too late to be of any use).

The validity of a needed change was accepted. A "new and improved" (N&I) plan was formulated, and many sheets of engineering paper were used to create text and diagrams I would follow. Something totally new was incorporated into my running—a goal race months out in the future.

How long does the test take?

I am not talking about the proverbial "how long does it take to get ready to run [insert an ultramarathon or distance]." I am talking about someone who is fit enough to run an ultra comfortably—whatever comfortably might mean. I was fit enough to get up on any given morning and, with only minor consideration for the previous day's run time or distance, head out for a long run of 25–30 miles. During the summer months I sometimes extended the after-work run on Wednesday evening from a couple of hours to four or five hours without any hesitation. The fitness base was there. All I had to do was the tweaking for a high-effort run. I fiddled with the N&I schedule, looking for a work-stress-rest cycle that appealed to me. I looked at a two-week taper and a three-week taper. The taper thing itself was somewhat of a mystery to me.

I finally decided I would need twelve weeks for the N&I training and two weeks to taper—fourteen weeks backed up from "the day." This could also be viewed as the preparation taking fourteen weeks and the test taking one Saturday in October. In other words, it will take a person approximately fourteen weeks to see the results of a change from one training method to another.

How do I measure progress? Some people need real events (pay a fee, run with or against the rest of a field, and get a T-shirt) to put themselves in competitive mode. I do not. I can just as easily push through a 4-hour time trial or see if I can complete a known loop in a time I know is a high-effort run and evaluate how I feel about whatever I did. There was a trail loop I thought of as about 34 miles long. I ran it in about five and a half hours about eight weeks into the N&I program, slightly under 10-minute pace. I was very pleased with it as a test of my endurance fitness. Three weeks before the 50-miler, on my last high-effort day, I ran a controlled-pace road marathon—a 26.2-mile tempo run at an intended seven-minutes-per-mile pace. I completed the marathon in 3:03:03. Those two tests were enough for me. I say "for me," because in the same way that some support back-to-back long-run sessions or weekly speed workouts at a track, others might not. Each person will need to find the test that both measures their fitness and instills confidence. It appeared from these two outings that I had the speed to go with the endurance. These two measuring sticks should have pointed to all being well. They did, for almost eight days.

The N&I program had one part I was unable to measure, mostly out of ignorance: the cumulative effect of fatigue, both mental and physical. I was tired, but I thought I should be tired because I was training at a high level, both physically and mentally. Sometimes, however, being tired has nothing to do with running and everything to do with not running. I had not given rest and recovery enough consideration.

How do I find the bail-out point and then scramble to meld the old with the new and still get to the starting line? This may well be the worst part of trying a new training program. I had decided I needed three four-week cycles to implement the new plan. There were no problems with it physically. I completed the running with no injuries and knew from the way I felt (strong as an ox, half as smart, fleet as the wind, and so forth) that progress was being made. There was no need to consider not completing the fourteen weeks of the "new and improved" program. The problem, if it should be called that, came to light on the Sunday afternoon of the last weekend. At the end of the last run before the taper was to begin, after a 14-miler that should not have even been a challenge, *I felt similar to the way I feel **after** completing a race, not a training run, but a race.* I had just entered brain-dead.

Since there had been no provision for evaluating the N&I at some intermediate point, I never considered that it might not be working. I had committed to it. There was no way that I was going to change the regimen midway. It would have been similar to changing tactics for a race. You keep on because you don't know that it might not work until you try, or that is how it worked for me.

What went wrong? I had paid attention to the training chart. I treated it as some etched-in-stone document and followed it to the letter (or to the mile might be more correct). The informal run fast, run slow, have fun with running, rest if you feel like it "plan" of the year before had been successful for me because my mind needed running to be fun. Even if I was going to race, the buildup had to include some gentle stuff. A lot of runners can do a "run exactly what is on the printout" program. I cannot.

I completed the 50-miler on the same course on a beautiful fall day with excellent running weather. The second one took 52 minutes and 35 seconds longer than the first, over a minute per mile slower. My legs were fine at the end of the day. As best I can recall, my mind never put in an appearance. Physically I was okay. Mentally? My mind never even got in the game.

Aren't you glad running is so simple?

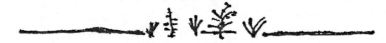

Blathering About Long Runs

Trying to figure out how cows got in this thread, I finally noticed I was one word high in the dictionary. Lucky for me, someone asked the following question: "Should I run Le Grizz for a first 50-miler?"

My answer: You've been running much longer than I have, so I don't know that I have anything useful to contribute. For whatever reason, laziness, lack of concentration, or fear of injury, when I trained for Le Grizz I started out with five-day run weeks. For tracking purposes my run week ends on Sunday. I have always rested on Monday and Friday—even when training for the hundred-mile thingies, I kept Monday and Friday as off-days...maybe a walk or low-effort bicycle ride, but no running.

I don't do traditional "back to back" (b2b) stuff. I don't even think of b2b as traditional, although it is a way of training for some. I look at the weekend total rather than "something must be done on Saturday and some other something must be done on Sunday." Sometimes there are weird splits for the weekend, e.g., 32/8, 17/24, 13/34, 44/4. Even if I run the goal for the weekend on Saturday, I still do some sort of loosen-up run the next day (that's where the active rest of a walk or bike ride on Mondays comes in).

Tuesday and Thursday were about equal—6 to 8 miles. Tuesday was easy; Thursday was easy plus speed play along the way, and maybe every third Thursday was a structured track workout. That "speed play" or "playing with speed" simply means making the run fun—run fast to the next big tree, go through the crooked section hippity-hoppity, turn around and sprint back for 53 yards. Running is not supposed to be all work; make it fun, too.

Wednesday was in the 12- to 14-mile range, always on trails, and was often a night run.

I seldom went past 60–65 miles per week even when racing. Racing training was different from running training. Running training was simply more running. Racing meant getting disciplined speed stuff, mostly those long-tempo runs, at regular intervals. Racing meant lots of headwork to keep the effort up. Paying attention to pace, to effort, to which side of the road you are on, to passing on the left or the right, to grabbing aid bottles and throwing down the empties instead of stopping to change things...racing was only done about once every three months.

In 1986 and 1987 we (wife and I) were doing an ultramarathon or a marathon about every third week, mostly running, occasionally racing. Running relaxes the body and the mind. Racing taxes the mind and takes a toll on the body. The mind gives out fastest, or at least mine does. When you quit paying attention, you get injured doing the wrong workout, pushing when you don't need to, eating poorly, and forgetting to refuel properly...silly little things.

Serious stuff here, this switch from running to racing, thinking, thinking, thinking—there was a tension with racing that was never there with running. The concentration needed to stay within a narrow effort window—the equivalent of running 90-second laps ±3 seconds. You need to know how far into your effort reserves you are at any point. How long can you do what you are doing?

Once I learned about Le Grizz, I knew it would be just great to go run. I have run it thrice and would love to go back. Just one of the most beautiful ultra environs anywhere. The Northern Rockies are for running. Le Grizz is 37 miles of rolling forestry roads and then 13 miles of pavement. There's a dam to cross at 47+ and a climb to the end. One year, we almost had unexpected guests as a mother moose and her calf swam across the lake during the awards ceremony.

While training, I kept close track of effort levels during runs and made sure there were plenty of rest days. A hard, long run might have been 6–8 hours of push on trails or a 4-hour 30-miler on pavement—followed by nothing hard for four or five days.

I stretched the Achilles, lower back, and right-side ITB fairly regularly (I have old injuries to live with).

I made sure there were lots of playing days while running, time to stop and see waterfalls and deer, new flowers and the dogwoods blooming; it didn't matter the effort of the day—nature is the gift we get to run through—there was always time to stop and see what's there.

I got comfortable with distances. I did not get complacent with distances. I never said the terribly flippant "It's only a marathon" or "It's only a 50k." The starting line always hid demons to be met, but I made friends with the distances. The watch quit ruling the runs. I often ran without it. I would put it on when I decided I was going to run a road marathon or a comparative time on some chosen loop.

Now this is definitely way, way too long an answer. Le Grizz? That would be great. Go to Apgar, see the salmon, see the eagles, and see the big brown furry...

Leadville Trail 100
or
on Becoming a "Real" Runner

The question came up again. A long, long, long time ago (similar to a very, very long time ago) the subject of ultras came up at a get-together of runner types. Kathy and I were the only runners there who ran ultras. The first question about ultramarathons that came up was have you ever run one of those hundred-milers?

A long time ago (not as long as a very, very long time) the subject of ultras came up as I was buying a pair of shoes at the local running-stuff store. A couple was looking at trail shoes. They looked at what I had just bought ("genuine" trail shoes, Montrail Vitesse). A few questions and answers passed back and forth, ultramarathons were mentioned, and, then, after all these years, came the same old question. "So, have you ever run a hundred?"

"No, I have not." Back then I had not. That exhausted their knowledge of, or interest in, ultras. I left the store. When I got home Kathy took one look at me and immediately asked what was wrong. I said, "Do you remember that time at Karen's house just after I had won the 100k, a bunch of us were talking about the 100k and so forth?"

"Yes."

"There was a new couple there. They had listened to the back-and-forth for a few minutes. They finally asked a first question. Do you remember it?"

Kathy smiled, nodded knowingly, then said, "The question again?"

"Yes. It seems you still aren't a real ultrarunner unless you have completed a hundred-miler."

Kathy smiled again and then said, "Well, go run one."

There is something silly to this idea. The fragility of the ego (mine) is such that the positive images from the many runs that went well (overall winner a couple of times [a 100k in the frightfully scary darkness of a Halloween night and a 34.5-miler with an incredibly steep and extremely challenging long climb], a course record in the old-folks division at 50 miles, several age-group wins, and years of experiences with ultramarathons that were all very positive are totally overshadowed by what should be a totally forgettable incident, an incident that barely fits within a loosely defined "peer pressure" moment.

I went in the back bedroom, reached up to the shelf that has the back issues of *UltraRunning*, and took down a half dozen or so. I found the information for entering the Leadville Trail 100 (LT100), filled out a check, did the SASE thing, and mailed the entry blank. There, that's that.

Could I run there? In late January "the card" arrived and totally changed a simple walk back to the house from the mailbox. I was looking at the envelopes, working my way through the mail, and finally I got to a simple postcard. Oops. My entry into the LT100 had been accepted. Oddly enough, at this moment the bottom dropped out of my stomach. When I got back in the house, Kathy looked at my face and then asked me what was wrong.

Holding up the card, I said, "I got in to Leadville."

"Yes, did you think you wouldn't? What's the problem?" she continued.

"I suppose it is the altitude thing," I muttered sort of halfheartedly.

The perennial joke about how easy Leadville would be if it were at a lower elevation has never been a joke to me. It is a weak excuse made by people who went there unprepared. Courses can jump up and bite you on the butt if you don't have any respect for them. The one thing you cannot prepare for is the altitude. You can get T-shirts with "There's no oxygen at Leadville" and other encouraging stuff. Physics and the atmosphere being what they are, the air at Leadville is thinner, less oxygen per bucket or breath and so forth. That is a physiological barrier for everyone. My sudden (groundless?) fear was that I might have some form of some sort of pulmonary or respiratory deficiency that would not allow me to run at high altitudes (high altitude being defined here as above 9,000 feet—I had completed the Crater Lake Rim Run, a marathon at between 6,000 feet and 7,850 feet, four times).

What to do? The answer would be to go to Leadville. Quite a few of the hundred-milers have training, orientation, familiarization, or some other introductory-sort-of-word weekends. Leadville is no different. I signed up for the three days of running on the LT100 course. I did not know it, but all my questions about running at Leadville would be answered a few hours after we landed in Colorado.

We flew out of Portland, Oregon, (almost at sea level) at about six o'clock Wednesday morning, arrived at the sprawl that is the Denver International Airport, picked up a rental car, and drove through the maze that is Denver. We found a grocery store, stocked up (our Leadville room had a kitchen) on food, and got back on I-70 headed west into the Rockies. We turned south on Colorado 91 and headed down an almost empty two-lane highway, quite happy to be doing the "ooh" and "ahh" as we drove along. We crossed Tenmile Creek, Humbug Creek, Clinton Creek, paused at Fremont Pass (elevation 11,318 feet), the East Fork Arkansas River—whoa! The what? Even though I had only seen it for the briefest moment, I was sure of what I had seen. I checked the mirror, slowed, and turned left onto a side road. The gravel road was appropriately named "Trail Road."

What is the importance of the (East Fork) Arkansas River? I was born in Arkansas and worked on the Arkansas River for several years. That river is a thousand and more miles downstream and easterly of us. I know of the Arkansas River as a half-mile- to a mile-wide, slow-flowing, muddy or murky body of water, not as a fast-flowing, gurgling-with-rapids-and-waterfalls, high Rocky Mountain creek. Kathy looked at the creek and asked, "Is this the same Arkansas River we know?" I said, "Yes." I knew the headwaters was up here somewhere but had not bothered to look up exactly where. We drove on up the dirt road about a mile, parked, and got out. The "river" had split into several small streams. Who knew which the river was and which was some nameless creek? We walked along a hundred yards or so, and then I saw what I was secretly looking for—I turned to Kathy and proclaimed, "I am going to jump across the Arkansas

River." I turned, ran, and jumped across the five- or six-foot-wide East Fork Arkansas River. As further demonstration of my manly physical abilities, I ran, jumped back across, picked Kathy up, and carried her across the now conquered river. We were glad to be out of the confinement of car or airplane and stayed for a while to run up the road to the end. At the end of the road we paused so we could strain our necks looking up at the mountains around us. The thought "Well, we can run here" crossed my mind but was quickly banished. The run back to the car was relaxed and easy.

During the next four days I logged about 70 miles on the LT100 course including a double crossing of Hope Pass, the 12,660-foot-high signature of Leadville. Kathy was busy putting in about fifty. We should have just paid for both of us. It didn't matter for the ultimate goal. The test worked. I (we) could run at the higher elevations of the Rockies. I would return in August still having great respect for the distance and the course but with slightly less trepidation.

The Run—Leadville Trail 100, August 21 & 22, 1999

Synopsis of (confidence-inspiring) training: A 3:12ish road marathon in June. A 5:02 trail 50k in early July. I had nine 40-mile (or more) weekends. For twenty-eight Wednesdays I did a night run of 12–15 miles. I had no injuries going into the LT100. The food and drink issues seemed to all be solved. All the logistical riddles were gone.

The secret goal that I had never said aloud: I thought I could run a sub-24-hour if (huge "if") I could control the demons in my head. That would be the issue—find a way to believe. I could look at the numbers, the miles put in, the marathon and the 50k times. I could look at them and think I could do it, but I could not cross over to the level of confidence I had when I thought I was ready to run a 6:30ish 50-miler (which I did).

The Start to May Queen: I had to be really careful here. The downhill start, the adrenaline surge, and the ease with which I could pass people all screamed in contrast to the voice that said start easy, run slowly, you have all day and all night, too. I had run enough to know I was much too close to the front. I needed to be back in the pack, maybe use the large number of runners to clog up the trail so I had to slow down. I listened to none of that and was in and out of May Queen with several minutes to spare.

On to Halfmoon: Bullheadedness, a blessing since childhood, and ego-enhanced stupidity continued as I passed several more people going up Hagerman Pass Road. I did not go to walking until we left the road and got on the much steeper Jeep trails and the Colorado Trail. One voice said I had been at the wrong effort level for over thirty minutes. I had decided not to have any splits or pace charts with me. This is misleading as an anxiety-avoidance tool because I simply memorized everything. I do that with numbers. The trip down from Sugarloaf Pass was done as if I was in a 50k instead of the reality of the LT100. Fear is only one voice away. The paved section is no help at all. It is flattish and runnable, so I ran. There were several dips between Treeline and Halfmoon. They were not steep looking, but I knew I should take some short walks as I flew through them. Light years from now I would find out I was running on an 18-hour pace. One of the internal voices finally won and I took a walk break. Unfortunately the next bend brought the Halfmoon aid station into view. Except for the climb up to Sugar Loaf Pass I had been running all the way. In the last hundred yards to the aid station tent, the screams and howls of the whole internal gang echoed with anger and fear. They all took a seat and were quiet and well-behaved as I refilled things, ate a turkey sandwich, said thank you, see you tonight, and turned to leave. I should have felt them arise as one as I looked at my watch. The numbers are still fried into my eyes, 5:42. The internal crowd roared something about being on pace for a 5:50 50k. One of the voices screamed, "Twelve-minute pace is a 20-hour finish!" Another just silently banged his head against the wall of my skull but found that to be of no use in getting my attention. He grabbed several cohorts and headed for my stomach. About a quarter mile out of Halfmoon I slowed to a walk then stepped off the forestry road. I walked into the trees and vomited without grace, good form, or silence. I threw up everything—fear had won.

Regrouping on the way to Twin Lakes: A little-known fact about ultrarunning saved me. Contrary to what people think of a run like the LT100 with its huge field of runners, a person can easily run alone. I needed to be alone to regroup. It would take me a couple of hours to get to Twin Lakes. I was going to need an hour or so to calm myself down. I needed the time to settle the debate about whether or not the cookie-coughing session was critical or just a minor inconvenience. I checked to see how much I had in the way of food and drink. I had just emptied everything. What was going to be an all-day battle to keep the calorie deficit under control was now a battle to find a way to be able to hang on between each aid station. The hundred miles was no longer an issue. The issue was using the gels, energy bars, and three bottles I had in a pattern that would get me to Twin Lakes. I guessed at two hours for the crossing from Halfmoon. I could eat all the food in the next ninety minutes; the water needed to last about ten minutes longer.

The change from a wide forestry road to the single track of the Colorado Trail reduced the size of my world and gave me a manageable length of trail I could cope with as I went. I sipped and nibbled my way. One pair of voices over in the corner whispered, barely loud enough for me to hear, "If he can make Twin Lakes by noon..." I slid on into Twin Lakes. The stop at the aid station was longer than planned, but I needed more food and drink. Kathy got me a plastic bag for takeout and I headed for Hope Pass. It was 11:54 in the morning. The pair of voices over in the corner noticed and chortled with glee, "See, I told you. He's still thinking about it. See. See?" They all climbed on my shoulders, and we headed up Hope Pass.

Noodles at Hope Pass: Even though some of the voices, feeling they had done their job, stayed at Twin Lakes, the remaining ensemble chattered in a worrisome tone as I crossed the river and entered the woods. I did no running up to Hope Pass. I had not planned on running, but I had planned on walking better than I did. The forewarning of just how fast I would deplete each aid station's food was in plain sight. The climb to Hope Pass from Twin Lakes is the easy side. I was out of energy as I got to the meadow full of tents and llamas. I ate several cups of noodles and bars, drank a bunch, filled the bottles and my takeout bag, and headed for the pass.

A Popsicle at Winfield: Somewhere up on the northerly side of Hope Pass is the fountain that comes out of the rocks. Water even Coors doesn't know about. I took a shower, drank several handfuls of water, and pretended to run on down to the valley. The cars on the road to the turnaround at Winfield kept it dusty. I was certainly thankful for having that third bottle with me. The normal two-bottle running would have left me at the side of the trail hours ago. I drained the last bottle as the circus tents of Winfield came into view. We had decided long ago that Kathy would not come to Winfield. It looks too much like a finish line. There are cars and people, music and kids playing, and many runners sitting in cars. The thought of sitting scares me. I don't know that I would get up in just a couple of minutes. I feared that I would not. I did the many-cups-of-noodles again, drank, and refilled the bag. An old guy was handing out Popsicles just outside the tent. I took one. Oh wow, that was good. I finished the Popsicle in about 17 seconds and asked for a second one. He smiled at me and said, "Time's passing." Hmmm, I looked at him, mindful of the gentle prodding he had just given. "Time to go home, thank you for helping," I said to him. I finished my second Popsicle on the road back toward Hope Pass.

The Downhill Slide off Hope Pass: The energy depletion game continued. One of the oldest tortures in running ultras came into play. If I stayed in an aid station for a half hour, could I eat and drink enough to replenish fuel and electrolytes? Realistically the answer was probably yes. The lost half hour could be more than made up by the time regained from regained energy. Psychologically, the answer is no. I am too fearful of stopping. I simply must keep going. My legs were tortured by the nutrition war. My arms had cramped a time or two—dehydration was asking for more and more attention. The paradoxes and problems of downhill running came in. I couldn't run fast enough to take advantage of the descent. I couldn't even coast—it was too steep. Since I could not coast, I had to hold back, and the braking with every step took a lot of energy. The descent from Hope Pass ends any flirtation, however remote, with a big buckle. It was the numbers thing again. I said I did not need to write things down. On one blackboard in my mind was the note "Last chance for sub-25 is to leave Twin Lakes by seven p.m. *and* be able to stay at, or below, 15-minute pace." I pulled into Twin Lakes at 7:10 p.m. The crowd cheered and small children threw flowers at my feet. Kathy and the always-wonderful aid station folks filled me with noodles and mashed potatoes and even a brownie in an effort to reconstruct me. I left Twin Lakes at fourteen minutes after seven, but there would be only a few 15-minute miles the rest of the way. I knew the flashlight would be out before I saw her again. Darkness was approaching, and it had nothing to do with sunset.

Off the Colorado Trail: The miles between Twin Lakes and where the Colorado Trail dumps the runners out onto the road to Halfmoon was completed without seeing any sign of any other runners. The stars came out. The stars seen from way high in the Rockies never fail to cause me to stop at least once. They are closer here. The air is thinner. The Milky Way is thicker. As the trail wound its way through an occasional meadow I would pause and look up. The fight for each mile vanished in the beauty of the heavens. The silence of that section of the LT100 was an absolute complement to the night sky. I was aware of the mental numbness setting in. Had there been anyone to hear, it would have been noted that I was telling myself things out loud. "Pick up your feet." "Relax the shoulders."

"C'mon, blockhead, get a shuffle going." The good part would be that it was a one-sided conversation with no voices offering retorts, yet.

Kathy's voice came through the night air, "Hi, John." What? "Hi, Kathleen," was my numbed reply, "how did you get here?" I had just come off the Colorado Trail. There was a small trailhead parking lot to cross and then I would head down toward the Halfmoon aid station. It was several miles to Treeline, the nearest place she could park. "What are you doing here?" "A guy was driving up this way and asked if I wanted a ride." "Sure is good to see you—terrible emotional down stretch back in there." We were walking on down the road toward Halfmoon. After a hundred yards or so, she started running and then turned and said, "Come on." I started to run and then told her, "I can't keep up with you." Fortunately for me she just laughed. I think any sort of joking about my condition might have ended things right there. We got to the tent and did the soup, noodles, turkey sandwich thing again. I got a laugh when I responded to "Anything else?" by saying I would surely like to brush my teeth. We said thank you and headed out for Treeline.

Potato soup and brownies: Just below Treeline was a paved stretch. It was now about pretty close to midnight. After the single-track Colorado Trail and the road down from Halfmoon, the course was now out in the open of the valley floor. I was again in awe of the stars. They had been breeding since I looked last. Darkness and a night sky like this lend spirituality to the run. There was a barely audible exchange as I passed someone. His pacer was a soundless figure at his side. A car came toward me and slowed. "Hot potato soup and brownies two miles up at Fish Hatchery" came from a faceless voice in the car. Brownies at midnight 10,000 feet way high up in the Rockies and a vision of a glass of milk suddenly came into my mind. I noticed the porta-pot and in true Pavlovian fashion suddenly needed to sit. I had not been off my feet for over twenty hours. The "throne" truly was a seat for royalty. The company Kathy provided for the four or five miles back near Halfmoon seemed to have lifted me. It could have been the realization that this was doable was sinking in. I was mixing walking with running in what felt like a productive proportion. The ten miles from Fish Hatchery to May Queen hold the last climb—the return over Sugarloaf. I was conscious enough to know to stay at the aid station and have a couple more bowls of their absolutely wonderful potato soup—and a brownie complete with milk. I left Fish Hatchery alternating one hundred right-foots of running then one hundred right-foots of walking. The concentration needed for this seemed to be bringing my mind back from the abyss I had teetered on for so long. The stretch of pavement that seemed so endless this morning, oops, yesterday morning was covered and the climb started. My mind was both refreshed and dead. I left the warmth of soup and brownies at about elevation 9,600 feet. I had to get over Sugarloaf Pass at about elevation 11,200 feet. I faced a climb of about 1,600 feet in the next four miles. I did what any self-respecting runner would do. I pulled the bill of my cap down to shrink my world into the flashlight beam on the ground in front of me. It was time to walk up this thing. I would not look up until I crossed the jeep road way up toward the top. Walk, John, walk. Walk, John, walk. The stars were no longer available. What concentration I could spare from walking was used to keep me from slumping over. Several eternities later I noticed I was going across a double-track trail—a double-track...? A road! The warnings of the false summits on the climb to Sugarloaf cried out. Don't look up until you are at the second one echoed vaguely enough to be ignored. I looked up and was rewarded. I had concentrated on looking down and walking as hard as I could. It worked. I was on top. I paused for one last revolving turn to look at the stars that had got me through the night and headed for Hagerman Pass Road.

The last climb done with, I even got to enjoy a moment of lucidity when I figured out the fireflies in the valley below were the lights of the runners as they traversed the trail alongside Turquoise Lake. They were inside a half marathon to run. They had a number that was totally comprehensible in their minds. I was chasing them toward sunrise.

Hagerman Pass Road: The only reason I bring up this barely-a-mile-long stretch is that as I left the jeep road I remembered it being a mile to where we left the road to return to the trail again. In some truly perverted twist of masochism, I thought it would be a good way to bring things back to life by running all the way down to the trail. I even put the light on my watch and pressed the "Split" button before starting to run, and run I did. I was surprised at the ease with which I fell into a comfortable foot strike. I had been out about 23 hours, and yet I was capable of running. I only had to concentrate a little to maintain form and speed. The cruelty of memory brought back the trip in July when I ran this in 6:58 just to see what a mile at speed would feel like. The reason I mention the cruelty of memory is because when I completed the one-mile sprint by arriving at the trail crossing I looked down and saw 13:34. I was 22 seconds short of doubling my last time on this gently downhill fully runnable one mile long. Apparently I can run twice as slow and still believe I am running—the blackness that humor can take was not lost on me as I turned onto the trail.

I am not going over there: There was a woman standing in the middle of the road. She had a flashlight. She was pointing to her right and had told me to go over there. I did not know her. I did not know what was over there. I looked over there and did not see any of the glow sticks I had been following all night. I could not think of what to do. I did not know what she was here for. Along with all those other didn't and couldn't things, I don't know how long I was there before Kathy showed up. She looked at the woman, muttered something, then smiled and looked at me.

"What are you doing?" she asked.

"I don't know."

"Why don't you go where she is pointing? May Queen aid station is just down that trail."

"It is?"

"Yes, that is where she is trying to tell you to go."

"Oh."

"Say thank you to the nice volunteer."

"Thank you, nice volunteer."

She smiled, sort of, shrugged, and went back to watching for the next runner.

Abandoning my fanny pack: The May Queen aid station was somewhere between *M.A.S.H.* and *Apocalypse Now*. My fear of chairs had extended to cots. There were cots with "Wake me up in ten minutes," "Wake me up in fifteen minutes," and so on notes—each with a runner asleep on it. I refilled one last time. Bottles then baggie, and out the door we went. Kathy said she could see me at the far end of Turquoise Lake. I turned to the trail and left the noise and lights behind.

It was still dark enough that up and off to my right I could see a light or two up toward Sugarloaf. I was now one of the fireflies I saw. Someone else could chase me. The second sunrise did not wait. It would greet me before lake's end.

One would think that things would clear up as the night unfolds. One would think as decision points are passed that things would be easier. Wouldn't one? I needed a porta-tree or bush. Modesty being what it is, I looked behind to see if there were any approaching lights. There were none. I found the tree of proper height with a handrail-like branch. In only a few moments business was taken care of and I was back on the trail. In only a few more moments I had turned back and was hoping I could find where I had stopped so I could find my fanny pack and get back on the trail. Good fortune (in addition to patience, whoever watches over me obviously has a sense of humor) had my fanny pack sitting on the ground with the reflective band toward the trail. My eyes locked on it when the flashlight beam hit it. A part of my mind thought about lost minutes, three? Four? Quit. Move. Sixth and Harrison awaited my arrival.

You ready to run it on in? There was pavement beneath my feet. I had just come off "The Boulevard," and things that had held together for so long were unraveling. A mile to go was a thought full of tears and joy and the need to pull things together one more time. A mile to go is not the end. I still had to cover that mile. I needed help. It came in the form of a stranger's voice.

"You ready to run it on in?"

"Sure, why not?"

And we started what we both thought of as running.

"Long night, eh? I'm Michael." And a hand is offered.

"Yes, long is a good word. Over is a better. I'm John." And a hand is accepted.

"First time here?"

"Yes."

"First hundred?"

"Yes."

The sheer beauty of laughter, a wonderfully open laughter with 99.5 miles behind us, was heard in the clear morning air.

"Why on earth would you pick Leadville for your first one?"

"That's a long story, Michael."

Like René Casteran of many years ago, Michael Ehrlich of Steamboat Springs, Colorado, slowed just a step or two as we got to the red carpet, graciously allowing me to cross first.

A hug from Merilee: If you watch the New York, Boston, or Chicago Marathon on television, you are likely to see the superneato shiny Space Blanket placed around the shoulders of each finisher just after the finish line is crossed. In Leadville, Colorado, on Sixth Street just a few yards downhill from Harrison Avenue is the finish line for the Leadville Trail 100. There are no Space Blankets.

In Leadville, Colorado, on Sixth Street, just a few yards downhill from Harrison Avenue, at the finish line of the Leadville Trail 100, I got a hug from Merilee O'Neal. There is no exchange rate of hugs versus Space Blankets.

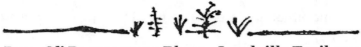

Dem Ol' Postpartum Blues—Leadville Trail 100

"I'm not sure. I'm exceedingly ignorant—..."

The young man laughed and bowed. "I am honored!"
he said. "I've lived here three years, but haven't yet
acquired enough ignorance to be worth mentioning."

—Ursula K. Le Guin, *The Left Hand of Darkness*

There are 1,731 treatises, essays, outlines, and so forth about how
to train for a marathon. There are somewhat fewer descriptions,
recipes, or prescriptions for training for ultramarathons. I read a lot
of them and then condensed, edited, and massaged the words until
I found something that provided me with a viable training method.
What I found missing, and puzzling once I noticed its lack, was information about the way I would feel after the endurance-run events.
I did find one or two brief mentions of depression or loss-of-moti-
vation themes but very little to describe what one might encounter
upon successful completion of a marathon or ultramarathon.

I started running in August of 1984. I had done several 42–44
minute 10k runs and two half marathons at 1:30:27 and 1:32:20—
both on hilly courses during the August-February training. Two
weeks before my first (official) marathon, I ran a last training run
of 26.25 miles. There was nothing really exciting about any of them,
certainly not any emotionally draining experiences.

I ran my:

> 1st marathon in Seaside, Oregon, Trail's End, February 23,
> 1985, 3:37:08

2nd marathon in Salem, Oregon, Phidippides, April 14, 1985,
3:23:12
3rd marathon near Weott, California, Avenue of the Giants,
May 5, 1985, 3:15:15.

My emotional state after the four marathons (without getting into the semantics of "marathon"):

1. The 26.25-mile (3:40) training run gave me a sense of confidence and a feeling that the training had gone well.
2. My first official marathon left me dazed and confused. It was a struggle from the 20-mile point on in. There were several stretches of cramps and walking in the last five or six miles. My goal had been a 3:10–3:15 window. The success of completion was overshadowed by analysis of the failure to run well. A large part of the failure could be attributed to my running alone all during training, overall ignorance of long-distance running, and being quite ignorant of how relatively well I had done. (I would come to my senses six days later and mail in the entry blank for the Phidippides Marathon in Salem, Oregon, on April 14, 1985.)
3. The second official marathon presented another challenge I was not ready for and had given no thought to—heat. I lived in Olympia, Washington, and we had not seen many days with a high temperature above 60°. When I got to Salem Friday afternoon the temperature was around 80°, and I was surprised at how warm that felt. A two-mile walk/jog/shuffle to loosen up from the drive to Salem caused me to change my thoughts of "warm" to "it's just plain hot here."
    The 3:23:12 time pleased me because I had adjusted my effort level in response to temperatures in the mid-eighties. The enjoyment of success was almost totally subdued by my wondering how much the heat had affected my running. I

still had more negative questions than positive thoughts. I got home and looked through the schedules. I found the Avenue of the Giants listing three weeks away and sent in the entry blank.

4. I finally get one right—a totally subjective view, but who cares? I ran "The Ave" with no concern for pace or time. I concentrated on two things while I ran, being comfortably aware of effort and staying relaxed. The 3:15:15 did not make me wince and wish I had picked off the "extra" 15 seconds somewhere. I did not have a calculator with me to figure out my pace. There was a momentary smile when I heard someone a step or two behind me say something about finally getting under 7:30 pace, but it was discarded—heard and immediately classified as unimportant.

What I found was an emptiness of thought beyond being pleased. I did the eat-and-drink thing, but since I did not know anyone and don't do the mix-with-strangers thing very well, I was in the car and northbound in just a few minutes after finishing. The inattentive part crept in. I drove through Eureka without stopping for the sandwich and drink I both needed and wanted. I stopped in Arcata, ate, sat there for a few minutes, then got back in the car and continued up US 101 toward Oregon. After a half hour, maybe more, maybe less, I was dead, simply not paying attention. I pulled off into Humboldt Lagoons State Park and was asleep almost before I was parked. I woke up wondering how long I had been asleep. There being no answer, I started north. This time I made it a while longer, and when I pulled off I was not sleepy, just inattentive, unfocused to the extent that it hampered my driving. I was mentally fatigued, brain-dead to what was around me. I had heard other runners talk about the physical fatigue, but no one had mentioned this, whatever "this" was. I found a place to spend the night. I napped, walked out to the beach, watched the waves, ate dinner, and went back to the room.

The next day the drive was a lot better but still dotted with pauses every couple of hours. I even got out and did the run/walk/jog/shuffle for about thirty minutes somewhere along the Oregon coast. That puzzled me. I was okay to run. There were no aches, no pains, and no physical stuff to keep me from running. My mind was just shot. I mistakenly attributed it to fatigue from four marathons in fourteen weeks (during my sixth through eighth months of running). The idea slipped from my mind—which was exactly the problem, I could not keep a thought in my mind. I had no more marathons planned. I had accomplished what I had set out to do, run a marathon comfortably. I was okay physically and enjoyed the stop-and-go nature of the trip home.

I did not experience the mental dead zone again as the next several years of running passed. For the most part I did not encounter it when I ventured into ultramarathons. I think this is because of the variety of goals. Each ultra was a trip into a new distance or a new place to run. The shift from a ten-lapper on a paved walkway in Seattle to six hours of mud on the Wildwood Trail in Portland, Oregon, to fifty miles of forestry roads to fifty miles of trails kept the mind occupied, but there was a continual transfer of thought to the next one as one finish line after another was crossed. In retrospect, there were no goal races, or at least none with weeks or months of planning. There were runs that became races with results (a master's record at fifty miles and an overall win at one hundred kilometers) that were totally unexpected. They resulted in finish line delirium but no descent into the emotionally and psychologically empty abyss.

The closest I came to it was when training ended for my second trip to Le Grizz, Pat Caffrey's incredibly beautiful fifty-mile run along Hungry Horse Reservoir just south of Glacier National Park. I had switched training methods completely. As the end of sixteen weeks of four hours on Saturday followed by two hours on Sunday neared, I became aware of the mental fatigue. On the Sunday afternoon when I completed that last 16-miler, I sat on the porch and was mentally dead. I had just finished the hardest period of training I had ever done. The physical part was okay, but mentally I was spent. That emptiness came before the race and did a thorough job of destroying the highly complex house of cards that holds my confidence.

A conversation Kathy and I had on the way to Montana for that second Le Grizz touched on the difference between the runs in the Olympic Peninsula and the training runs of the past fourteen weeks. We could finish a 40-mile run in the forests and get to the car wishing we could head right back out on the trails. I would finish a training run and either be thinking of Sunday's run or just be glad another weekend was over. We were on the right track, but at that moment a bear crossed the highway, and we never returned to the conversation. Well, okay, almost never.

In 1999, I completed the Leadville Trail 100 (LT100) run. Outside of the standard convictions a person has while training for ultramarathons, each of us often has one, two, or a variety of unique promises made to ourself that are outside the training regimen but still an integral part. If any of them happen, the whole dream is swept away. I have no anterior cruciate ligament (ACL) in my right knee. I am a card-carrying member of the orthopedic surgeon of the month club, several of whom have suggested that I might want to consider quitting running. I have certainly paid the dues but often failed to attend meetings or heed their advice, it being easier to just continue to run until the day my right leg fails. My primary thought associated with the LT100 was that I would finish it unless my right knee finally gave up the ghost. From January of 1999 through that last 26-mile-long (although by then I thought of 26 miles as a medium-length run) run two weeks before the big day in August (of the same year), every twinge or ache received careful attention, short of including a visit to the orthoped. I had promised myself there would be no need for anything more than the usual poking and prodding of my knee. There would be no incisions, none.

The concentration going into the LT100 was of a different sort than when I decided I wanted to run a 6:30ish 50-miler. The almost-fast 50-miler had quite a few relaxation moments in it. A mental weakness of mine was the relaxing I did at 47 miles down. I knew the 6:30ish time was well in hand, so I relaxed, quite probably costing me a 6:28 instead of the 6:30 and a small handful of change. It was far different from the time going into my first 100k. The "less than ten hours and I am done" environment was not that demanding. I did something similar at the 100k. I relaxed early rather than pushing hard at the onset, obviously adding several minutes to my time. A lapse in concentration at Leadville was not to be considered or allowed. I was going to enter the longest extended period of concentration I had ever experienced. The one-hundred-mile events ask a lot of a person. In particular, the hundreds ask that a person think a lot, dedicate a lot of mental energy to the event, and not let the mind stray far, if at all.

Without going into detail about the training or the drive to Leadville, suffice it to say it all went well, and there I was on an almost rickety bed in a motel room in Leadville, Colorado, on the morning of August 21st of 1999. The thinking did not go away when the alarm sounded. Try as I would to just let Kathy take care of things so I could relax and think about the hours away, minutes away, seconds away from the four a.m. start. The thinking did not go away when the alarm sounded. The sound that sent us off into the predawn darkness of the Rocky Mountains did not end the thinking. It only shifted areas of concern. Now I had to think about effort or think about intervals between drinks and nibbles. I had to think about passing, not passing, or holding steady.

I got to think about eating brownies and Popsicles. I had to think about walking with a purpose and not strolling along in the warmth of the sun. It was relaxing to look at the meadow at Hope Pass aid station with the llamas scattered around. That relaxation vanished as I looked up toward the last few hundred yards to see the saddle of Hope Pass. I started thinking about the trail full of switchbacks down, down, down to Winfield Road. I had to think about time. I thought about the still reachable 25-hour finishing time and its pursuit all the way to Winfield. I thought as I climbed back up Hope Pass. I finally quit thinking about the big buckle as the ever-thoughtless watch said it was gone.

At Twin Lakes on the way home, I looked at the lowness of the sun and thought about how soon I would be running in the beam of the flashlight. I thought about food and how critical it would be at each aid station. My head hurt from thinking about the time I was taking at the aid stations. One part of my mind said, "Hurry, you need to be moving," the other part said, "Stay and eat or you will move no more." All through the night I thought about the footsteps, about the food, and about the beauty of the night sky above me. The thoughts of a time goal had vanished. I was concentrating on moving forward. The constant drain on energy was on my mind and would not go away. The 100k point was over twenty miles behind me. I had been in virgin distance territory for hours. I had to think about my energy level, about hydration, and about really good brownies at Fish Hatchery. That was a nice surprise. I thought about how it should not have been a surprise. I knew about it but was thinking only about the course, the miles done, and the miles to go.

The night wore on. The miles passed. I thought of the coming of a second sunrise. I could not bring up the quote where someone expressed the thought of being lapped by the sun. May Queen was behind me. Now I could break the remainder of the run down into small parts—to Tabor Boat Ramp, to the end of Turquoise Lake, down the power line, across the railroad tracks, up the "Boulevard" and, presto, I am done. I think. A lapse of thought meant I had to retrace footsteps to find the porta-tree where I had left my fanny pack. Sunrise and single-digit numbers of miles to the finish made my thoughts lighter. I never thought about not finishing. There was no time to allot to thinking about things like that. Sixth Avenue and the unraveling of all that thought started to take flight. Within those last few blocks of climbing to the red carpet, my mind was being emptied of things to be concerned with; things to think about were flying away, their job was done, a blankness came in.

On the two-or-three-blocks walk to the motel, Kathy has to turn several times to see where I have gone. The simple act of walking alongside her takes thought, and I have no thoughts left. The room, a shower, a nap, some snacks. It will all be better in the morning. I think.

I recall breakfast the next morning being a collection of smiles and quiet. Two or three people were eating in an obviously absent-minded manner as they looked out the window. Stan Jensen came in. I had met him at the training-run weekend in early July. He was here in pursuit of the Grand Slam, or that is what I thought he was doing. He asked if we minded sharing the table. I motioned for him to sit down. I commented that he must feel good just having the Wasatch Front 100 left to do. An almost infectious grin was followed by, "No, there are two more to do, Wasatch and Angeles Crest." Oh. He was doing what is known as "The Last Great Race"— Old Dominion, Western States, Vermont, Leadville, Wasatch, and Angeles Crest—six one-hundred-milers scattered from one coast to the other and among some of the most widely varied mountain terrain a person can find here in the US. My satisfaction with having completed Leadville vanished. The thought of running those six, actually any six, hundreds in one summer was mind boggling. And there was that thing again. I asked if it was harder to regroup physically or mentally. Stan smiled again and with almost no hesitation said, "It's the mind. The running is always there if the mind is willing. It's the mind." I thought of the thinking part again. An enjoyable breakfast ended all too soon. The Monday-morning breakfast and "until next time" was taking place just as it does in the many little towns across the world of hundred-milers. Smiles, waves, a few handshakes, and we were outbound, back toward Oregon. (Stan would successfully complete all six of the hundred-milers to finish "The Last Great Race"—a truly amazing feat.)

As always, we avoided the major highways as we drove back to the Pacific Northwest. This proved to be beneficial as I twice stopped at an inviting creek to go stand in the knee-deep waters as part of the recovery week. Both times Kathy was content to get out the folding chairs and read for a few pages as I took a nap after the *Jacuzzi au naturel*. We only drove about 250 miles that day. The next day was better, but I still had a tendency to daydream—driving required more concentration than normal, and I was glad we were using deserted roads leading out of Colorado into Wyoming. The physical side of me was fine. We stopped as we crested one pass. I told Kathy to drive down a mile or so and I would walk or run down to her. My legs reacted just fine for about a hundred yards, and then, without any consultation whatsoever, I was walking. Hmmm, what had happened? I had to pay attention to keep running. It was not a pain issue. There was nothing physically stopping me. It was just an encounter with a mind that had paid attention for all those months of training and now wanted a few days off.

I ran or walked or stood in a creek here and there along the route back to Oregon. Our conversations by a campfire as we watched the sunset changed from monosyllabic to something coherent. The threats to leave me at every nursing home we passed diminished. My ability to concentrate returned, not with a flash or a suddenly-clicked-on light in the blackboard of my mind, but running without needing to stay aware of each step returned. It would be October of 2004, at Cabo Fisterra in Spain, before the topic would become part of our conversation again and finally make sense to her.

What I Have Learned

If you run only trails, you will lose some of your road speed.

If you run only roads, you will not have trail agility and strength.

Variety is almost always good. It also keeps the mind game enjoyable.

You start out training to attain the endurance to run a long time.

Endurance → Strength → Speed

You need to (not "have to," almost nothing within the world of running ultras is etched in stone) become comfortable with the long training runs that are twenty miles or more in length. The marathon distance should become a friend. I started feeling that way when I could run a marathon and only be comfortably tired afterwards. I would be tired but willing to run another one the following weekend, or, as time passed, the following day. Marathons had become long tempo runs pointing at an ultramarathon somewhere. The respect for the distance was still there, but some of the intimidation was gone, on most days.

Once you can run for a long period of time, you start doing strength (running, not weights) training so you can run a long ways for a long time at a higher effort level than when you started.

When you reach the point where you can run a long ways at a fairly high effort, you do speed work to be able to call on higher leg turnover to take advantage of downhill stretches, to be able to pass someone, or to pick up the pace for some desired period of time. On trails, high leg turnover is invaluable for those same downhill stretches plus the twisty-curvy sections.

That's it. That pretty much sums up what I have learned. Beyond that, each person picks his or her own training program. Some like to run seven days a week; some prefer low mileage, high effort for all runs, track workouts, fartleks, or any number of variations that suit particular goals. This takes time, time in the form of practice. It takes time to find the training program with the stress-and-rest cycle that fits you.

What if you want to try a new method? Changing training programs in marathons or longer distances is an unforgiving idea if it is wrong. It takes approximately 14 weeks to change methods. The 14 weeks of change is made up of 12 weeks on the new program, two weeks to taper, and then only one day to run, or race, and find out if it worked. It takes a lot of courage to switch from one method to another. Trying a new program takes commitment, because if you don't believe in what the "new and improved" is doing for you, things will not go well. The sole judge of whichever program works will be you. Within ultramarathon circles the often-heard "we are each an experiment of one" contributes to the widespread diversity in training.

It isn't just the distance you run, it is also the frequency of doing those runs. Generally, in the training and running of road marathons, there is still an entrenched attitude by most roadies of only one, or two at the most, hard-effort marathons a year. Many recreational runners still look aghast at the thought of two or three weekends in a row of 30-mile runs. That kind of running is superhuman only when viewed from within the confines of the marathon or shorter environs. Running a 30-miler on consecutive weekends does not mean you are some sort of fitness freak, it simply means you have found a comfortable training regimen for training for ultramarathons. You don't run at high-effort level during training runs. Training runs are to develop strength and endurance—ditch the watch, relax, and enjoy the run.

Regardless of which training program ends up being your choice, remain flexible in application; understand that training programs are guidelines, not etched-in-stone rules. Be open to at least trying some of the following practices—variations in training help both the body and the mind.

The Tempo Run

The exact definition of a tempo run was tossed back and forth by four of us some years back as we wound our way here and there on the trails of McDonald Forest in Corvallis, Oregon. If you cannot define a particular drill (and its intended purpose and result), how will you know what to do?

Once you have an endurance base, you might include fartleks, speed sessions, or tempo runs. They are defined relative to the distances for which a runner is training. The problem that arises with defining any of these for ultras is the distance involved. There are lots of training books for the marathon and shorter distances.

The purpose of the tempo run is to get your mind and body comfortable with extended high-effort running. You want to be comfortable while running at something close to your aerobic threshold. That "extended high effort" is the catchphrase. Just what does "extended" mean when you are fighting the ups, downs, roots, rocks, and the many twists and turns of an ultramarathon? Note: I run mostly trails, but a lot of this was written when running an ultramarathon could just as easily mean road or track as well as trail. Trail and ultramarathon are not synonymous.

The variety of venues of ultras as opposed to the relative flatness of marathons causes most typical training guidelines to be useless. For a road marathon you can go to the track, do some number of mile repeats, then go on the road, do some 3–5-mile, 80–90 percent effort or lactate-threshold or marathon-pace (assuming you know what each of those means for you) stretches, and you are somewhere in the ballpark.

So what do you use for a distance for the tempo or speed or high-effort run for an ultramarathon? Just the idea of needing tempo runs points at wanting to run for time instead of running simply

156

to finish. You are now training to maintain a certain effort level rather than just to get to the trailhead before dark. Now you need to evaluate how you can combine your current fitness level with your physical skills—talent level comes into play. Numbers are necessary. An occasionally tossed around rule of thumb is to try 10–12-mile (or longer) runs at hard-effort marathon pace, and you have a good tempo run for a 50-miler. It was fairly easy to find people who felt the tempo run (high-effort run?) for a 50-miler should be in the 16–20-mile range. I used time or distance, i.e., run for X number of minutes or for N number of miles, depending on how I felt that particular day. I mixed miles and time to fit how I felt on a particular day and what was the purpose of the training. A mix of time/effort/distance for me might be any one of the following:

- Run at a perceived high effort for two and a half to three hours for the longish tempo runs
- Do an 8–10-mile hard-effort stretch in the middle of a 25–30-mile training run
- Run 3–5 easy, then 6–8 hard, 2–4 easy, 6–8 hard, 3–5 easy
- Do the ugly one: an easy 12–14 in the morning, a hard 8–10 in the afternoon

The hardest part is deciding what is hard, medium, or easy effort levels. There is no rule for it. Books, blogs, and Web sites are only guidelines that tend to suit each runner relative to their own ability.

There is also the thought that if the course you are going to run is difficult, a challenging single-track trail for example, then you are going to need strength rather than speed. Ultras demand more versatility in training than road marathons. You could come off a 3:53 50k and two weeks later be real happy with a 5:02 50k, one being just a little hillier than the other. Often the initial problem is how to start the speed stuff. By running ultras in a nonracing mind-set, we tend to rarely run fast. There is that "what is fast" question almost immediately. I don't use a formal definition for "fast," because for me, like most others, fast has its own definition with each passing day.

On any old training day, throw in some playing-with-speed sections: run at faster pace to the next switchback, to the next park bench, to the next oak tree, whatever. "Faster" can be just an increased speed, could be steady acceleration until you are just about as fast as you can go, could be just above aerobic, just below anaerobic...just almost gasping...this is all on trails or paved pathways or something other than a track.

If you are on a paved road or even a well-graded dirt or gravel road where you have all low-effort hills or surfaces, no hard ups or downs, no ruts, roots, or pigsties to deter or distract, you can do a speed workout. Any course where you can concentrate on running form, a course where you have no need to check the footing, a course where you can simply relax and run, is a speed-workout course. You have to be able to quit looking at the terrain so you can relax and concentrate on what the legs are doing.

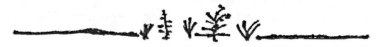

A Starter Track Workout

Do something or other to get warmed up, just warm enough to run, not midsummer hot, then, in the listed order:

1. Run four laps of run the straights, shuffle the curves
2. Run four laps of run the curves, shuffle the straights
3. The weirdo (you still run four laps): run half a lap, shuffle the straight, run half a lap, shuffle the curve, run half a...

4. Run a lap, shuffle **half** a lap, run a lap, shuffle **half** a lap, run a lap, shuffle half a lap, run a lap... it takes six and a half laps to complete this set
5. Pretend to cool down

An alternative to the certain-number-of-laps plan is to go to the track for some period of time, say an hour. During that hour, run fast, run recovery pace, run fast, repeat. Somewhere there is a coach with credentials that is cringing. I am not offering any sort of rigidly structured program. It is just a way of training that kept the tedium out and the fun in for me.

There are easy variations on the track workout. I often pedaled to the track, making a twenty-minute bike ride the warm-up portion of the day. Some days I would run a hard lap, shuffle a lap (recovery lap), and just repeat that simple pattern for an hour. This is running with nothing to distract the mind but paying attention to effort. This is not maximum speed. I suppose 75–80 percent of other runners might define it as speed. You don't do it at an effort that you perceive as hard. I used to do this about every other week (often ending with a four lapper on the inside lane).

In the first few speed sessions, the hard part is starting hard enough to get a workout but easy enough so as not to strain or pull a muscle. If you feel any twinges, quit, go back to easy running. You might need to warm up more, might need to do the "playing with speed" for 50, 60, or 100 yards two or three times a run once or twice a week for a few weeks just to get the legs used to the faster turnover.

Be creative. Find a route that gives you a chance to "play with speed" as you do your regular run. This evening I used the power poles as I ran the service road that parallels the power line. I was running three power poles (two spans), shuffling two power poles (one span) for about two miles.

It is hard to judge effort, especially during the early stage of a running life. I have a feel for the effort level I am at while running. That sense was developed over the years. That sense and the underlying experience is more important than any numbers on the face of a watch. The face of a watch, GPS, or HRM will not tell you how long you can sustain whatever you are doing. Only a well-developed sense of effort will be a reliable guide. You need to develop this awareness so you can feel what you are doing during a run. Right now I am running comfortably at about nines (on sort-of-nice trails). I am probably at about 7:00–7:30 on the "speed" stuff. This is just a "that's about what it feels like" thing. I know I could go a little faster, but I am holding the effort for about 30–45 seconds for the short stuff.

In today's world of technology there is a trend away from knowing your effort level. There is a tendency to look at the heart rate monitor or GPS and see a number displayed. There are also complaints about batteries dying during a run. It is still a tremendous benefit to be aware of your effort as you run and to know how long you could sustain that effort—without looking at an electronic instrument. You should know your body.

I better stop here, let you read this and then think about ways you can incorporate some speed stuff into your running without falling prey to the injury bug. This is all out of order (my running always was—I had speed first, then built endurance, then built strength).

For training to work,

- dogmatic tones must be undone (there is no "one size fits all"),
- the gospel of training isn't gospel, and
- flexibility, rest, and adaptation will be crucial to success.

CHAPTER FIVE

We often take for granted the very things that most deserve our gratitude.

—Cynthia Ozick

Volunteers don't get paid, not because they're worthless, but because they're priceless.

—Sherry Anderson

Silent gratitude isn't much use to anyone.

—G.B. Stern

I am only one, but I am one. I cannot do everything, but I can do something. And I will not let what I cannot do interfere with what I can do.

—Edward Everett Hale

God has not called us to see through each other, but to see each other through.

—Author Unknown

Too often we underestimate the power of a touch, a smile, a kind word, a listening ear, an honest compliment, or the smallest act of caring, all of which have the potential to turn a life around.

—Leo Buscaglia

Volunteers: the Event Variety, Not Your Crew

They are almost universally needed, always appreciated, not always overworked, and the simple reward of having helped must be important, because many people who have never experienced what we are doing volunteer year after year. They will stand around in the rain or heat, snow or wind, alongside a dusty dirt road or next to a gate in a barbed-wire fence that keeps both cattle and runners contained for care and feeding. They will camp on a remote mountain pass with just enough shelter to keep a camp stove burning as they wait. They will stir soup or pasta, pass out cookies, and find a way to keep cocoa warm as they wait for the next runner. Volunteers can be trained to put T-shirts in bags, separate safety pins into small groups, and other stuff as needed or to be defined later.

They will take their own cars off down dirt roads hoping to find a gate they have never seen before and then recognize where a trail crosses an even fainter dirt road. Once there, they will disregard the wind, rain, snow, and even darkness of night to set up card tables, unfold those weirdo folding canopies, and then move the car so it is both handy and a windbreak. They will set up a stove of some sort to get soup or coffee or tea or hot cocoa or grilled cheese sandwiches or chili dogs or almost anything else a weary runner might want. Someone will slice oranges and bananas. Bowls will be filled with potato chips, pretzels, crackers, and who knows what all else—somehow it makes its way to the table.

Volunteers will stand at remote trail intersections deep in the woods in the pouring rain, smiling and pointing (usually correctly) the way for the paying public. They will count laps for hours and hours for someone behind a number that they might have never met. "Did you get me?" is a question they will field time and time again through the hours as you run. Volunteers from local radio clubs often form the backbone of most ultramarathon communications systems—go to almost any major ultra and you will notice a group of "they don't look like runners" over to one side. They will be standing near a bunch of mud-spattered vehicles with tall whip antennas. They are getting ready to babysit electronically, track us through the day and night, tell of good news and bad, and willing to respond—almost always—to the "Can you tell me where number such and such is?" posed by crew members of the runners. They are well worth talking to before the race starts. Most of them are locals and can tell you about what the weather might be and how the trails are, and their concern with the day going smoothly passes on a sense of comfort to you—there will be a lot of folks out there today, many of them just there to help you get through the day.

Their generosity, care, and concern are pushed to the limits as the hours pass. The leader's passage is a distant memory and the middle of the pack has gone on around the bend. Now they wait for the stragglers—the back of the pack.

Scattered, but not random, memories of volunteers or volunteering along the way:

Coast Hills 50 Mile, Siletz, Oregon: What's the Chevy doing way up here? On a day when whoever was in charge of the weather failed miserably, there was an unexpected bright spot. I had seen clear skies, rain, sleet, freezing rain, snow, and wind as we covered the trails in the first 42 miles of the run. Most of us had misjudged the weather and had spent a lot of energy turning various colors of blue as the cold came and went, accompanied by the previously mentioned rain, sleet, freezing rain, snow, and wind. The several miles of climb were over, and I was finally in the "last" downhill section. I had been assured of this by the smiling medical person on top of the "last" climb. He had told the truth to the extent that the climbing had ended just a hundred steps past where that aid station was. I had revived enough to warm myself up by running. Greg Marbett had caught up with me, and we were in the part of a hard trail ultra where conversation is a mixed bag of grunts and a hand that is sort of raised and sort of points.

He pointed off to the right at the sun glinting off a windshield down below us. We thought it was probably the last aid station and started talking about the need for some chocolate chip cookies. Greg, being an uncouth sort, was hoping for some dry, crisp ones. I, being the more sophisticated, was already picturing some gooey, half-baked cookies. We rounded a last curve, and there was a familiar brown Malibu and Kathy. She explained they were short on volunteers so she had driven up here to be an aid station. Oh—got any chocolate chip cookies? Yes, you want dry or gooey? Heaven is an aid station that caters to individual tastes. We nibbled and drank and finally noticed she was pointing down the hillside. Leave some for the rest? Sure. One more? Sure. Get out! Okay, see you in Siletz in a while.

Mudderfell Six-Hour, Portland, Oregon: The Mudderfell run was Warren and Patti Finke's now-defunct mudfest on the Wildwood Trail. I was recovering from surgery and Kathy was running. I volunteered (Patti noticed my monstrously big bowl of Chex Mix and assumed I wanted to share) to help at the second aid station out (Mudderfell was an out and back—aid station, aid station, then turn around at the aid station about 8.6 miles out). The first time through, about six miles done, everyone was bright and shiny, smiley and happy, full of vim, vigor, and enthusiasm. The "big dip" was just past my aid station. The slipperiness of a muddy downhill and the climb up and then out to the turnaround aid station waited.

The next time our intrepid adventurers arrived, about eleven miles were done and the "big dip" had been crossed twice. There were no more clean shoes, socks, or legs. The appropriateness of the run's name, Mudderfell, was indelibly stamped on all runners. Still, they smiled and laughed and accepted our chips, oranges, bananas, and...discovered my big bowl of Chex Mix. Some were slow to leave until I moved the Chex Mix back to the car.

On the third pass a sense of urgency was visible. They needed to get back to our point of refuge in the wilderness in order to qualify for a T-shirt. Our aid station was at the 28.1-mile point when reached on the fourth pass. In addition to the highly-sought-after, and much-needed, T-shirt, the reward for two crossings of the "big dip" and venturing into ultraland was also access to the Chex Mix.

McDonald Forest 50k, Corvallis, Oregon: Mud, smiles, hugs, then tears—Clem LaCava's McDonald Forest 50k trail run had done what many suspect trail runs of being able to do. It had assumed a personality of its own over the years. But on this Saturday late in April of 2003 it outdid itself. Six years I had been there, either running or helping, and this was the muddiest I had seen it. The rain made the decision to volunteer rather than run a lot easier. Kathy and I left the house at about 8:00 and headed for our point-this-way-or-that positions. I left her down on Dan's Trail near Jackson Creek and headed up the trail, looking back to be smiled at once more before I disappeared into the falling rain.

I climbed Dimple and headed down the road to Baker Creek Trail. Baker Creek Trail is a place I avoid during the wet season. The mud is sticky and has been known to suck the shoes from an unsuspecting runner. It is a steep trail, and the switchbacks will make you slip and do butt slides, think unkind thoughts about Clem, and question your reasons for being here or just for being. I arrived at my home for the next several hours—Sander and Dale came by, trail markers and direction givers most excellent. We smiled and discussed both the quantity and the quality of the mud on the trio of trails coming together here: Baker Creek, Lovely (not so lovely today) Rita, and Waddayaknow, and so on—my smile partly because I was not running today.

Early starters came through; lead runners came by. I pointed thattaway, smiled, muttered something incredibly witty, and watched them cross the log bridge and disappear across the wetlands. The familiar faces passed by, folks from Ashland and Portland, West Linn and Seattle, Bend and Corvallis, smiles and greetings, Scott McQueeney came through for the first time with a familiar smile of hello (certainly not because he had just exited the Baker Creek mudfest, eh?)—I thanked him for an unusually poetic birthday message from a few days earlier and sent him off into the muck of Lovely Rita.

The lead runners were returning from the loop then, causing some conflicts of right of way on the bridge but never any trail rage, just smiles and cheerful encouragement of runners passing by. The mud was taking its toll; more and more often I heard, "How far to the next aid station?" or, in a hopeful voice, "Is this the last hill?" I smiled and said there was one more smallish hill. Veterans of the Mac smiled back knowingly, newcomers smiled back not knowing... they headed off generally toward where I pointed.

"Hi, John."

"Hi, Marilyn." Marilyn Bailey was up from the Siskiyous to get away from the snow.

"Hi, Peter." Dad (Peter Idema) tried to stay ahead of daughter (Ashley).

"Hi, Pam." An escapee from the Oregon State University bookstore.

166

"Hi, John, I need a hug." Hmm, who was this person?

"Hi, Glenn." How many recognized Glenn Tachiyama without a camera?

"Hi, Marlis." Marlis Dejongh's always-present smile warmed a cold and wet trail junction.

The parade of strangers and friends continued, smiles and laughter, words or silence, hugs, pats on the shoulder, or simply a nod as they passed by and I was left behind in the rain and mud of Baker Creek.

Scott McQueeney came back, a serious set to his face as he slipped and slid down the trail on the far side of the creek. As he crossed the bridge I managed a straight face and said, "Just like Badwater, eh, Scott?" The smile came back. We joked a bit, only a few sentences, one last smile as he told me how bad he felt about leaving me here alone. Hugs all around and he headed off into the mud and rain and the climb out of the bottoms.

Hugs and smiles are good on a muddy day in the Mac.

The time between runners was longer then. The fatigue was showing more on the faces of the runners. I provided lies and encouragement. The young and the old, the new and the veteran, I'd tell 'em anything to get them down the trail and on up the hill in good spirits. The mud had brought out new levels of challenge that were met by newly found determination.

The sweeps appeared. The flags and ribbons were taken down. I collected the things to carry out with me. David and Steve went off up the course, doing their housecleaning. I smiled and headed the other way, up Baker Creek Trail. As I made my way up the half mile of mud on the uphill side of the mountain, I smiled at the thought of how little of the mud and trails I had to cross compared to the runners today.

Later that evening I would be totally shocked to learn that Scott McQueeney, friend, runner, occasional poet, and veteran of many of these excursions had died of a heart attack at the finish line.

I want people to remember the smiles of the day, the good times; we never know which run will be the last. We never know which smile will be the last we share with someone. We lost someone good that day.

McKenzie River Trail Run, McKenzie Bridge, Oregon: At a beautiful run in central Oregon, Kathy and I were the finish line crew for five years. Phil Vaughan's run was known for keeping the finish line open until the last runner was in. We were proud to be part of that tradition; welcoming those last few runners was always worth the wait as the smiles came to tired faces when they saw us. Doing something like that is just as hard to leave as a run you have participated in as a runner for many years. We really disliked breaking the string, but we were going for a walk across Spain, and it was time to go.

Volunteering is so many things that a person can do to help out with our sport. There is the evening spent stuffing bags in the 6th Street gym in Leadville, looking in tired eyes and finding the words needed to encourage someone to continue, taking on the task finding the food for a 12-hour track run, introducing volunteers to what they can expect on the first organized run in the Turtle Mountains of North Dakota, fixing a few pounds of baked potatoes to leave with the RD, explaining to someone that no one gets behind the sweep, and 1,739 other things that volunteers get to do to contribute to our sport, hobby, avocation, or whatever you might call it.

The Stressful Side of Running—Crewing

(A special thanks to Lynn Ballard, Letha Cruthirds, Kent Holder, Lisa Henson, Chihping Fu, Lisa Bliss, and Erik Moortgat for passing or pausing at the Cascade Crest Classic 100 Mile in 2007.)

It is the last hour before the start of another ultra. I am watching the greetings of old friendships being renewed, the handshakes and smiles, listening to the hellos and stories as a shared trail somewhere else is remembered, when I start noticing the tension in faces scattered through the milling crowd.

A sleeve is tugged. "The drop bags are out," a crew member says, her face that of a harried mother on the first day of school. A nod from her runner and she returns to her task list.

Three people are talking animatedly as they walk amongst huge piles of water bottles, ice bags, 5-gallon containers, and an assortment of food. Items are checked off the list on the clipboard. A pause and a sudden return to a pile, bags shoved this way and that—where?—searching hands—here. It's here. The three turn to the next pile; only a slight relaxing of furrowed brows shows.

Seemingly outcast from the runners, off to one side is another group, mostly older people, all wearing identical jackets, all driving vehicles with long antennas. They look at maps, point at spots, check watches, drink coffee, talk, and point up into the hills—a glint of excitement shows on several faces, calm commitment on all.

A runner pauses from her conversation and slips into the jacket held up by a young man. I ask if he runs, too. "Yes," he says quickly, "but today is her race. I'm just crew." These last words were tossed over his shoulder as he separates the pile in the rear of a van into three groups—hands moving with urgency but not with haste.

People separate, runners moving near the starting line, crews stepping back to better viewing points, the radio folks driving off to their places in surrounding mountains. An appointed time is near. Laughing and shouting ring out from the smaller crowd as they approach the line drawn across the old dirt road. Faces are photographed from this side and that. Four runners join hands to look at the lens. A baby is held in Mom's arms as Dad snaps one last picture. "One minute!" Shuffling, quiet, and then the startling blast from a

169

RUN GENTLY OUT THERE

fire truck's air horn shatters the morning—the race is on—the runners are gone.

"Do we have time for coffee before...?" Some say yes, some say no, many just head for cars and drive off into the mountains. Breakfast will be after they get to where their runner expects them to be next, knows they will be, must be.

Tall cedars and firs filter the sun's light high on the mountainside at a point where the trail crosses the road. The morning quiet is broken as cars arrive. Chairs and tables are unfolded. Lists are consulted. Bottles and belts, shirts and scarves, pills and powders, a collective sigh as arrangements are completed. Now they wait.

Books are read, sort of. Conversations are held, sort of. Everyone's eyes and ears return constantly to the still-empty trail.

"Runner!" Eyes search for a remembered shirt or cap color, for a smile or a frown. What will he need? What will she want? Does she look tired? He shouldn't be here this soon, should he? A printed sheet is consulted; a frown forms, disappears; smiles, only smiles for the runner. Cloak the runner in smiles and good thoughts, replace gels and bars, and refill water bottles quickly. As one runner turns back to the trail, her crew is already checking the map for the drive to the next aid station.

The drizzle comes in the afternoon. The seemingly simple task of getting a rain jacket brings worried thoughts—what if he comes while I am at the car—will she need a jacket—will he want to change shoes—will she need a cap—what kind of warm food is at the table. Adjustments are made and the many and varied portable runners' supply stores open and close and move off down the twisty, hilly road.

Nightfall and changing faces—eyes trying to pierce the darkness as each flashlight appears in the distance. Is it mine? Can you tell who it is? She looks tired. He's shivering. He is early. Where is she? Shoulders are hugged, soup is offered. Bottles refilled, hearts reawakened, too soon a runner's back is watched as it disappears into the darkness, so alone and fragile looking. I saw smiles and frowns, tears and laughter as some pack to go home, while others reload to go to the next aid station.

With the dawn comes hope and concern. If we can get a bite of breakfast in her, she'll perk up. If we can get him to stop long enough to refuel, he can pick up the pace. There are climbs ahead. It will be cold up there. Can I get him to stop long enough to change shirts, he's way ahead of schedule, he won't want to stop. She needs gloves—we don't have gloves. Here, I have an extra pair, give 'em back at the finish. When is cutoff at...

Cutoff? Agonized looks. The unspoken just came to life. Dawn is to bring hope, not some demon on a taut leash. Here, drink this and go. No, you can't wait for him. Yes, you can catch up on the flats. The mixing of silence and nervous conversation as goals and setbacks are being realized churns the morning air. Could we have done more? He sure liked the soup, eh? She still looks strong...doesn't she? Doesn't she? When do we see him again?

The gaps between aid stations seem endless. Drive safely, but hurry to get there. As the run nears the end, each gap brings a disconnect just when crew and runner want contact. The self-doubter needs a familiar face, a trusted voice to say the same encouraging words strangers have been saying. Death-warmed-over needs another smile from a loved one to keep going. It's only five miles to the next aid station, isn't it? One runner, twenty-seven minutes ahead of schedule, barely slows as bottles are topped off for the final leg. Cars are reloaded one last time. Another runner, cold and drained of energy, slowly pulls on a jacket and stares at the numbers being unpinned. "Other days," someone offers. "Other days," is softly replied.

And the crews gather at the end and wait, not patiently, not well, but they wait and look at where they know the runners will appear. It is on Sixth Street, it is on a track, it is a trail coming out of the maple trees or firs or out of the sagebrush. What color shirt? What color cap? Go ask the radio people if they passed through the last station yet. Well, go ask again—nicely. Where is she? Do you think they will still be together? Can he...there!

There's my runner.

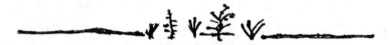

Is the Gamble Worth It?

So here I am again, sitting here at my pretend typewriter (it's really a word processor on my laptop) glancing at an electronic background of CNN, MSNBC, the ultralist (aka "the 'list", ultra-list, or...), and three or four other connections to what I think of as the news of the day in topics all across my interest scale with so many side trips that whatever I was going to write about quickly vanished. I am my editor's worst nightmare.

Oops! Huh? I hit the "back" arrow on the browser to reread. Hmmm, really? *And why one would go out into that heat...The gamble isn't worth it.* Of the many comments I have read during the several days of a "runners lost, runners found'" story, this one stands out. *The gamble isn't worth it.* An appropriate response in French is *au contraire!* Even with all the (potentially) inherent dangers of trail running, endurance running, ultrarunning, or whatever you call our running, that phrase sums it up for me. *Au contraire! Quite the opposite!*

It is worth it. The slow steps and the fast steps. This year, via the Internet in one form or another, we were treated to following an astoundingly fast run at Wasatch—another side trip. Was it really only 2002 that Nate McDowell put things together to become the first to break the 20-hour barrier at the Wasatch Front? It seems like forever ago, such was the giant step he took. If we didn't take the chance to go out there, we wouldn't have any understanding of what Geoff Roes has accomplished. If we didn't go out there, we would not know that although his footsteps may have long grown cold, it is the same trail for Wendy Holdaway, and her finish held just as much value as his. It was well worth being out there.

At the Watershed Preserve 12 Hour, I was happy with my 32.25 miles and was done for the day. Kathy was just heading out for her "50k" lap. She smiled at me and said, "This may take a while." But, as with others who face the challenge of one physical barrier or another, who fight one training interruption or another, who see cutoff times as almost insurmountable barriers, she turned and went back out there for that critical one more lap. That last lap is a gamble only to those who don't value being out there running. For the rest of us, it is a sure thing. It might take a while, but that plus side of 30 miles has a value all its own, and that makes it worthwhile.

The love of competition is the stage for what are often thought of as the biggest gambles. *He really laid it on the line today. She gave it her all. The runners left it all on the trail this weekend.* Generally those are descriptors used for the frontrunners. But, as Dan Baglione pointed out, "You never know for certain what lies ahead on the day you stand at the starting line waiting to test yourself again. If you did know, it would not be a test and there would be no reason for being there." That premise leads us away from the gifted elites and the light-footed nimblies to that motley group just a few paces, minutes, or hours behind. You know, those midpackers, back o' the packers, and their ilk. They have come to the starting line to roll the dice again—training regimes crowd the dots on one face of the die, diet and nutrition on another, while the weather comes dressed as the jester crowding out the snake eyes. Past injuries, sleepless nights, and last night's double-chocolate mocha seem to be on more sides than are possible on the remaining faces of the cubes.

At a recent ultra, as the rain continued to fall and the coastal breeze became a legitimate wind, I could hear several conversations. "It's going to be a crapshoot today," said one as she pointed at the dancing limbs and darkening sky. "Six hours," someone else muttered, "I just want to break six hours here; give me a dry trail just this one time." The changing sky was pairing, or mismatching, runners and clouds and the ease or difficulty of running to the probabilities of the weather screen they had watched the night before. "Maybe we should just run today and save the racing for next month?" We should know by now that starting lines are always gambles that we hope are worth the time we've spent training and the miles we've driven to get somewhere.

We always gamble with whatever it is we've been ignoring. I remember one little gem heard at a starting line.

"We can't not run, right?"

"Right?"

What? I leaned toward the couple, wanting to hear their conversation without appearing to eavesdrop.

"We drove 400 miles, we have to do this run."

"Do the shirts say finisher on them?"

"Uh, no."

"Well, I'm not going to wear it if I didn't run it or work an aid station or something to earn it."

"Okay, but you're the one who thought you would feel better by the time we got here and felt the gamble was worth the drive..."

"Go see the RD, find out if they need any more help at an aid station or somewhere."

"Okay."

Somewhere, as each season turns, the gamble begins anew. An entry blank is filled out. The commitment that goes with filling out the entry blank perhaps brings the intent of reaching a previously unheard-of level of fitness. As darkness falls earlier each day, we are soon to be robbed of the easy running time and driven into the night. The layers that let some of us run in the fall become inadequate as winter edges closer with each sunset. For some it is time to train indoors, gambling that the effort will be high enough to counter the lack of rocks and roots and hills and dales. For others it is a time to read running reports and nutrition books, a time to exchange e-mail and flog dead horses. A last side note of distraction shows up in an exposed corner of the screen—it is in a forum, a request for information on how to train for the Arrowhead 135 with the subquery "Is this a foolish gamble for a newbie?"

Foolish? No. A gamble? Yes.

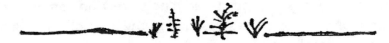

How Long Does It Take and Which Is Harder?

Quite often the mix of people making up the crew at an aid station will include veteran ultramarathoners, novices at the sport, folks still thinking about dipping a toe in the waters of ultras, and folks who follow the sport from the chair of an interested fan with no desire to run down the trails. The conversations of the day are a cacophony of introductions, "what do we do here," vocation and avocation discussions, "where have you run," "why did you volunteer," "where will the runners come from," and the many branches of interest that each response brings.

I looked around at the aid station personnel. Lary Webster, Lynn Yarnall, Kathy Morelock, Karen King, Amy Sproston, Heather Anderson, and several more that darted here and there. There were winners of road marathons, trail hundred-milers, 75 kilometers of pavement pounding, and a 5k and 10k or two; a through hiker of the Appalachian Trail and Pacific Crest Trail with dreams of the Continental Divide Trail still dreamt; a 24-hour round-and-rounder; a pedaler of humongous distances; and a draft choice to be named later. They were from the youngish twenties to the still-young seventies. It was a day of dangling conversations interrupted by filling bottles, fixing and handing out sandwiches, passing out electrolytes, and responding to smiles and thank yous as the travelers up above Easton in Washington's Cascade Mountains passed through.

Pacers, Should I Have One?

Having a pacer does not mean "learning to rely on someone else." The pacer only accompanies—assuming the pair stays within the rules. This generally means no muling (carrying the runner's stuff) and no pushing the runner up the hill; runner still has to run, runner still has to take care of resupplying at the aid stations, etc.

Running a hundred-miler does not require a crew. To the best of my knowledge, Badwater is the only self-supporting—i.e., each runner must have a crew, there is no reliance on race officials or expectations of aid stations—ultramarathon of a hundred miles or more out there—although an argument could be made for Barkley. Everyone on the course is "reliant on...scads of volunteers." Well, duh, everyone out there is relying on the volunteers. Even the fat-ass runs have transitioned to where some of them have aid stations. It isn't like you are begging for help so you can continue. You still have to run. No one is going to cover the distance for you. Generally, the pacer is not going to carry you or your stuff. There are exceptions. There are runs that allow muling just as there are runs that allow the use of trekking poles. If the rules say yes and you want to, then do it.

Pacing was introduced, and is often still thought of, primarily as a safety issue. I'll ignore the speed aspect of it, because that is a different type of pacing—it is more "rabbiting."

There are threads about the hallucinations during the long hours of darkness. There are stories of runners turning left even though the junction was clearly marked, well marked, and even had a person standing there pointing in some cases. Fatigue sets in and does strange, sometimes funny afterwards, things. Some people are completely unaware of what they did during the last many miles of an ultra. There is no recollection of several hours of that long night. They reach a point where they look at a volunteer and simply do not believe what they are being told until another runner does the same thing. It is part of the world we insert ourselves into when we run an ultra.

Pacing can add to a run, maybe provide the psychological kick to get you through a bad stretch. If that will cause you to offload your achievement to the pacer and fail to understand what you did, there is another problem to solve. There is no weakness in having a pacer. There are rules for pacers and runners. If the rules are followed, it is accepted that no unfair advantage has been gained.

If you feel you must do it by yourself, some purity-of-individual-effort sort of thing, then you must also ignore all the other runners or set some limit on conversations and running in groups or pairs as you go down the trail or else you are violating your own rules. What would you do with the people who enter an ultra with the intention of running together? Cast them off as weak-kneed whimpies because they can't do it alone? It isn't a reliance issue. It could be a sharing issue. My wife and I ran together when she did her first road 50-miler. It wasn't to use me as a crutch. She had won a couple of ultras (frail-gender division). We just enjoyed the run together. I did nothing during that fifty miles that was any assistance. In fact, my babbling is sometimes a hindrance to her concentration.

In the end, if the rules allow pacing, it is each runner's decision. There is no defining rightness or wrongness to it, as if there were some higher morality just for those who want or need company out there.

On Crewing, Pacing, Hanging Around...
(Notes to Someone About to Crew and Pace)

This is the experience of the crew on racing weekend. It will be more tiring, in many ways, than running.

Be with your runner every step of the way, from check-in to post-trace, especially before the start of the race on Saturday or Sunday. Take as much of the mental load away from the runner as you can. Your runner needs to know that you are all there and ready. Send your runner off with cheers and laughter, never with doubtful faces.

Limit the choices of food, beverage, clothes, et cetera, at the aid stations. Runners are, most of the time, not up to making decisions. Talk about this beforehand. Always have Vaseline, ibuprofen, et cetera with you. Crackers, too, for the occasional nausea. Decision-making ability will probably diminish as the run wears on.

Unless you like soda pop and Twinkies, have food for your crew in the car. There aren't many grocery stores out in nowhereville—where you will end up spending most of your day. If you are going to do any pacing, you have to be fueled to run.

By the time pacing can happen, as your runner tires, watch for behavior that wastes time—long stays in the porta-pot or behind the porta-tree (unless, of course, there is a real problem), lengthier rest stops in the camp chair, stopping with the crew and at the official aid stations for longer periods of time. Keep them moving. Pacers, remember to take care of yourselves, too.

I have crewed at three different hundreds and couldn't sleep at any of them, but if you can sleep, do so. Most importantly, enjoy the experience. It is as much your race as your runner's—but you are second.

Recognize that the runner will get tired, i.e., will look like death warmed over—be ready to empathize and sympathize, but also be ready to kick them back out onto the course. Understand the difference between fatigue, discomfort, and pain. The first two will happen to almost every runner. The last one could be cause to stay for a few minutes to evaluate.

Do as many training runs together as you can. Do as many night runs as you can. Do as many night runs as you can. Do as many night runs as you can. Do as many night runs as you can. Do as many night runs as you can. Do as many night runs as you can.

Make sure he eats. Make sure she drinks. Make sure he or she eats early. Decide before the run how you will refer to your runner. He, she, or it?

No experimenting with anything on the "day"—no sudden cooking surprise from your great-aunt. It ain't her day. It's his or hers or its.

Umstead is a lapper. Talk up the "another one done" each time. Learn something about the running of a hundred, i.e., late in the race, what is being called running may not look like running to the uneducated. Just being out there moving after 20 hours, after 70 miles, after the sun comes up... is quite an ordeal in itself.

Stay positive for your runner. That sounds so simple, but this also means to remember to check your runner for essentials (lights and batteries—LED lights have sort of eliminated the batteries, but have a backup light of some sort, one for each of you—ya just never know, bottles—should be carrying at least two), and so forth.

Know your runner. Is it better for you to be in front? Do you run side by side when possible? On her right? On her left? Talk to each other before the run. Find out if your runner wants silence or lengthy stories during the run. Be honest but positive. Everything you do is to be pointed at getting her home. Minor inconveniences for you are just that—they are to be tolerated without comment.

Know the course. You can print and laminate (or cover with Scotch tape) enough information (how far between aid stations, cumulative mileage done, name of aid station—that's about all, just enough to be able to assure and reassure) so you can look it up in just a few seconds.

Know the course markings. There may be times when you cannot see a marker in front or behind you. Be careful at junctions—you must pay attention. If there is any doubt, stop. One of you stays still. The other runs ahead a couple of minutes until you are sure you are on the course (or off it)—go back for the other runner.

Do not separate other than for recon reasons. One of you stays in one place while the other searches. This includes for potty stops. Stay in flashlight sight of each other. Your runner will be getting more and more tired; you will be the alert one. Don't go off the trail any farther than you have to (need to). The hell with modesty, stay close to that trail. It is your lifeline.

Make sure your CamelBak has the big lid—the aid stations have ice. They can just dump ice in there, top it with water or whatever, and you are done. Your runner might like a sip of chilled water, too. Operate with a sense of urgency, not haste. Haste will cause you to overlook something. Urgency is organized speed. Don't leave an aid station without whatever you need.

The nights I paced, I lived on potatoes, potato chips, and melon. Have a plastic bag with you so you can slip a few pieces in the bag, put the bag in your pocket, and eat on the move. Check your runner—make sure she eats and drinks at the aid stations. If she is in trouble (fuel trouble, running out of energy, etc) one of the hardest decisions to make is to stop, not just pause, at the next aid station for refueling.

Have her stop. Eat. Drink. Take a few minutes for it to get in the body. Eat and drink some more. Then go. It will only take a few minutes and will save many minutes later on. You must stay aware of whether she is getting food, drink, and electrolyte replacements (salt, salt pills, Endurolytes, SUCCEED!, whatever)—try to see her take them. Don't just depend on her saying so. She is going to get more and more tired. She has been up and running since 5:00 a.m. Saturday—it may be Sunday by now.

Get her in and out of the aid station as quickly as you can. The aid stations will be more and more like big warm fuzzies as the night wears on—they are places with lights, people, chairs, food, warm things to drink, people laughing and waiting on you hand and foot— that is all well and good, but get out of there. Think how much better the next one might be.

Most of the progress is going to be walk/shuffle/jog. Keep it going. Don't get into trudge/stumble/shuffle stuff. You will be up all night covering those last 40 or 50 miles. It is a distance you can both be very confident about covering, but it will take a continual mental effort to maintain an awareness of pace. Keep pushing. Walk the ups, get into shuffle on the flats, and go to jog (it'll feel like running) as you get on the downhill sections.

Know about clothes. As the miles go by either you or your runner might want to change shirts, shorts, shoes... whatever. Tell the crew what to have ready at the next meeting point. Sometimes the car will be nearby, sometimes it is several miles away. Avoid time-consuming changes, if possible. I changed shirts several times at Leadville. I didn't change anything at Western. It was warm all through the night. No gloves, no jacket. I ran Leadville in one pair of shoes.

Nag, pester, goad, prod, joke—whatever works, but keep her going. Try to feel for when the pace slackens. Try to figure out what is slowing her down—mind going away for a few minutes—getting tired—too bad, everyone is going to get tired. Linda and I loved to chase people. Chasing other runners gets you farther down the trail, makes the time pass without thinking about yourself.

When you pass someone, pass him or her or them and be done with it. It will be natural to want to slow down and socialize, especially as the night drags on. You have been running them down, don't slow down to talk to them—maybe for a few steps, but only a few—they are running slower than you have been—get on with it. The sun is coming all the time. Where will you be when the sun comes up—keep moving.

As dawn comes over the horizon, run. Laugh about making it through the night. Joke and enjoy the trail. Run and enjoy the trail, but pay attention. If you relax too much, you risk stumbling, maybe falling. After all, everyone is tired. Pay attention and run; face-plants are never fun and sometimes they are showstoppers.

Your runner may get sick and throw up. Stomach problems, not enough salt with the drinking, nerves, who knows what causes them? Be prepared. Throwing up can come suddenly. Step to one side of the trail. Help her bend over so she doesn't dribble all down the front of herself. I had a packet of Wet Ones or Handi Wipes or something like that in the pack—sometimes to wipe my face, sometimes to clean up my runner. Get her cleaned up and back on the trail. Now, throwing up is a dehydrating sort of thing; she must get some food and liquid in her, while staying on the move. I also have TUMS or Rolaids in the pack. When Linda threw up (twice), I had a few Wheat Thins for her and told her to take small sucks of Hammer Gel. We kept moving.

Injured? Blistered? Discomfort? Pain? Ideally there will have been some runs together (runner and pacer) so conversations about what might happen as the miles go by could take place. There is a need to understand the difference between discomfort and pain. We all need to know about the discomfort we will experience. We need to know when something needs to be done, but we also need to know when there is nothing to be done. We were at about the 95-mile point when Linda decided a blister was bothering her. There we were in the middle of nowhere so I said we can't do anything about it, it'll hurt if we go back or ahead. But she needed to do something. She pulled the insole out of the shoe, and we went ahead. Maybe earlier, maybe at an aid station we would have done something else, but with 5 miles to go and time being of the essence, she simply pulled the shoe back on and we continued to run toward No Hands Bridge. All through those last forty miles, you have got to differentiate between pain and discomfort.

Time? Will there be a time goal? Be realistic and truthful if you are to keep track of being able to make a certain time. The 24-hour thing drives some people; it slipped away for us out around the 80–85 mile-point, but we kept pushing to keep the time as low as possible. Your runner might be more interested in finishing than in having a fast time—know that beforehand, run with that in mind.

Say good things to all people you pass or are passed by while out there. You are all in this together. Smile and tell lies and keep moving toward Auburn, or Leadville, or wherever.

Eating for you. During the day you will be sitting around, twiddling your thumbs, and waiting. I ended up eating most of a loaf of some sort of whole-grained brown bread. You have to remember to eat for a long run that will start at about seven or eight o'clock in the evening. Do some afternoon and into-evening transition runs, preferably with your runner.

There will be some emotional down points. It is a long way to run. Try to keep her pointed toward Auburn. If things go bad, try to keep her walking toward the finish area. "Aha, it's downhill here, let's try to run a hundred steps." Anything to get back into the relentless-forward-motion (RFM) mode.

You are to be bulletproof. You don't get to be sick, lame, lazy, forgetful, or in need of a manicure. Make sure your CamelBak is filled at each station. Make sure you eat at each station. Make sure she knows you are there taking care of her. It is quite a privilege to have someone believe in you enough to ask you to pace for her. I think I was more nervous than Linda (we have a father/daughter age relationship). I simply had to get her to Auburn—this was an absolute.

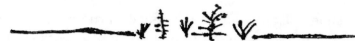

A short bit I wrote about someone else pacing to illustrate the scattered thoughts and actions that somehow will coalesce into the single goal of getting a runner (with crew in the background) from the start to the finish.

A year ago today we woke up in the tent at about 7000 foot elevation up on the Siskiyous just north of the Ohryghun/California border. We were an easy day's drive from Squaw Valley, California, or "Squaw," in the wonderful world of the 100-miler parlance. Just as Auburn is known as the finish line, so Squaw is known as the starting line. The event is the Western States 100 Mile Endurance Run. We were on the way south to pace (run the last 38 miles with) a friend on her first effort at Western. Generally, runners get to the starting area a day or two ahead of pacers and crew. The runner will need to attend prerace meetings and medical checks. The crew and pacer can often flounder around on their own, arriving bleary-eyed and frazzle-tailed an hour or two before the start and still function as needed.

Sarah, a friend of mine who will be pacing a friend of hers, is on her way to Squaw today. Today, mixed in with looking out the window as she travels, working her way through the airport, and finding her way to Auburn and on to Squaw, one thought is going to continually jump to the front—getting her runner to Auburn.

Oh, she may enjoy the flight, she may be seeing Lake Tahoe and the Sierras for the first time, she may stand in awe of that many runners and the energy emanating from them, but as 5:00 a.m. Saturday gets closer and closer, she will find her thoughts getting narrower and narrower—what do I do to assure my runner she will finish?

Friday will be a circus; the meetings, the information briefings, the long looks up the valley—you can see the first 3 or 4 miles climbing up from the ski resort area. She will see faces to go with the names we know as legends in ultrarunning—generally the potential top-10 finishers are called up for introductions. A lot of people are surprised at how "normal" they look.

A certain air of nervousness is apparent. My runner had to do the blood pressure twice—the first one being a bit high. She went to a darkish corner and sat there thinking calming thoughts and was fine the second time through. Lists and piles of equipment are checked—again, only to be checked again in the predawn darkness of Saturday morning.

Crew and pacers are already taking over from the runner, trying to remove as many cares and concerns as they can. All the runner's energy is to be directed to the course. The runner has to cross the Sierra Nevada, on foot, alone—at least to Michigan Bluff (55 miles) or maybe even to Foresthill (62 miles) before the pacer may finally join in. That will be late Saturday evening, maybe even after dark, depending on what time the runner gets to Michigan Bluff.

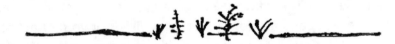

More Rambling, Scattered Thoughts on Pacing, Crewing, and Running—in This Case, at Western States Where Sarah is pacing Letha

When last we heard, Sarah was to start pacing Letha at Foresthill—38 miles to go to the finish line in Auburn. The rules of pacing vary with the event. Some events let the pacer start at the closest aid station to the halfway point with no concern for time (except the dreaded cut-off time). If Letha comes in fastish, you will start at Foresthill. If she doesn't get to Michigan Bluff before 8:00 p.m., you can start pacing at Michigan Bluff. What if it is 7:50, hmm, I do not know.

We had heard people talk about how Western was so strict about the rules. No crew accompanying the runner outside of the aid station areas. No muling. No carrying the runner's bottles into the aid station. No this, that, and t'other. All the sanctity of Western vanished as our visit there confirmed that it is just another big race—it is more rumors of rules rather than rules that are enforced to the letter. There is enforcement to prevent an unfair advantage, but there is understanding of what needs to be done, too.

Stay positive for your runner. That sounds so simple, but last year we were a few miles out of Foresthill and Linda said, "I only have one bottle." Yeeeeek! In the excitement of getting to Foresthill (62-mile point), feeling decent, and having company to run with, she had only taken one bottle with her. I wanted to just scream at her. Somehow I managed to just hold out the mouthpiece of the drink tube (I had the 100-ounce CamelBak on just in case she needed an extra bit of drink, which she did) for her—I nursed her through two aid stations until we met our crew at Rucky Chucky and got her a second bottle.

Pills, food, and things that water will ruin because we aren't all the "right" height. The water was about crotch deep on me. I am 6 feet, 2 inches tall, about a foot taller than either of you. That means the water will be close to waist deep on you and Letha. Whatever is in your pockets is going to get wet—check it all before crossing. There is a cable to hang on to, and there are lots of people there to help you get across the river. Let them help you. They are there just for you. Let them help you. Say, "Thank you, nice person," enjoy the cool refreshing water, get across, and get on down the trail.

Heat—you two should be okay coming from Texas, but it is a different sort of heat. The bushes close in and the heat just sort of settles on you, but it goes away as the sun goes down—thought you still need to be careful. Take the Endurolytes or whatever, enjoy the evening coolness, but stay aware you have a long ways to go.

Pacing at the Western States 100-Mile Endurance Run

"John, would you pace me at Western?" Linda Samet, a runner and friend in Corvallis, Oregon, asked that question one May, just six weeks before the Western States Endurance Run, her first attempt at a 100-mile trail run. "Sure," I answered, knowing that pacing someone in those last miles (at Western your pacer can join you somewhere at or after the 55-mile point) of a 100-miler can be the make-or-break part of the run. Did I really want to do this? I found out at 7:36 p.m., Saturday, June 29th, 2002, in Foresthill, California. Sixty-two point two miles down for Linda, thirty-eight miles to go, accompanied by her wise and stalwart pacer—me.

Being from Oregon, we don't get much practice for the heat and dust of the California trails—always a challenge for trail runners going south. The afternoon temps hovered in the low 80s on the ridges, 95 and up down in the lower canyon elevations. I had told Linda to hang on during the day and I would push the pace as dark and the coolness of night came in. She, of course, didn't listen, coming into Foresthill just a few minutes over the coveted 24-hour pace. That's good; she didn't feel too bad. A little dried out, somewhat hungry, not eating enough, and gaining a little weight. My pacing chores began in earnest.

We tried to stuff some food in her as she changed from CamelBak to fanny pack at the crew aid station. I worried about how much energy she had used, how much the three canyons had taken out of her, how dehydrated she might be, and a lot of other things. I did know she was a tough kid. And so we left Foresthill, sixteen, mostly downhill, miles before we would see our crew again.

After leaving the pavement of Foresthill, we entered the manzanita thickets surrounding the horse trail (the Tevis Cup Western States Trail) heading for Auburn, our final destination. As we wound down the gentle slopes, I started pestering Linda to eat the potato chunks. She was having trouble eating. A hint of more troubles to come? I continued to pester her to eat. We had a nice pace and kept going down.

The aid stations would appear out there in the middle of nowhere, islands of colored lights, volunteers refilling your packs, giving you food, and always offering encouragement. We refilled, grabbed some food, and continued into the approaching dark. Another runner passed by, moving well. "'Scuse me, trying to get as far as I can before dark." We all were, for with the dark comes a slower pace. The three dimensions of running become the two dimensions of light and shadows. Shadows have no depth. Shadows hide holes, rocks, and roots—run-stopping ankle turners.

Dark came as we continued the ups and downs, hearing creeks and the American River, watching the stars come out. We had the whole night in front of us. Another aid station popped up. Some are hidden just around a bend, and the movie *Apocalypse Now* comes to mind time after time. Lights, people moving, aid tables, food, drink, caring hands and smiles. Linda turning. "You ready, John?" "Yup." Time to run. Off we go into the dark again.

We began the long grind to Rucky Chucky—the river crossing at Western, a phrase known to most ultrarunners. Rucky Chucky: surreal, light sticks in the water so we could see our footing, waist-deep water, the American River, 150 feet wide, volunteers to grab if needed. We laughed more nervously than I liked and crossed to Kathy (for me) and John (for Linda) on the other side. With Rucky Chucky behind us, we climbed toward Green Gate.

A bad stretch passed, and Linda started waking up—"I'll lead on the next leg." The runner always has that option. Good. She seemed to be coming out of the doldrums from the past few miles. Those low periods come and go several times in 100s; the trick is to control them. I had told stories, talked about the stars, geology, cooking, lied about mileage, and we continued to run. Running, not shuffling, running. Linda, again, dug deep and found some energy. The earlier problems of not eating enough, not taking enough salt while not drinking enough, had built up, but (as I was to say more and more often) "Thassa a tuff little kid up there," and we ran on. Ten-minute pace at two o'clock in the morning. Wow!

The eternity of the uphill climb on an ugly rocky stretch got us to the Highway 49 crossing just before dawn. We tried to get in and out of the aid station fast, such a mixed thing. You want to stay because there are friends there. You have to leave because you are not in Auburn yet. Daylight is coming. 6.5 miles to go. A 10k away.

And then...a horrible blister stops us. Tears and laughter in the middle of nowhere on a trail that winds on forever. Linda asks, "What can we do?" I cheerfully point out, "Nothing." But we try something, redo the sock (ugly, dirty sock)—nope. Take out the insole. Ohkeigh? No, but bearable. It'll be better uphill. Moving. Time is slipping by. No Hands Bridge awaits, more cantaloupe, a cup of Coke—3.1 miles of gentle grade. Go. Push. Hard walking, houses of Auburn on the sides of the canyon, cars, trail ending. We are on pavement.

Robie Point—1.2 miles to go, pavement, arrows to follow, really sick of yellow ribbons, football stadium, Placer High School, the backstretch of the track—300 yards (or is it meters?). The PA blaring "Linda Samet of..." and it's over. Pacing? Nothin' to it.

25 hours, 48 minutes, 42 seconds. A hundred miles have been run. A great time for a tough course on a hot day.

Thassa tuff little kid.

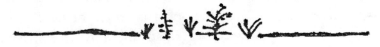

Moving Trail Markers

"What on earth?" I whispered quietly to myself, or I thought I did until I heard Linda ask, "What's wrong?"

I have many times said that pacing at an ultra is more stressful than running the thing yourself. We were somewhere between Ford's Bar and Rucky Chuck on The Western States Endurance Run. I was pacing Linda Samet. The idea that I would even be doing that was hidden in the short conversation between my wife and me some months earlier when I returned from a run.

"Linda called. She wants you to call her."

"Oh? Do you know what about?"

"She wants you to pace her at Western."

"Oh?"

That was about all I could say out loud. My mind opened lebenty-teen doors, all at once. Pacing is responsible running. Pacing is excitement even from this far away. Pacing Linda would be fun, but the fun would have to be carefully tempered—kept inside the challenge of taking care of a friend while making sure...

"What?"

"Are you going to call her?"

I picked up the phone.

Time, being what it is, passed slowly, too quickly, agonizingly slowly, and suddenly it was time to throw one of everything in the back of the car and head south.

I had started running with Linda at about 6:30 in the evening in Foresthill. That brief island of cheering, pavement, and daylight seemed an eternity behind us now. We were within two or three miles of Rucky Chuck, the river crossing at mile 78 on the Western States course, when I whispered, "What on earth?" One of the guiding rules (ruling guidelines?) of pacing is to never do anything to upset, distract, mystify, rattle, or raise any sort of alarm in your runner. Linda's response was quick and just enough decibels higher than other grunts and mumbles to let me know I had just done all of the above.

I started to explain that I had seen two glow sticks just a minute or two ago and now they were gone. The frequency of appearance of whatever sort of trail markers are used varies from course to course, of course. There is certainly no guarantee that some sort of trail marker will always be in sight, but as the night wears on, being unable to see the next point of reassurance almost always raises the fear of having missed a turn. I was sure I had seen the markers. The idea that I had seen two so close together did not register at first.

"Did we miss a turn?"

"No."

I had been running with both headlight and flashlight turned on. Both were on bright settings—two lights on high beams was something I normally did only on technical, rocky, rooty, porcupine-hiding trails. Two bright beams of light were not needed on this part of the course—unless you were pacing and wanted to be sure not to miss any junctions. We had joked earlier about my blinding anyone I happened to look at during the night. Now the brightness and this circle of light we ran in, however small it suddenly seemed, was my reassurance—no, I had not missed a turn. There were no glow sticks, no flagged points I could have passed without seeing them—not in my mind's eye.

The fragility of the mind as midnight approaches when a runner is on a strange trail can erode confidence quickly. We had only been running for a couple of minutes in our new apprehension-laden world when Linda asked the worst-scenario question, "Should we stop?" I was just about to answer when the two glow sticks were magically out in front of us, again—sighs all around as we relaxed. Two hundred yards, maybe three hundred yards out in front of us, who knows? I could not tell. All I knew was they were there and we were back inside the comfort zone. And then they were gone.

"Whaaa...?"

The groan that came from our two voices was barely audible above the roar of the night rushing back in to surround us. For a moment our minds ignored the beams of our own lights. Those lights so bright just a few steps ago. For a moment we were alone on a dark trail on a hillside just above the waters of the American River—the river's reflection, beautiful in the moonlight those same few short moments ago, was now small comfort. It meant (assuming it *was*, in fact, the American River) we were still on the way to the river crossing. Had we found the so-often-mentioned hallucination phase of these ultramarathons? I paused to look back. Aha! I pointed to two, maybe three flashes of lights behind us—more runners. Surely we were still on course. We turned to continue running...and a couple of minutes later the two lights were in front of us again. What was usually the warm welcome light of the glow sticks was now a ghoulish yellowish green that beckoned us in a silence that held way more drama than any trail had ever given before.

"John, the lights are moving."

"Hmm, yes, they are."

The lights were moving. We had not noticed it on first glance, but they were moving, and we were getting closer to them. Them? It? Runners with glow sticks? Then, just as my headlight beam was about to reach them, one disappeared, then the other. Oh me, this is, oops, there they are—this internal conversation was starting to get to me. What on earth...great big huge furry clippety-clop things? Clippety-clop? Horses? Horses with taillights? Seventeen not-quite-disconnected thoughts come together at almost the same time. Long before ultrarunners knew this trail as "Western," there was a horse ride on this same trail. The horsey folks are heavily involved with the Western States Endurance Run. There were a lot of volunteer safety patrol folks out there, and many of them were on, ta-da, horses. Yes, indeed, those were the rear ends of two horses complete with those leather belt thingies that go all the way around the horses (does it hold the horse together?) and—another ta-da moment or aha moment or, oh, never mind—each horse had a glow stick hanging from the belt thingie. I suppose it was so we (runners) could slow down in time to avoid running into the horses, which now looked really big.

A voice came out of the dark.

"Please pass us on the left, plenty of room for you."

"Thank you. Do you folks ride all night?"

"Yep."

"Wow—thank you for helping."

"You're about half a mile to the river crossing. Have a good run to Auburn."

Our attention turned back to the now-empty hallucination-free trail.

CHAPTER SIX

Heaven is under our feet as well as over our heads.

—Thoreau

Memory is the best of all gardens. Therein, winter and summer, the seeds of their past lie dormant, ready to spring into instant blossom at any moment the mind wishes to bring them to life.

—Hal Boyle

A rainy day is the perfect time for a walk in the woods.

—Rachel Carson

There is a muscular energy in sunlight corresponding to the spiritual energy of wind.

—Annie Dillard

Running With Strangers

Oaks instead of Douglas firs.

The almost flat plains of Texas instead of Washington's Cascades and Olympics.

A lake—a reservoir really—instead of the Strait of Juan de Fuca.

No eagles, only a few grebes and a cormorant or two.

Four strangers at a trailhead.

Several hours of trails—not my cedar- and fir-needle-covered trails but their twisting, turning, up and down and around, rocky and rooty trails.

Shadows chased, roots dodged, questions and laughter of stories exchanged.

Are your trails like these? Yes. No. Sort of. Not really.

Names put with faces. Strangers fading.

How do you run in so much rain?

How do you run in the heat?

Recollections of once-shared trails—oh, I've been there, too—came forth.

Their sun and my sun became our sun as we ran.

Four friends returned to the trailhead.

"Come run in our rain and salt-sprayed wind," I told them.

Homeward bound, I looked down at the Rockies from 34,000 feet.

Leadville, then the Wasatch passed far below, then our Cascades—runners' mountains all.

Friends and shared trails tugged as strongly as the mountains.

Fortune smiled down on that early fall day.

Fortune still smiles through memories.

Mosquitos and PB&Js

This time of year is partly spring, partly summer, partly patient, and partly totally, irrationally, uncompromisingly impatient to get to trails not trod since last fall. Gnarly, rocky stretches need to be crossed. Thin air needs gasping. Ascents and descents and...We look to the mountains and for several mornings have assured each other that the snow is much higher. Surely the *lower* trails are clear of snow by now. Right, yeah, sure.

There wasn't much to pack in the predawn darkness. The big box with one of each of various things was back there. It pretty much stays in the back of the car the whole year round. It only took one July snowstorm a few years ago to convince us to always carry a little extra. We left in the half-light of false dawn, stopping at the drive-up window of the last-coffee-for-58-miles coffee shack before the highway started winding upward toward Santiam Pass and that snow-free trail.

The beauty of a coming dawn made us suddenly reluctant to leave the coffee-enabled, Deborah-Boily-CD-playing, reclined-and-heated-seats. The last dregs of coffee accompanied the first few minutes of the sun glistening and sparkling on the many snowcapped peaks. We were at about 4,000 foot elevation, and only a few flecks of frost had been seen. Encouraged by the snow-free parking lot and drawn from the car by the sun, we put on running shoes, a layer or two, and the well-traveled fanny packs.

We headed south so the sun wouldn't blind us coming back. A mile in, we could see where the trail crossed an old avalanche scar and a meadow about two miles out in front of us. Kathy said something about the trail turning up steeply just past the meadow. That's okay. If we found snow, we'd turn around, go back to the car, cross the highway, and run north for a while. Light and shadow and warm and cool alternated as we ran through patches of trees. We were overdressed, moving barely above a jog, not even thinking about changing effort—listening to our breath, footsteps, and an occasional raven or stellar jay—just happy to be out there again. The parking lot was empty when we left; this trail was ours this morning.

Almost. We'd reached the meadow we had seen. I stopped. Why are you stopped? I turned my head, lifted my hand, and pointed toward the stirring mass in the meadow—seven million five hundred eighty-four thousand two-hundred and six mosquitoes, give or take a handful. They were also thinking the trail was theirs this morning. Actually, they thought they owned the trail this morning, and the buzzing and humming we could hear was them talking about the intruders. We looked at the two hundred yards of meadow, the two hundred yards of mosquitoes, and recalled mouthfuls and eyefuls and earfuls and red welts from trying to cross early-spring meadows full of mosquitoes one or two other times, the memories vivid enough to cause us to turn back.

We topped the bottles off at the car and crossed the highway. Our altered plan called for running northerly to a forest road, following it across to another trail, and then turning to complete the triangle back to the car. The low sun and the sky's pale blueness highlighted black and white peaks a hundred miles away, starkly contrasting in the early dawn light, changing by the minute, pulling at us to look, creating a danger of stumbles and trips when our focus needed to be on the trail. We started north, crossing ancient lava flows in their many forms and colors: pumice, basalt, and andesite; grays, reds, and black. The *crunch crunch crunch* of our footsteps was amplified and played back until we got to a rocky stretch that lasted until the forest road.

Four or five miles in, running easily, thoughts and conversations about how well we were running, how this was the earliest we'd run up high, and about picking up the pace were stopped when we came to a clearing beside which lay a small mirror-surfaced lake with a ring of still-frosty grass around its edges. Focus during these late-spring runs, these first trips to the mountains, was fragile and so easily diverted. I spotted two osprey perched near their nest on the far end of the lake. We stopped running and watched. One of them left the limb, flew out about twenty yards, and hovered for a few seconds, head turned down, eyes locked on the lake's surface. We held our breath. Then it dove, wings folded back, head forward, eyes locked on something beneath the surface. Just before it hit the water, the body tilted back; talons were extended toward the water. We had a memory of an osprey completely submerging to catch a meal. This one just skimmed the water, and then the wings were fully spread and lifting. Lunch was on the way, held securely in those locked talons. We'd seen it before. Amazing. We finally turned away. There was still a trail to be found somewhere up the road. And the road was rising.

We hadn't paid much attention to how steep the climbing had been since leaving the lake, busy talking about the osprey and arguing about which of the distant peaks was farther away—always fun when we aren't even sure which peak we are seeing—later, back at home, we'd get a map out and argue again about which peak we thought we saw, and we still wouldn't know. We rounded a corner, found the trail, and headed up again. Oops. Snow. Snow? A short discussion about how we had climbed up to the snow followed. We agreed the trail *should* drop as we headed toward the car and would *probably* be clear of snow in just a short distance. The snow was only a couple of inches deep there, and I have done this sort of misjudgment enough times to be pretty good at sounding like I know what I am saying. Up the trail we went.

A while later we reached the point where the snow was now knee-deep, and "post holing" is a kind description of our technique. Kathy did one last face-plant and the conversation turned to "Is it farther going back or farther going this way?" I countered by pointing at a large rock and saying, "That rock is big enough to sit on and eat a PB&J." PB&J? Yes, hi-tech clothing, old-timey PB&Js, and rare quietness. After lunch, I got up and wandered about fifty feet up the trail, slowly turning and once again marveling at the beauty of these mountains we get to run in. I finally looked northerly and smiled. I turned back to Kathy. Saddle up.

Saddle up? Yup. We had stopped just short of the ridge's edge—where the snow stopped and the trail dropped down to the parking lot. The mosquitoes won the first round. We won the second round. We talked about next weekend and round three while the sun warmed our backs as we dropped down the ridge to the car.

A Long Conversation at Winter's End
or
50 Miles of Pavement, Briefly

The cast of (dubious) actors: Lary Webster, Chris Hart, Rob Volkenand, Vic Harris, Ray Atleson, Del Scharffenberg, and René Casteran plus another twenty or so persons of questionable background and intentions—most of whom seem to be concentrating on the large bowl of fresh strawberries on the serving cart.

The setting: The banquet room for the postrace meal after the Greater Oregon Health Service 50 Mile ultramarathon in Grants Pass, Oregon, March 12, 1988.

Lary: I'm surprised they didn't go off in a ditch.

Vic: Yak yak yak—they didn't even notice us passing them.

Chris: René, just what all did you two talk about?

René: We were...

Rob (interrupting): They missed one turn because they weren't paying attention to the course. I yelled at them to come back, or they probably would have gone on to Crescent City.

Lary: Their eyes were sort of glazed over on the second lap.

René: We were just...

Del: All I could hear from them was something about baking muffins. I don't think they even saw us.

Ray: Someone said they overshot an aid station. John never misses an aid station.

Vic: I still want to know. What were you talking about?

René: We were just talking...

A hush falls over the room, and all conversations pause as Kathy and I enter.

[Earlier that same day, much earlier, like, maybe about the time the sun rose]

In today's world of ultramarathons, there is no problem finding a run to enter. In fact, the problem might be that there are too many to choose from—the difficulty lies in selection, not in a lack thereof. In the late 1980s, if you lived in the Pacific Northwest and ran ultras, March would find you thinking only of Grants Pass, Oregon, and the Greater Oregon Health Service (GOHS) Ultra. GOHS offered both the 50-mile and 50-kilometer distances. That was it unless you wanted to cross the Siskiyous and venture way down to California.

Quite a few of the runners have California on the mind this morning as we line up in front of the Fort Vannoy Elementary School in the Rogue Valley just west of Grants Pass. The early morning start, deserted country roads and an almost flat course provide a near perfect setting for those needing a qualifying time for Western States. I am in the minority. California is not on my mind, nor is a qualifying time. The worst part is that along with a qualifying time not being a concern and California not being on my mind, neither does running seem to be foremost in my thoughts.

Kathy and I had arrived in Grants Pass late Friday evening. We had run this together last year for her first road 50-miler. A lingering late-winter cold sidelined her this year. The crispness of a cold, clear sky greeted us Saturday morning. As we drive out to the starting line, I am haunted by indecision over which distance to run today. All

I have to do when we get to the starting area is walk over and tell the volunteer to switch me to the 50k. As luck would have it, I am starting that way when Steve Heaps hollers hello. He is from Spokane, Washington. We know each other from Le Grizz, Pat Caffrey's 50-mile offering to the ultramarathon world from just south of Glacier National Park over by Hungry Horse, Montana. We talk for a bit. The disjointed conversations of the ultramarathon world are prized possessions of mine. A person might share some words with a stranger along some trail new to both of them and then months later and hundreds of miles away renew the conversation. Steve and I did just that. In the parking lot of an elementary school, next to an almost deserted country road in southern Oregon, a conversation born in the Rockies is renewed. Montana trails or Oregon roads, as someone said, "It's all good." The timing of his greeting distracts me from the registration table. All of a sudden it is time to run. I am registered to run fifty miles. I have a day full of running in front of me, like it or not, and run into the brightness of the morning sun with the rest of the herd.

I start the day's inventory of cows, check the fields of hops, and even though still not in any sort of mood to run manage to cover the three and a half miles to the first aid station without going astray. The GOHS run is a three-loop course. It is also the setting for another series of disjointed conversations. This is my third consecutive year of running the GOHS event. Bits and pieces of conversations from last year are renewed, plus conversations that will come and go today are started with the aid station volunteers. I offer thanks, grab what seems appropriate food and drink, and start on my minute or two of walking out of the aid station. This short walk isn't a fixed time or distance, just a minute or two that assures me I get a handful of calories in and a good drink or two—it starts the refueling process that will be a battle all day long.

Footsteps coming up behind me register just as I hear a not totally unfamiliar voice say hello. I glance over to see René Casteran pulling alongside. He is the former race director of the GOHS ultra.

"Good morning, John!"

"Hi, René. How's it going?" The simplest questions sometimes unravel the half-formed tapestry.

"Not so good."

Uh-oh? We are way too early to externalize bad stuff. "What's not so good?"

"I need to run under nine hours today, wanted to run about eight and a half."

I glance at my watch; 38 minutes since starting. We are just past 3.5 miles plus the aid station. We are dead on an eight-and-a-half-hour 50. "Yeah? Looks like you've got a good start." Maybe he forgot his watch?

"I don't feel like running."

René is obviously trying to steal my lines. "Would you like to tell me about it? I could maybe hum 'Eye of the Tiger' as we go." It is always good when you find someone who feels worse than you do. We might be in business here. If I play things right, René might get things going and get me into a running mood.

"No, I just wondered if you minded my running with you for a while." Whoa! Say what? This is head-swelling stuff. René is a veteran of Wasatch, Western, 6-day events, and stuff like that. I am on the second anniversary of my first 50-miler—a veritable rookie. I briefly consider discussing my standard fee of six cents a mile for a day's accompaniment and then decide to offer today's company free. "That sounds good to me. Why the time goal?"

"I need it for my qualifier for Western."

"Oh. Won't you need to be running trails a lot?" We are on a road 50-miler.

"I'll be on trails almost all day long for a week or two at a time starting next week."

"Wow! How do you get to do that?"

And thus started a conversation whose topics included horticulture, being a back-country ranger, cooking, cows, coaching running, the Resume Normal Speed sign, cloud reading, are you from here, running long, bakeries, running fast, flowers and plants alongside the road, aid station fare for the discriminating ultrarunner, how did you get to Oregon, how did you get to Washington, and other stuff.

The GOHS course is sort of *J*-shaped. There are three laps, two of 17 miles and the final lap of 16 miles. The two "legs" of the *J* shape make for a lot of hellos, waves, smiles, and general comings and goings as the hours, and miles, pass by. The shoulders of the road are wide enough and the traffic volume low enough that running two or even three abreast is the standard pattern. Runners on automatic pilot somehow notice oncoming runners, and the opposing groups shift to single file, exchange smiles and the standard lies about each other's appearances, and then re-form into the preferred conversation-enabling formation after the pass is completed.

As the morning comes and goes, René leads me through the Siskiyous and along the upper parts of the Rogue River—his storytelling is simple but full of realistic detail from the eyes of someone who loves being in the forests. Pictures are painted on the easel of my mind. I bring in the Olympic Peninsula of Washington and the Ozarks of Arkansas. The ankle-twisting quality of rocks and roots on both sides of the Mississippi are debated, and a ranking system is born.

Oops, "Runners!" We scramble to get to single file as an oncoming trio is very close. "Hey! Wake up and pay attention," Jim Sapp, Lary Webster, and Del Scharffenberg come at us with laughter and cheers—and waves of good-bye.

I sneak glances at my watch as the miles pass beneath our feet. Some people want to know the time gone by, some don't. I almost shake my head in disbelief as 34 miles are completed and we continue to "sit" on ten-minute pace. As we leave the start/finish aid station for the fifth time, I absentmindedly make the comment, "It's the thank-you-and-good-bye lap." René looks over and asks what I mean by that. I explain that we are on the last loop, and I try to be sure to say thank you, good-bye, and see you next year to the volunteers as we go through the aid stations.

"Last lap?"

"Yes."

"You sure?"

"Yes."

"Last lap" is said one more time, and we both smile. At the start of the day, 50 was a totally unmanageable number. Now we have less than 16 miles to go. Sixteen is a manageable number. We exchange one last "hello and lookin' good" with Paula Patee and Mary Edwards as we move aside for them to pass. A rope connects them, but an invisible bond stronger than the visible rope connects a sighted ultrarunner (Paula) to the blind ultrarunner (Mary). The riddle of "how do you explain ultramarathons" falls by the wayside as I wonder what words and thoughts have passed between those two women today. They will grace the cover of the May 1988 issue of *UltraRunning* magazine.

We ignore the Resume Normal Speed sign on Upper River Road for the last time and turn off to parallel the Rogue River once more. The waves and smiles that we exchange are becoming less frequent in these last few miles. The dogs that barked noisily at us this morning don't even look as we make our last trip to the turnaround aid station on Lower River Road. The frost that coated the roadside grass this morning has disappeared in the afternoon sun. A last bit of joking takes place as Ann Whiting calls out from the shady side of the road and kids us about how hot it must be way over there on the sunny side. Almost everyone has dropped their gloves, caps, and long-sleeve shirts hours ago as the chill of this morning's 26° was replaced by an unseasonably warm 70° on this late winter day. We are out long enough to remember worrying about frosty spots this morning as we now think of how the sun will beat down on us and will feel like a furnace when we turn our back to the sun at the last corner—such is this world of ultramarathons.

We reach the corner of Lower River Road and Hunt Lane and make the final turn onto Hunt Lane. Fort Vannoy Elementary School; the finish line that was a starting line awaits us.

"Apple pie sure sounds good," René offers with a smile as we make the turn. There is a double-crust apple pie, home baked and kept warm for the finishers—a benefit of small ultras?—waiting for us just seven-tenths of a mile away.

I look at my watch; 8:25 on the nose. "We are going to be just a little bit late."

"Doesn't matter, there was a 30-minute cushion. A bad start turned into a good run; thank you."

"No, I owe you one. Good run, good day, good conversation. Thank you."

We do the look-both-ways and cross the highway and enter the school parking lot with fifty miles done. Marcus Mayfield yells something at René. René looks over at Marcus and hesitates just for a step or two to reply. That causes the results to show us finishing four seconds apart. That four seconds of separation in the results completely hide over eight hours spent together, matching strides, and sharing stories. It was a day of full immersion in some of the hidden truths of running ultramarathons—we often run to enjoy the day, the conversations, and friends.

Salvaging a Hundred: Cascade Crest Classic 100, 2002, DNF

The prelude (or why my confidence was not real strong): June 29/30, did a pretty good hamstring strain pacing at Western States; July 13, rolled my ankle about four miles from the finish at the SOB 50k;

Thursday of last week, I got stung by something, presumably a bee where we were camping. My hand and forearm were quite swollen Thursday and Friday. I took several Benadryl to get things back under control. All in all, not a real positive last few weeks, but it was such a beautiful course, and you just never know what Saturday morning will bring.

All climbs have been exaggerated to enhance the effort and accomplishment.

Thursday night we camp at about 4200 elevation on the Keechelus Ridge. We get up several times, waiting, checking, looking to the south—finally the clouds clear away and there, about forty miles in the distance, is Mount Rainier under the light of the full moon.

Earlier, we ventured into the 2.3-mile-long ex–train tunnel that is on the course (52.0 to 54.3), trying to figure out how Kathy could pace me through that part just because it would be fun to go through together. My son, Scott, was supposed to pace me from the 70-mile point on in to the finish.

Friday passes quietly with some walking here and there. We go to the "trail from hell" section—not that bad when viewed without 70 miles behind you. I can remember Hope Pass at Leadville—the 21-mile double crossing took less than six hours on fresh legs during training weekend. That same 21 miles took almost seven and a half hours on race day in August. Things change a bit as the miles add up.

Saturday morning—we leapeth forth from the tent and start folding things up only to stop and watch a large (15+?) herd of deer wander down the hillside and to look at the receding layers of mountains watched over by Mount Rainier once more, and then we continue. We stop at the pay shower in Hyak and finally head for Easton and breakfast, still casting furtive looks at the ring of mountains beckoning on all sides.

Breakfast—one of my weaknesses this year—I never did get myself trained to eat a good big breakfast and then head out running.

This time it is even more difficult, as there are several people I want to meet, e-mail acquaintances from the ultralist. Randy and his Kansas flatlanders. Dan B. from Maine, but no lobster. Kendall, Rob, Robin, Geri, and a host of others. As always there is not enough time to say all you want to say—seems Randy is herding us toward the certified fireplug for some reason. Something about heading off for Goat Rock.

It seems like a nice enough idea. We leave Easton on a flattish stretch for about three miles and then, yeeeeek—climb about 2,800 feet in the next three or so miles. Ron has Fred and I pose in front of Goat Rock (if you look in the background, you can see some of the course; we will pass behind those lakes) as we go by. Ron and I have fond memories of chasing each other at the Siletz, Oregon, 50-miler in the late 80s. Oh my, how time has slipped along and we are still out here.

The first hint of doom makes its appearance. I feel like I am dragging my right leg through water; no sharp pains, no cramps, just a weariness in my head. We start down the five- or six-hundred-foot drop of the next mile or so. Leon Draxler, veteran of many 100s, Badwater, Iditasomething, and so forth, passes by. He is a day younger than I am and flashes a wonderful smile when I mention how little respect he has for his elders. He slows, and we talk about Badwater for a while. He has done it the past three years. This year was the good one; he had enough left to summit Mount Whitney, finally. He soon leaves me behind as we cross the top of the 1,400 feet of the second climb. My leg drags on through the syrupy environment it lives in.

I am working my way though a PB&J when a voice says, "Oh, no. I can't see you. I don't see you. Oh, John..." It is Melissa Berman. In a very loose use of the word, I have been coaching her on how to run her first 100. We did lots of night runs and hard walking sessions—in all honesty, she should not see me today. I should be gone, long gone, and far ahead. I manage to laugh, give her a last lecture on how fit she is, how strong she looks, and tell her to get on down the trail—Easton is waiting. She is gone.

I walk up the last grade to Blowdown with Marie Boyd. I had met her in the parking lot. When she said she was from Bishop (CA), I said, "Oh, I went to kindergarten in Bishop in '47." She introduced me to her husband. We might have been classmates in kindergarten many long years ago but have no proof, and our parents are not anywhere around to ask. At the next aid station (15.7 miles), I admit I cannot even walk decently. Ratz. It is over.

Well, not really. My son, remember him, is there to pace me. I ask him if he wants to pace John Lebeskind instead. Sure, why not? We ask John if he wants a pacer, and the smile he gives us tells us that is a good idea come to seed. I ask Randy if there is someway, somewhere, Kathy and I can help. He asks if we want to help at the Keechelus Ridge (62 miles) aid station. Oh, boy—that's where we had camped. We head back for another full-moon rendezvous with Mount Rainier.

Pat Hinds and his wife are there setting up the aid station and welcome us. We watch runners pass through from just after seven in the evening until about five thirty in the morning. The lead runner and pursuers, the midpackers having a suddenly good run, the survivors just trying for under 32 hours—just a finish. We dish out chicken noodle soup, hot chocolate, Cokes, Mountain Dew, PB&Js, turkey sandwiches, advice, encouragement, and even sarcasm—anything to get 'em out of our aid station and on down (yup, finally down, we are at the top of a seven-mile climb) to the next aid station. That is all you do at a 100-miler, go from one aid station to the next one.

Death warmed over comes in several times. We coax them back to life, all but two of them. Josh falls prey to youthful inexperience, Reinhold to bad shoes. They can go no farther. We rent the tent out for fifteen minutes of sleep to Clem LaCava while Curt Ringstad, his pacer, paces anxiously. I wake Clem at fifteen minutes, not a second more. They grab a bite to eat, a sip of something, and they are gone into the night.

John Lebeskind shows up. I wake Scott up. It is 1:44 Sunday morning and time to run. Scott has only run farther than 14 miles once, a 28-miler with me. Cautious smiles and waves—they head off down toward Kachess Lake and the trail from darn.

The Kansas crew shows up to wait—flatlanders a long ways from Dorothy and Toto with only a big green LED light to guide them. Their runner, Randy A., arrives. We all poke and prod, feed and water, and off he goes running. Their runner taken care of, the Kansas crew goes back to their car and follow slowly, trying not to stir up the dust.

There are fewer patrons now. Kathy Welch is greeted with cheers from her three anxious and concerned crewfolkses. Marlis looks at the false dawn and leaves her "big" flashlights with me. Time, the ever-fleeing time, is becoming more important. There are cutoff points that have no feelings, only the harshness of sand passing through the hourglass, slowing for no one, certainly not for weary legs in the morning's dawn.

We are done. The last runner has gone. The ham radio people turn off the equipment—they have given us information all through the night. But now they are done, and they drive off to a bed somewhere in one of the Kittitas Valley towns. We drive about five miles and pull off for a nap. We are done, too.

Maybe not. We awaken about an hour later and notice that we could get to Easton in time to see the lead runners come in. Off we go. We get there in time to see Tim Halder win. It is his first hundred and his first win. I kid him about how he cannot improve. He starts to agree until I point out there is still the course record to attack (he was about 16 minutes, uh, slow?). Ah, youth...something to come back for, after all, eh?

The runners come in, sometimes over an hour apart—a night of running alone over those last miles. Kendall and his magical

22-and-some-change run. We check on where John and Scott are—we project a time using 16-, 17-, 18-, and 19-minute miles. Oh my gosh! They have cleared the 97 and are on the way in; we didn't consider them running under 15s during the last 18 miles, but they did. All that is left is to wait for Melissa. We know where she is. We know she is having blister problems. We wait. Linda, whom I paced at Western, John A., and Pam (Melissa's earlier pacer) head out to the 97—we wait.

Suddenly they are back—we look at the watches. The 32-hour barrier is no longer an issue. Melissa and Rod come into view just after 4:00 p.m.; just over 30 hours on a challenging course, and her first 100-miler is a done deed. My day of defeat and misery has been overshadowed time and again by people I got to help through the night, by smiles and thank yous, by the good spirits of the participants and the beauty of the mountains.

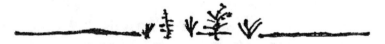

Still Trying to Explain This Stuff

As some more examples of the difficulties of explaining the nature of trail running or running ultramarathons, I offer the following real-world events:

At the Daybreak Climb a Mountain Run in Spokane, Washington, the 24 or so miles of rolling pavement were behind me. The first six miles of the climb were wearing me down. Four miles to go. Running way too hard, John. "Way too hard," echoed the demons.

A car passed, little voices yelling and hollering, "Hi, Grampa! Run, Grampa, run." Grampa staggered on.

A few switchbacks up, the steepness now telling, I walked. Oops. There's Kim (daughter) and the grandkids. A small voice was heard, "Mom, why is Grampa walking?" How do you explain 31 miles down, three to go on a ten percent grade to a five-year-old? It's all good, their last chorus was, "Grampa won! Grampa won!" (I was first overall. At age 55, I had snuck in another win.)

I came up alongside Sally one evening as we rounded the lake. "Hi, howzrunnin'?" I asked her. She responded with, "Well, I thought pretty good, but I guess not." "Uh," asked I, "what do you mean?" She explained she had finished as the first female at a recent 10k and came back to town all excited, heartwarming little trophy in hand. A weekend's adventure to cherish. At work Monday morning she told a coworker about her victory and had to answer the query, "So, how many entrants were there?" "About 84." "How many women?" "Twenty-eight." "Well," he pointed out, "you didn't beat a very big field, did you?"

Drat.

There was the ignominious question asked when I had told someone I had just set a masters' record and finished second in a 50-mile run, "Who beat you?"

Ya goes 10–1 and all anyone will ask is, "Who beat you?" The tale of your grand effort will not be heard.

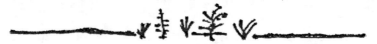

Full Moon and Winter Solstice, a Night Run

Winter solstice passed a few days before Christmas, almost at the same time that the moon was in perigee—the closest it gets to earth during each orbit. At perigee the moon appears to be some 12 to 14 percent larger than usual. Winter solstice is the unofficial start of our regular night runs on Wednesdays. As others are sitting down to dinner, we are looking for lights, gloves, and fanny packs.

This particular evening, we had left the house about thirty minutes before dark to get into the woods to a trail on the easterly side of the mountain. Frost from two mornings ago still sparkled in shady areas. We crunched along the trail, running upward toward a meadow crossing, checking watches frequently. Stop, I whispered, we'll wait here. How soon? Soon.

We had barely gotten still when the show started. The top of the rising moon was almost red as it caught the setting sun's last rays. The shadows that had run from the sun not an hour ago were now being reborn by the moon. The moon's shadows—always magical, even more so in the woods—would let us run without flashlights for a while.

We started up the trail and turned onto the first forestry road, striding our way through pools of moonlight. The thickly wooded forest would hide the moon on the trails, keeping it dark away from the road. So we ran on the open road for a few miles before finally deciding to turn off down one of the trails. We stopped then. It was time to go to work. We had to decide what to start using.

We each had on a headlight and each had a flashlight in a sheath on the fanny pack belt. I had two more headlights and several more flashlights in my backpack. The early sunsets give us time to do night runs without staying up all night. The night runs give us time to test all the new *things we might need* for later-in-the-year night races. Kathy had a green 3-LED to try; I was trying a handheld with green LEDs, too (but with the choice of 4 or 10 LEDs lighted), and a new headlight.

We had finally become comfortable running with our headlights after those first runs when we took turns blinding each other before we got used to the idea that you don't turn to look at the person you are talking to—unless you turn your light off first. Headlights are also great for seeing things that aren't on the trails. You hear a noise, you turn to look directly at—wow! Look at all the eyes staring back at you. The record (held by Kathy) is finding five pairs of eyes belonging to a family of raccoons crossing a road.

We turned on the handhelds and started down the trail. I was switching back and forth from 4 to 10 lights, headlight on, headlight off, just doing some serious evaluation when I ran into Kathy. Why are you stopped? I hear something. Is it big? I don't know. I turn off my lights. **What are you doing?** I hear better in the dark. Turn the light back on. Look, over there (as if I can see which way she is pointing). No, over there (see, I told you).

Bobcat? Bobcat! Wow. A glimpse of something spotted and short-tailed is all we get. Gone, I say calmly. All gone. We listen and hear nothing but our wildly erratic breathing. We adjust things; I change to a single-bulb blue-white handheld, turn the headlight from bright to medium, and we head on down to a well-used creek crossing.

At the creek crossing, we can see several sets of footprints: deer, elk, raccoon, and a largish one we pause over. In our woods there are two things you should recognize: poison oak and...

Cougar? I think so. You want me to pretend I can tell how long ago it passed through here? Maybe feel the print for warmth or something? It is about the same size as my hand. It is on top of one of the deer hoofprints.

We start up the trail away from the creek, reciting all the things we know about cougars, mountain lions, panthers, catamounts, pumas, and woolly mammoths (just in case). We can hear our heartbeats above our footsteps as we move. You always remember the wrong thing. I point out that they are predators, that predators are stealthy; therefore, we won't hear one if it is stalking us. Oops, that didn't help.

We run up the other hillside, undoubtedly the fastest we have ever run getting up that stretch, back onto the road, and pause to catch our breath. We assume we've left the cougar, or whatever, far below. We decide which way to go and start on around the mountain to the next cross-trail back to the other side. I change to my dual-bulb headlight because it has a light-up-the-sky switch and get the new flashlight back out. Of course, the green LEDs lead to the question of which lights would a cougar see better: the white, blue-white, or green?

About two hundred yards later, we both hear something moving through the brush just uphill from the road—recalling the won't-hear-the-predator theory—a remarkable calm is exhibited as we shine the lights on the hillside. Another first for us, a small porcupine comes meandering through the brush. We laugh, watch it for a minute or two, and then, just as we are about to start running again, we hear something big just down from the edge of the road. Big? Sounded big. Yes. How many lights are in the backpack? Two more headlights and three handhelds. Get 'em out. All of them? Yes.

Imaginations are strange things to have with you in the woods. We have often wondered what the animals in that part of the forest thought about us as we passed through the night. Two strange creatures with eyes that light up the road both frontward and rearward, and in their paws, eyes on both sides, too. One green one, one white one. It was just after solstice on the night of the full moon...

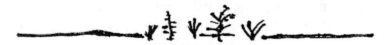

An Early Spring Venture

Separations and work schedules being what they are, our weekends are relegated to just being outside together for a while. We reached a new level of sloth-like behavior yesterday—late getting up, an even later breakfast, late late late getting out the door, where we were delayed along our way by first one thing and then another.

A mile or so across the prairie, the trilling song finally penetrated. I paused and looked around, finally finding the red-wing blackbird that, having returned from his trip down south, thought it was time to officially begin mating season. We looked around at all the empty bushes and thickets—no audience of prospective brides had he. Kathy commented on his lack of audience and continued on toward the bluff.

We turned right at the *T*-bench and started up. A hundred yards or so of climbing and we would be on top. From there the trail wandered along bluff's edge, rolling up and down for the next couple of miles before dropping to the beach. Suddenly two large shadows crossed on the ground in front of us. Our heads jerked up, eyes searching. Kathy saw them first. She exclaimed, "Eagles!" trying to do so quietly, as if you can. It is the time of year for the established couples to return to last year's nest and a time for this year's mating to take place.

Two adult bald eagles, wings and feathers extended fully as they rode the uplift of air at bluff's edge, went past—so close that we pretended we could feel the air those huge wings pushed. I have never become used to the sound—the air pushed so forcefully we could hear it a hundred feet away as they flew on. They were so unmindful of us we didn't even get a glance. Our climb was delayed several times as we watched them pause on wind's unseen hand, then climb, following the curled contour of the wind, finally to turn toward their nest. Their arrival meant we "needed" to pass that way more often to watch for the arrival of another generation.

Trills and gwaks and scwraks from a raven tree chased after us as we dropped down the zigzags to the beach. The lagoon had a scattered population of mergansers, scaups, and buffleheads, ruddy ducks with their blue bills, and a few Barrow's Goldeneyes—all of them moving away, pushed by some unwritten definition of safe distances from people. Duck-like birds of black, white, blue, brown, and yellow—they get along together better than we.

Harlequins! Harlequin ducks, down from their summer homes up in the mountains, were scattered amongst the waves. They knew we couldn't run out there to get them, and we got to see them from only ten or fifteen yards—the males are slate colored with patches of chestnut and white. They easily rival the wood duck for beauty with the sculpted swirling patterns of their feathers. We found a log of the right size and in just the right place to sit and watch the many winter visitors. They were from the Arctic, the North Cascades, and one year there was a stranger that took several hours with the books—it was a traveler on the way from the Antarctic regions back to the Arctic—an Arctic tern—a crosser of hemispheres. Do the various birds with their many places to come from and go to discuss the routes and the aid stations as we do?

We reached the end of the beach part of today's route and turned inland at the Pacific Northwest Trail to start the climb up and into the forest and onto the Kyle's Kettle trail—no major climbs, just a winding series of ups and downs through a small section of old-growth forest. One more pause—a pair of kingfishers chittering and chattering about where she wants the nest to be—and we were on our way inland. Between the birds and the driftwood we had taken over an hour and a half to cover five miles. This would never do. A determined jog took us up the quarter mile of the Pacific Northwest Trail and the junction. Our sudden success with the climb led to the bravado-laden "Let's run across Kyle's."

Kyle's Kettle trail twisted and turned and had roots and...a...reason to pause again. A pileated woodpecker was starting on a new home or just trying to get a headache by banging its beak against the tree. Down, then up, then down, then up, past the Douglas fir that we took the time to measure one day. It is just over 27 feet in circumference. It is called "the Grampa tree"—guesses of 800 years of age seem to be agreed upon by all us experts.

Seven miles and we were just passing Spencer's trail when Kathy raised the question, "When's the last time we did Spencer's?" What? Go down there? Yes. Why? Why not? Because, it is getting dark. Ah, c'mon, we can get across there before the sun is across the yardarm (I always like it when a situation arises where I can say that).

I have heard there is one biker that crossed Spencer's without putting a foot down. One rider out of how many in how many years? Most just laugh and don't go down there. You don't run it. You hop along, skip step along, grab a tree, slip, slide, and pivot along, and duck your head along. It is barely a mile. In a fit of manly challenge and an overdose of ibuprofen, I crossed it one day in 18 minutes. Today there were three fallen trees to climb over or under. A voice I sometimes recognize mentioned flashlights twice along the way.

A chorus of cheers from a throng of purple finches in a blackberry thicket greeted us as we climbed out of Spencer's. I felt obligated to check the time. "We are down to (up to?) 24-minute miles," I half grumbled as we got to Pigeon Ridge trail.

"Take off your watch," she said, "just run," smiling and turning in the direction of the house.

CHAPTER SEVEN

I like these cold, gray winter days.
Days like these let you savor a bad mood.

> —Bill Watterson, author of *Calvin and Hobbes*

Laughter is the sun that drives winter from the human face.

> —Victor Hugo

Winter Variations in North Dakota

Twenty-four winters have passed since I started running. There have been winters with no new T-shirts, but only a few. Without meaning to enter into the was-it-an-official-ultra discussion, there have been no winters without running an ultra. If asked, "What would it take to keep you from running?" I would generally respond with a blank stare—I did not think anything could do that if I was healthy (vague illusions of being bulletproof and emotionally stable notwithstanding). Surely I could always run, couldn't I?

Then came winter in North Dakota and many weather patterns that various Web sites assured me were anomalies, outliers, or aberrations in the grand scheme of climatological history. The first snow came early. It was October, and the scattered flurries scattered in a fourteen-inch-thick layer over the Turtle Mountains. We donned layers and boots and shuffled here and there, eventually ending up over at the high school track one afternoon, where enough other desperate souls had gathered. By walking abreast, we soon had pounded the snow into submission and, presto! There were two lanes available. The first, but I hope not annual, Turtle Mountain 3-hour track run, snow clearing, and tall tale 'fest was done.

The local residents assured us the snow was unusual (probably using the same misguiding Web sites as I had as a resource) and would be gone soon. As "soon" passed, or stayed, we managed a few miles around the cemetery, then another track session, and finally I trimmed trees and bushes to make a loop that was about eight minutes long, still laps but much more enjoyable, in the woods behind St. Ann's. One afternoon, in a nearby wildlife area, we found our plight was shared. We topped a rise, and a large white something was moving across the road into the meadow. We paused (the mythical white moose?), looked closer, and when it moved we both said, "Snowshoe hare." Kathy laughed at the idea that the hare was dressed for winter, for the change of seasons, not for the anomaly of an early storm. The same white that would render the hare almost invisible when winter did arrive was now in stark contrast to the browns and grays of the late-fall woods, making its camouflage all too visible. No wonder its movements were so skittish.

As the various hunting seasons made the game-management areas off-limits to us, we looked for other places to run. That first October snow was gone, and someone told us there was a Rails-to-Trails over toward St. John, about 15 minutes drive away. We headed that way, found the familiar railway bed, parked, and got out, feeling the wind as soon as we opened the door, blustery and coming down from Manitoba—cold Arctic wind. I reached back inside the car to grab another layer or two and a Windbreaker for each of us. We have tried to become accustomed to winds that drive the temperatures to 15, 20, and, finally, 40 degrees below zero (a number that used to be only a math trivia number: At what temperature do Celsius and Fahrenheit become equal?), only to meet with failure. "The tree must have fallen over," I muttered under my breath. Kathy looked at me. "What?" I explained it's an old story I first heard in Missouri. There's only one tree up north to break up the wind between Missouri and the Arctic. On mornings when the wind bites and just won't let go, someone always seemed to say, "The tree must have fallen over." We continued northerly, leaning into the wind, shuffling from one cleared patch of ground to another. Fence posts alongside the trail barely poked through the wind-driven snowdrifts. We turned back after thirty minutes, Windbreakers crinkly from the layer of developing ice. What to try next....

Twelve days later the mercury climbed into the positive numbers—when would I have believed 12ºF could feel warm? On the third day of this heat wave, I noticed there was some pavement showing through. The fourth day and it was now patches of snow instead of patches of pavement. Where to go? When we first got to Belcourt we had driven out to the new school, the Ojibwa Indian School. It has a big parking lot and a paved perimeter road. Off we went in pursuit of the perfect patch of pavement.

Arriving at the school, we drove the perimeter road—nine-tenths of a mile long—where is the missing tenth of a mile? Oh well, that's what happens when you have a nonrunner for a site-design engineer. An engineer who is a runner would have snuck in another curve here or there to make the loop an even mile, maybe. Okay, so it wasn't a trail and there weren't many trees, birds, animals, creeks, or porcupines; it gave us good footing, and there were no cars or snowmobiles (they outnumber the cars up here in the wintertime) to worry about. We ran laps, together and separately, clockwise and counterclockwise; I even did some walking-backward stuff just to stretch whatever muscle that stretches. The movie *Fargo* came to mind as I looked at the snow-covered fields stretched off endlessly to the south and east. I am fascinated by how a land so flat can have such distant horizons. It isn't just the snow effect; the green of the flax, soybean, corn, and grains that were here in August gave the same strange infinity of distance.

An old game that Kathy and I played when running with lots of passing or meeting each other came to mind. A song title would be spoken at each meeting; the name of the artist was the challenge. An answer was to be given by the next meeting. An acceptable artist was decided by unspoken rules, usually made up by the song pre-senter, i.e., "At Last" would be okay by Etta James or Diane Schuur but not by Michael Bolton; "A Little Help From My Friends" would bring up Joe Cocker or Ike & Tina Turner acceptably, but Barbra Streisand's version would start a call for the never-present referee. Joan Baez, Toni Braxton, Billie Holiday, Sting, Roger Miller, Willie and Waylon, and the afternoon sun—the occasional lap with no challeng-es because one thought or another had caused a mind to wander—rocks used as lap counters were moved from one side of the road to the other—all to the irregular sound of our footsteps. It wasn't an ultramarathon-distance run, it wasn't a trail, but as with many other runners plagued by severe winter weather, we were out and moving and, as we waited for spring, that was enough.

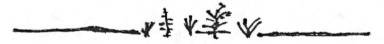

Once Around the Block Under a Full Moon

As darkness falls earlier each day, we are soon to be robbed of the easy running time and driven into the night. The layers that let some of us run in the fall become inadequate as winter edges closer with each sunset. For some it is time to train indoors, gambling that the effort will be intense enough to counter the lack of roots and rocks and hills and dales. For others it is a time to read running reports and nutrition books, a time to exchange e-mail and flog dead horses—or run to watch the seasonal astronomy shows.

We are in Belcourt, North Dakota, on the Turtle Mountain Indian Reservation for the coming winter. Almost everything we read or hear makes us think we will not be venturing out for any long periods of time as we progress (is that a good word?) into winter. Will this be the year we get snowshoes? A treadmill? Just bag it for the duration? Surely we can still go run around the block. I decide to go do a run around the nearest block. It is on the outskirts of town but still in the Reservation. I'll do it just to find that forgotten feel of things along the fog line, just to see if it will work.

The road system around here is basically a series of north-south or east-west blocks—not many diagonals. A typical block is one mile to the side; it will be four miles to run around the block—a long enough test. Halfway down the first side and the lowness of the horizon creeps into my consciousness—stars and planets all the way down to the ground—way way down. It's flat to the south and east of us—really flat—and the moon is really small looking. That thought jogs my memory of a recent Web page—apogee? The moon is almost at apogee (recall from the Greek *apo*, away from, + Greek *Gaia*, Earth), giving a visual appearance of a 12 to 14 percent decrease in size. One distraction leads to another, and I start thinking about the north-south by east-west grid I am running. What is in the quadrants of the night sky above and in front of me as I go around the block? Oh boy, haven't done this in a long time.

Okay, that's the moon off to the left—might as well get the easy one first. I'm on a westbound leg of the block, and there isn't anything real bright in front of me, at first. The ancients used a lot of imagination when they saw the constellations, but the longer you look, the more you see. I finally sort of spot Cygnus, which means I can drop my line just a bit and there is Lyra, maybe. At the corner, eyes full of unnamed stars, a left turn onto a southbound leg.

Wow...another easy one. The bright spot about thirty degrees up and right in front of me is Jupiter. The crisp clearness of the cold night air makes me wish I had binoculars with me. Several of Jupiter's moons (There are over thirty? Forty? Why think of that when I'm out here?) are visible with only average binoculars. Galileo's discovery of the moons of Jupiter through his telescope in the 17th century was a major stepping-stone into the Scientific Revolution—just recalling that would make a certain 10th grade teacher proud of me. I know Pegasus is somewhere up high and to the left, a little bit into the southeastern sky, but tonight I cannot connect the celestial dots.

The next corner comes up, and the turn points me right at the Pleiades—the seven sisters. There is a comfort in finding all these *friends* of the night. For years we have done running at night—sometimes just after staring at a star map for a few minutes—with certain trails in mind. The trails would point us toward the section of sky we were running to explore that night. The Pleiades have a place in the history, myth, and culture of many countries. Once discovered and placed in the mind's eye, they are easily found, even from places far distant from home. They serve as a landmark for me. Just up and a little left is Perseus; farther up is Cassiopeia. This part of North Dakota suddenly feels less strange. We are in almost the same latitude as we were on the island in Washington State, and with one well-known reference point found, I stop and slowly turn around with head turned up, eyes searching for bright points.

Aldebaran, Capella, and Betelgeuse are found—finding Betelgeuse means if I go out again, but start later, Orion will be up, maybe. Maybe I need to wait a few weeks for the fall sky to turn to the winter sky. The Winter Hexagon and the smaller Winter Triangle are there, but who is missing from my view? Rigel and Sirius are still below the horizon, but I can use Betelgeuse to point to Pollux, hmmm, parts are missing. Yes, I will need to wait for the heavens to turn and then leave an hour or two later. It isn't that cold.

My thought of leaving must have traveled to the nearby lake. A great rush of wings and honking means a flock of geese are lifting off the lake's surface, heading into the night sky to go farther south on their yearly migration. They probably know the night sky better than I ever will—some scientists think they navigate using the stars. I have a flashlight with a green beam of light. I can see about seventy-five feet and am comfortable with my four-mile run. They have no lights but will cover many miles, happily honking along as they have for many seasons. They form up, gaining height with each loop in their slow climb to cruising altitude as I turn back and head for the last corner.

Ursa Major is low on the horizon in front of me. Its pointers send my eyes straight upward to Ursa Minor with Polaris on the end. I am northbound. Draco is in between the two Dippers, still following almost the same circumpolar (it never sets) route as when Ptolemy listed it in his sky map about 1800 years ago. The lights of Belcourt start to rob me of my night sky. An awareness of the cold returns, and I realize that running under the distractions of the night sky has kept me warm, or at least unaware of the cold.

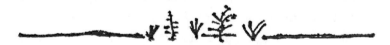

Nature's Webs

It was strands and ripples and numbers again. It was one more recollection of an environmental engineering professor expounding on how we must drop the idea of linear relationships and start seeing that all things are related. He often used a spiderweb for a pound-it-home hammer. Touch the web at any point and all points of the web are touched—some more than others. As the frost becomes part of each morning's run and I pass the many spiderwebs glistening with their diamonds of dew, his words often come back. My recollection of intertwined relationships was stated aloud and, as with most conversations, Kathy had a differing view. She saw relationships as those of the ripples on the surface of a pond. It does not matter where the stone strikes the water's surface, all points along the shore will be affected—some sooner, some later, some more than others, but in the end, the ripple, whether wind or stone created, is everywhere felt.

We only have one pond to throw stones in, at, or across, but there are lots and lots of spiderwebs. The pond, created by a glacier about 10,000 years ago, remains fixed and not subject to anything I can do. Once I accepted that I turned my thoughts to the spiderwebs. I cannot move them, but I can adjust my view of the spiderwebs without touching them. If I time a run right and use a certain trail, I can recreate sunrise five, maybe six times on a single run. I just have to be out about thirty minutes before the sun peeks out from behind the Cascade Mountains. I have to be out early enough to run to the end of one of the bluff trails so I can turn and run into the rising sun. The earth is inside the seasonal window when the earth's orbit puts the sun directly in my face even though the trail points me to the southeast. For the next few weeks I can create a new sunrise as I climb each rise in the trail on the return trip.

The variety of spiders—big or little, shiny or not, ground dwellers or high-limb jumpers—all contribute to the show this morning. The single strand of silk from an orb weaver drops from a limb ten feet above my head. It leads my eyes to a web that spans and encloses an opening between a tall fir and a wind-twisted shrub-like spruce. The idea of that spider climbing up one tree, going out to the end of the branch, and then jumping with a particular lower branch in mind causes that pause of casual observation to lengthen. Maybe on the next pass it just climbs up the strand just made? I never seem to arrive at the right time to see how the second strand is made. No one is around to tell me how the spider knew which branch to jump from.

Did it wait for a quartering wind to guide it to the lower branches of the waiting spruce? Is it truly just a happenstance thing done as many times as are needed and a hope for success is not really held (sort of like running here and there and hoping the fitness needed to complete an ultramarathon is achieved)?

The frost-coated grasses that my fingers had brushed on the outbound trip are now silhouetted against the sun's glow, and an almost invisible curtain is revealed. Spider webs barely two inches wide and not any taller span the now-still stalks of prairie grasses. Unlike the orb weavers' webs, these webs appear almost solid, though frail looking. The gossamer webs, now covered with dew, have all the properties of a prism, as a rainbow reveals itself to my lowered head. As I continue along the trail, slower now so as not to miss this reception of tiny mites, I see a web wind torn and tattered. It lasted the summer and fall; now winter calls it to its end. On this web or that, an egg sac wrapped in silk awaits winter's turn. Another of nature's cradle of thousands so a few might survive and the species prolong. This same funnel web design will show up a few months from now in a thousand and one locations as the various spiderlings that make it through the winter continue their life cycle. The sun is providing light but not much warmth—not for me or for the many dormant spiders and insects. While I put on layers, they sleep and wait for the sun. When I finally start shedding layers, they will wake and come out in the sun's warmth. For now I enjoy a frosty morning's reflections and wish I had worn thicker gloves—or mittens.

Some days I run out to the park from home and spend some time on the woodpile, splitting and stacking firewood for the winter visitors in the campground. As I work my way through the woodpile, I am distracted by the lethargic movement of the insects I have uncovered by moving a piece of wood. They are, for the most part, the same insects or spiders I have seen for months on my running trails. They are just very slow to move—some sensory guide tells

227

them to go back under the protective leaves and wood litter or, on a day when the sun is high, the many curled up "things" may slowly come to life and scurry about in a few minutes of warmth. In the twisted corners of my mind, I think of the relaxation in my body as I leave the cold of the shaded portions of the trails and run out into a sunny stretch. A gazillion years removed from the life forms that I uncovered, but we both enjoy scurrying about in the sun.

I finish my time on the woodpile, notice, as always, that it does not look appreciably smaller, and change clothes to run. It is late afternoon by now, and the wind is making its presence known, moving the tops of the trees. Down in the bottom of Kyle's Kettle the air is still and cool, the wind's presence known only by its whispers in the upper branches. As I climb out of that hole the glacier sculpted so long ago, the scent of salt is in the moving air—the wind now a felt and scented presence. The trees along the PNT trail are quiet on the near side of Lake Pondilla but dancing on the far side—a sign the wind is out of the south. A few minutes later and the whitecaps of the waters off Partridge Point show the force of the wind. The wave line is at right angles to the wind—it will be strongest farther along the bluff.

As winter deepens the spiders no longer ambush me with their webs on the trails. The trail spanners are gone for the season, their lifespan so short it might not even fill a full year. Those that remain are deep in the thick moss and layers of leaves alongside the trails I am running or in the woodpile I use for cross-training. As with most other of nature's creatures, I scurry across the open trail overlooking the beach and then return to the dense woods, out of the wind, where the shadows of late afternoon remind me to hurry. My mind clears of its own webs as I pick up speed, heading home.

Spring Cleaning, Too Many Shoes

I sit here on the porch looking at my shoes and thinking of the places we have been, the places they have taken me. The places were okay, but the "they" is becoming a bit of a problem. A few minutes ago, I picked these shoes out of the closet next to the back door. I go to this closet almost every day, stop, pull open the door, pick out a pair of shoes, put 'em on, and head out for the day's folly.

Today, however, when I opened the closet door, all the shoes came tumbling out, dozens of them, hundreds of them. You don't suppose shoes can breed during the winter if left in a dark closet, do you? I know neither you, nor I, would ever buy that many pairs of shoes, right? But there in front of me were hiking shoes, trail shoes, bicycle shoes, road shoes, patent leather high heels—oops, wrong column—anyway, many many shoes. I stood there for a moment, contemplating; I don't seem to be throwing away shoes as they get old like I'm supposed to.

I picked up a pair I hadn't seen in a while. Why do I have these old, beat-up Sauconys? I got them in 2003 for that road marathon somewhere along the Yaquina River. Why are they still here? Judging from the grass stains, they have been relegated to being work-in-the-yard shoes, the last assignment before the trash can. So why aren't they in the trash can? What else is in here?

That pair, the newest-looking ones—gray, blue, and silver Montrails—those are my *racing* shoes. The ones I only take out when some *serious* training has been done, some interim measures of fitness have been met, and, most important, some reconciliation with my head about the difference between running and racing has settled in. Their laces haven't been all twisted from mile after mile on the trail. The heels are still even, not yet showing the asymmetric beating my body gives the soles. Nope, no signs of Shoe Goo on this pair. They don't see the light of day very often.

The Cascadias, all prettied up in yellow with black, red, and orange trim (who decides these colors anyway?) are for *friendly* trails—trails with no pointy-side-up rocks, trails with lots of pine or fir needles or soft sand and grassy spots. Thin soled and flexible, they don't care if they get wet. They find traction in mud and creek crossings. I changed into these shoes at a creek crossing twenty-five miles into a 50-miler along the Rogue River a few years ago. My first DNF, that grand creator of self-pity and analysis, came ten or fifteen miles later. The shoes were at fault. It wasn't me—had to be the shoes. Not sure why they're still in my pile.

And these? They don't even look like running shoes—more like house slippers now, dull gray and navy blue. The soles have been worn down to where my toes can almost grip the rocks and roots. I can't wear them for running anymore. The support is gone. One eyelet is torn loose and hangs across the tongue. One heel is worn thin, while the other is deeply canted. But I can't just throw them out. The Vitesses were new when I laced them up that morning in southwestern France, slung the big red backpack into place, and started walking westerly, over the Pyrenees, into and across Spain. Six hundred and some miles those shoes saw, fifty-two mornings and more. They should be bronzed.

The ASICS, the yellow and silver ones with the strange lacing pattern, bring back memories of the many attempts at solving the "how to run downhill and not lose toenails" problem. As with any shoes, after you have solved the size issue, then you have to find a style with toe-box room combined with heel snugness; then, finally, you have to learn how to lace them, all with the toes in mind. I tried ladder-lacing, cross-twisting, even two strings for each shoe, and then I experimented with thick socks and thin socks. There had to be a way to run the descents without blackening or losing the toenails, just had to be. Finally the day came when I laced up these shoes, ran that four and a half miles of quad-burning downhill all the way to the gate, and didn't even wince. The last time I wore these shoes was on Sixth Avenue in Leadville—can't throw them away.

I reached for the Hardrocks, still almost new looking, and remembered I had worn them on a trail when, being rather full of myself that day, I told someone, "The runner gets the shoes to the finish line more than the shoes get the runner to the finish line." That day slowly turned into a run gone bad. When I paused and bent over to untie my right shoe so I could remove a boulder that was causing me some discomfort, I was long gone into dehydration and out of fuel. That little act of bending over to untie my shoe locked up every muscle from buttock to ankle on one side. I had untied my shoe but now could not bend down to take it off, shake out the humongous rock, slip the shoe back on, retie, and continue to run. I did finally manage an unchoreographed hop, slip, slide, and stumble to a nearby rock, lifted my foot up onto said rock, leaned against a tree, did the aforementioned tasks, and then set off down the trail, determined to get those blue shoes to the finish line. They did not seem inclined to help me that day. Guess I'd been right after all. So here they stay, waiting for me to get them to another finish line.

I stand there looking at the pile of shoes, Vasque, Reebok, New Balance, Keen, and others still hiding in the closet, wondering if they knew that with the approach of spring I would feel some urge to organize, to restructure, to rededicate—to, maybe, clean out the shoe closet. I wonder if it is a bad thing to wonder if my shoes know what I am thinking. It's not like I talk to hand bottles, too. Hand bottles? How many...um, best not go there.

I take two pair out of the pile for inspection. Their midsoles are wrinkled from being compressed too many times; one has a hole where the big toe on my right foot always wears through. I set them aside. Once you decide which pairs are to be discarded, the rest can go back into the closet. I look at the two pair sitting by themselves, beginning to have second thoughts. They can't be that old, can they? So what if they have holes and bad soles. They deserve more than an ignoble end in the trash can, right? I'll decide after my run. For now, I'll just shove, er, stack them back in the closet. I'll decide who goes and who stays when I get back. Or maybe I won't.

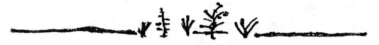

A Three-Bottle Run

I am not in my own room. It is a good room in which to sleep, an almost totally comfortable place—just not my own. I can see just enough by the subdued light of the full moon so the room has only a slight feel of unfamiliarity. The bed is a good bed, but the pillow doesn't fluff just right, and the mattress isn't molded to the shape of my body. I need to run my hand along the wall as I walk down the hall to the bathroom. As I walk back to the bedroom, I pause before the window that has no curtain and look out toward the upper edge of the valley. The brightness of the moon in the north-facing window lets me see the outline of the mountains ringing the valley. I can see the outlines of several of the peaks that make up the Rattlesnake Hills. I can almost see the tower.

Kathy's voice comes sleepily from the bed, "It will be there in the morning. You know you're going to try it again. Come to bed." "Yeah, in the morning," I say to myself, adding, "I'll get up early and beat the heat."

But I sleep in. A truly strange house would wake me, but this is a home for us, a home that Kathy's aunt has lived in for over fifty years. It is a big blanket of comfort that hasn't known a stranger for many seasons. I doze until the smell of coffee and breakfast fill the room. I finally pull the curtain back. Instead of our usual gray and cloudy morning on the island, a pale-blue sky greets me. Instead of a day that might reach 55 degrees in the afternoon, this clear sky of morning foretells a hot afternoon here in the lower Yakima Valley.

There will be no cooling ocean breeze. The grasses alongside the canal are barely moving.

I help myself to the remaining toast and bacon, pour a cup of coffee, and go outside to the patio, where all the voices are. Aunty Pat kids me for sleeping in, adding, as she points, "You can still get up there and back before dark." "Good grief, I can walk up there and back before dark," I say weakly, recalling how late in the day I started last time—having totally misjudged how long it would take. Over the years I have been known to misjudge the same route several times, savoring each lesson as I went astray. I had better try it if I am going to get done without frying my wet-side-of-the-mountains brain.

Kathy has put three bottles in the freezer. I put two frozen bottles in the fanny pack and carry two hand bottles, one frozen and one chilled. The memory of suffering through a day of trying to make it a one-bottle run is still clear. If I can get to the top in two hours, I will have something cool to drink on the way down. I holler, "Bye, see you in three or four hours," at the laughter on the patio and start running up the road.

I run easily up to the canal, cross the bridge, and leave the road to head into the open sage and bunchgrass of the upper valley away from the dairies and apple orchards. This is open-desert running. There are few things more relaxing than running out here. The snowy shoulders of Mount Adams and Mount Rainier are behind me, an arm's reach and sixty or seventy miles away at the same time. Blue glints and glimmers reflect from the Yakima River a few miles south of me in the bottom of the valley. It is quiet out here with only the barest whisper of wind. The sand quiets each footfall as I work my way toward the foothill shelf, over an hour of gradual climbing away.

It is warm, only seventyish, but that is warm to me. We haven't felt fifty-five on the island yet this spring—warm is always a concern when we leave the "wet" side of Washington and cross to the

Palouse, the "dry" side of the state. There is no trail to follow, just the glint of the sun on the tower up on the skyline—also just out there at arm's reach. I pick a draw to start the climb, feeling a bit sneaky for following an old game trail that winds along the face. Even though I see lots of scat or droppings, the mountainside remains empty. It is steep and slow going as I work my way up and around the distant shoulder heading for the easterly end and the spine of a ridge that shapes the top of the mountain. I empty the first bottle as I reach the ridge and the old road. It isn't a road really, only the barest trace of where the workers at the tower once passed. The last of the morning breeze had cooled me as I climbed; now the air is still as I follow the spine toward the tower. I had the sun off to the right as I climbed. Now it is straight onto my neck and back as I shuffle up along the ridge. The warm gives way to heat.

I get to the tower in slightly less than two hours, actually a bit ahead of "schedule," and start thinking about going farther along the ridge before starting down. The tower never gets more than a brief pause. It snaps and crackles menacingly as it sends out however many millions of wavy bits and pieces of communications that pass through each second. What it does and what I do are at opposite ends of the spectrum of speed. I usually run on past for a mile or so to get away from the noise of whatever those steel arms and dishes do. When I am far enough past that the snaps and crackles are gone and I can hear my breathing and heart again, I pause to look around—westward to the snowcapped Cascades; easterly I can see bits of blue, reflections of the once-majestic Columbia River; southerly, with just a bit of imagination, I can see Oregon. Height and distance distort perspective so that all that I see is downhill from here.

A cooling breeze tells me I can go farther along the ridge, past my usual trail down to the valley. I run to the end of the ridge. Now all I hear are wind whispers. I stop and look today from a place where I am sure that someone must have stood at some time long ago—perhaps a Native American or an early explorer stood here, slowly turned, looked, and, using names I would not recognize, saw the same things I see now. Turning for one last look, I pick a game trail to follow back to the valley floor and start running again. I have one bottle left and an hour or so of running to get me back to the laughter and voices on the patio.

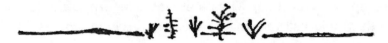

Old Men on the Trails

Fall in the Pacific Northwest and the running gets quieter as the rains soften the leaf-covered trails. I parked the car and started running down the Kettles Trail. I was headed for the old men up on Cedar Grove Trail—cedars and firs that have been shedding needles for two, three, or maybe four hundred years. One old man, limbs bent from seeking the sun those many tens of years, always brings me to a stop.

Eight feet thick he stands. Most of his limbs are bare. The six-inch-thick bark is deeply grooved, fire scarred on one side. Many times I have asked him what happened those summers and winters gone by. Just as many times no answer was offered. Three ravens were perched on his lower limbs one day. They told me tales from the many seasons gone by, years of snow, wind, and rain, of hundreds of summers long ago.

Today at the fork leading to the old men was another old man—white-haired and bent at the shoulders. He looked up, and an easy smile greeted me. He had a walking staff and stood to one side to allow me to pass. I pointed to the left, saying he was okay. He asked where my fork led. I slowed. You never know which interruption will turn out to be an "important" one—which one becomes a memory—but the woods are not to be hurriedly passed through. I paused to answer.

I told of the loop I was heading up, to the old trees, the "old men" as I called them. He said he was walking the trails trying to remember them from before the war. They weren't trails then. They were logging roads. Oh. That war. His war and my father's war. He spoke of living and working out here, days at a time, never thinking of returning to town. The sounds of the axes and steam engines would stop in the evening. The quiet would return to the forest, and the bluffs would call to him. He told of watching whales and ships and sunsets from the bluffs.

He asked of my running. I said it is not really running. I pause to talk to trees and ravens and listen to the songs of early fall's migrating birds. I told him I run the bluffs answering those same calls he did those many years ago. Perhaps some of my whales were his whales before he left for less peaceful lands.

We talked of Vermont and of Georgia, of France and Germany, of the Pyrenees and the Rockies, of scattered families and friends, some gone, some remembered, some somewhere ever unknown to us.

He looked at his watch, smiled; "I must go and find my car," he said.

I gave directions, offered my hand in thanks and farewell. The twists in the trail separated us quickly as I headed for the old men to tell them of an old man.

Perhaps they would remember his earlier passing.

CHAPTER EIGHT

Sunshine is delicious,
Rain is refreshing,
Wind braces us up,
Snow is exhilarating;
There's really no such thing as bad weather,
Only different kinds of good weather.

—John Ruskin

It is one of the secrets of Nature in its mood of mockery that fine weather lays heavier weight on the mind and hearts of the depressed and the inwardly tormented than does a really bad day with dark rain sniveling continuously and sympathetically from a dirty sky.

—Muriel Spark, *Territorial Rights*, 1979

Running is real and relatively simple...but it ain't easy.

—Mark Will-Weber

The wind shows us how close to the edge we are.

—Joan Didion

Bad weather always looks worse through a window.

—Author Unknown

The Wind's Many Faces

Wind but no windchill this morning. That in itself is good. The difficulties of picking clothing while considering that relative humidity, wind speed, and sunshine will affect our idea of coldness have been left behind for a while, back in the spring that hung onto winter. Wind, at my back or in my face? Outbound or coming back? Simple.

I glanced at the upper limbs of the red-barked madrone trees. They have broader leaves than the firs. They can catch the wind and like tattletales or weather vanes tell me which way to turn. Sometimes, a whisper of wind promises to hide the noise of the highway for the mile or so to the trailhead; sometimes wind seduces with swaying branches, with rustlings in the leaves, with fences that sing and funnel me to the end of the pavement again.

Winds stir memories. We runners are amongst the fortunate—getting to go out onto the trails, feeling nature change as we go from valley floor to ridgeline, watching for the telltale signs of wind, listening to sounds too far removed from a world of electronics for most to hear. One day as I climbed, I passed a cave without knowing it. I ran on up the trail for about a hundred steps or so, and then I paused. I had felt a coolness brushing my face back there—why? I turned and walked back down the trail, watching the uphill side. There! A ghostly brush of coolness was felt. I left the trail and went up into the aspens. A few hundred feet up the hillside and there was the cave, its mouth exhaling cool air that I now felt fully on my face and legs. I looked at the many bones near the cave, some old and sun bleached, some not so old. I turned and with adrenaline-charged senses let that light wind carry me back down to the trail.

We camped at Great Basin National Park in Nevada on the way to or from nowhere one year. The winds we listened to there, at Great Basin, first strike land on the Pacific coast. There we were, several hundred miles inland in a tent almost 10,000 feet above that far-distant ocean listening to the sound of its waves carried by the wind. All through the night, crashing waves would wake us and then lesser waves would put us back to sleep. In the morning as we ran the trail to one of the stands of bristlecone pines, a word that had been rattling around inside my mind suddenly popped out, "Anabatic!" What? Anabatic. The wind coming up the steep sides of the mountain is an anabatic wind. It's caused by...

Kathy interrupted with some nonsense about plants awakening and how their rustlings in the morning air as they opened their leaves searching for the sun were causing the air to move, and the movement of the air woke up the ravens, and they were flying to their daytime perches, and the movement of their wings made the air move even more and...

Okay.

But there were no ravens when we stopped in Death Valley at Emigrant Campground. We had come in from Beatty through one of the Nevada entrances, paused at the one-way sign to the ghost town of Leadfield, wished for more time, and headed on over Daylight Pass. Our thermometer showed 112 degrees Fahrenheit when we put up the tent that evening. At first there was no motion anywhere. We put the tent up, changed to running stuff, and headed down the hill to get rid of several hours of sitting-in-the-car stiffness. We ended our run coming back up the valley to the campground in gently moving air.

Kathy commented on the wind we were starting to feel—the hot breath of the air still heated by the sun was in conflict with the valley's shaded regions. As the sun slid behind the distant Sierras and the nearby Panamints, newly formed shadows cooled the heated air of the day. These fingers of relatively cool, heavy air pushed down the hillsides to the valley floor, displacing the hot air. An evening wind was being born.

Flying grit and sand drove us inside the tent as the wind increased. Lying inside a small tent listening to the wind, when the wind starts rocking the tent, does not put me to sleep. I was sure our tent, with us inside, would soon be a blue and silver tumbleweed rolling down the jeep road we had run just a few hours ago. I could see the couple in the RV from Illinois recording us on their camcorder as we bounced and tumbled out toward Mesquite Flat. I got out and placed car-sized rocks on the corners of the tent. We slept the same as we would the night before an ultra—fitfully and with one eye toward the coming dawn.

We crawled out in the predawn quiet only Death Valley knows, the quiet of the last few stars winking out, the quiet of air so still we were sure we would hear the sun coming up over the Amargosa Range. The wind of last evening was gone to wherever winds go, one of those places we sometimes try to run to so we can find out where the winds go. I rolled the rocks back as Kathy packed sleeping bags and tent. The sun cast long shadows that we chased toward Lone Pine in that windless quiet of morning.

I often wonder if our shadows feel the wind, know more of what it brings than we do with our civilization-diminished senses. Wind-driven rain on a warm summer day is better than any shower I've ever had. Wind-driven rain on a trail cooled and darkened by January's heavy clouds cannot be warmed by any jacket I've worn. Breezes not yet winds gently chase us down winding trails in early fall. Winds soon to be gales make us clumsy and hold us back from the protection of the woods in winter. Which wind awaits?

240

The winds that cause you to stop and look, to notice the blackness out there just beyond arm's reach, to make you wish you had learned a bit more about reading the sky, have as many names as there are countries—abroholos, austru, barat, borasco, etesian, and levant, the fictional "Maria," and our Chinook, Diablo, and the Santa Anas, the Knik Wind, and the Kona storm.

Those winds whose names we know welcome us, beckon us to run In their familiar patterns. They become friends we run with because we know them and what they bring. It is the misbehaving winds, the coyote winds that give us so much trouble. There are winds that are full of mischief and wile; winds that shift from temperate coastal winds to dry, cold Arctic winds; winds that become thunderstorms and pelt us with hail; or, in the heat of a summer day, winds that go away and leave us to suffer in air that doesn't move at all.

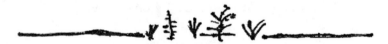

Fog Running

Wisps and whispers,
this morning's companions.
A breath of fog's
gossamer wrappings
hiding my trails.

This bypath or that,
padded footsteps pausing, asking.

Around and down I run
into the bosky kettle,
through tunnels of branches,
across carpets of fallen needles;

how many winters old?

Shadows shape-shift as I pass,
changing into trees,
trees with hobgoblins and fairies
and kobolds in the roots.
All watching.

Wait!
There!
Pausing, peering...

Unseen wings, muffled, beguiling,
for no songs do I hear
nor forms do I see,
only wisps of fog stirred by unseen wings.

My padded footsteps on the forest floor,
the hushed rustling of cedar boughs—
the only sounds as I pass by.
Wisps of fog close in behind me,
silently taking back their trails.

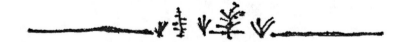

Just Outside the Fog Line

On a prairie that gives no echoes
my footsteps fall in morning's solitude.
Every trail around is soggy or frozen.
Bare trees, pavement, and a fog line.

Prairie crossroads, a mile apart.
Turtle Mountain roads put the sun
at your back or in your face, off to
the left or to the right.

A sun too far away for warmth,
good for long shadows but
not much else.

Must be two hundred geese lifting off
a frost-edged pond to my right.
Climbing, turning,
on a due-south heading, no wavering now.

The last wheat is being harvested.
Four Chippewas stood, breathing fog,
waiting for the combine's next pass,
huddled in morning's conversation,
clutching hand-warming cups.

They waved as I approached.
One held out a steaming cup.
Windchill is well below freezing.
Good coffee,
just the other side of the fog line.

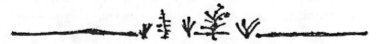

Orion at Two a.m. on a Cold March Night

Early May
    A late arrival in the Klamath Basin of southern Oregon
    We put up the tent in the dark in a snow shower

The next day we start a walk through one of Mother Nature's holding pens for migratory birds

Our first reward is four golden eagles in a single tree

Geese and duck-like birds and white pelicans are everywhere seen

Approximate elevation 4800

43.23N

121.77W

Camping that night

Empty campground

Run in the high desert with no noise but the wind

Sunset and the campfire

Fire dies, stars, stars, and ever more stars

It was going to be one of those cold, clear, high-desert nights, cold, crisp air when the stars have been lowered to where you feel you could reach out and touch them.

Somewhere around two a.m. I awoke and lay there for a few minutes trying to decide if I really needed to get up and go outside— two a.m. bathroom urges are okay at home, not so much when the temperature is below twenty (not twenty below, just below twenty). I unzipped the tent flap and peered out at the clearest night sky I had seen in quite a while. Overhead the darkest black imaginable spread above us. The often-described unending field of diamonds of the night sky sparkled, winked, blinked, beckoned...Orion pointed to the Pleiades. I pulled on sandals and jacket and crawled out. I looked for a while, finally turned, and woke Kathy. "The stars are out." We pulled the ground sheet out, moved the sleeping bags out, and lay there watching another of God's screen savers for a while. We could pick out the nebula in Orion without binoculars. Conversation about what is the mnemonic that tells us the planets ensued; three were finally dredged up from memory.

Men **V**ery **E**asily **Ma**ke **J**ugs **S**erve **U**seful **N**octurnal **P**urposes

My **V**ery **E**ducated **M**other **J**ust **S**erved **U**s **N**ine **P**izzas

My **V**ery **E**legant **M**other **J**ust **S**at **U**pon **N**ine **P**orcupines
Mercury, Venus, Earth, Mars, Jupiter, Saturn, Uranus, Neptune, Pluto

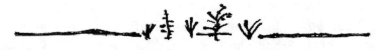

Downwind from St. John

For several days the windchill has caused what we feel on our skin to be about 14 degrees colder than the actual temperature. Yesterday it was 36 and it felt like it was 22; today is just a couple of degrees cooler. Yesterday the wind was out of the southwest and bit and stung as we returned to the trailhead. Today it comes out of the northwest pushing moisture-laden clouds that are totally willing to bury us in snow if only the wind would let them pause. We are out on the edge of the many miles of North Dakota farmland. The nearest wind-shielded forest trails are several miles north of us, full of hunters.

The hunters are out doing whatever season is calling. There are pickups parked at almost every trailhead; boxes that transport dogs are empty—somewhere a master is being served by pointing at a grouse or something. The empty pickups are a bigger deterrent than the muddy trails. I've been muddy and I've been cold—an extension of that is that, in a general sort of way, I've been shot at, too. Given my druthers I'll take a windswept prairie Rails-to-Trails route far from the empty pickups. I can pick the route that lets the wind blow me back to the car much better than I can pick the route that hides no hunters.

The wind seems determined to play with my senses today. I can hear birds and the trees are empty—emptier now than last week, when they were empty of leaves with no green. The leaves are gone and the birds that used the trees are gone, too. The songs come now from the rushes and reeds, the cattails and scrubs along pond's edge. There are finches of some kind, as total strangers to me as I am to them. They will pause through the midday wind, gain southerly miles before sunset, then rest for another day of travel.

There are benches every so often along this long-abandoned railroad bed. Some point at the empty fields, some point at the Turtle Mountains. Small plaques dedicate the bench to someone's memory. I wonder why she liked to look at the cropland that goes to infinity rather than the oak-covered hillside. Will he get a bench when he goes to join her? Does anyone know he put this bench here? Would I like a bench? Yes, but not out here in the open; hide mine deep in the woods.

Burnt leaves? Another intrusion into the senses—no wisps of smoke tell of a fire, just the smell—probably from the two barns off to the left. Two horses stand between me and the barns. One is standing, facing into the wind, the other is not. I wonder if they change positions every so often or if there is even a pattern to discover. How do you find out if a horse understands random acts, Poisson distributions, or even fuzzy logic? Just as I decide it isn't something to be worried with, they rotate. Now the paint is tail to the wind—waiting for a gust to play some sort of perverted wind-broken song?

Thirty-four geese lift off from a nearby lake. Canada geese maybe, but they look too dark. Duskys? The wind gives us something never encountered before, geese quiet in flight. Usually geese need constant reassurance of each other's presence; two flying geese are as noisy as seventeen ducks. As they quarter around, the wind brings the honking to us. They take roll call, vote on a leader after several caucuses, finally form a semblance of a vee, and, hugging the hillside, turn southerly. It is only the first of November; soon our footsteps will have no ears to fall on—everyone seems to understand the need to be south of here.

Mist lifted from the lake is carried by the wind to water our eyes and make the decision to turn after only forty-seven minutes easier to make. The turn is made, arms outstretched, and the downwind parasailing run back to the car is started. Some zippers can be loosened now. All senses are shut down as the wind shadows carry everything past eyes, ears, and nose. The crunch of the gravel is felt but not heard on the downwind run to the green dot we left just down there, a little ways downwind from St. John.

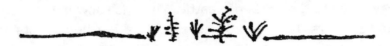

Late Getting Out

A meeting that should take only twenty minutes lasts an hour. One o'clock becomes almost two in the afternoon.

I am pulling on a Windbreaker and heading for the door at three p.m. when an unexpected phone call comes—just a minute, I'll check.

Just after four, sun sinking fast, an old database-design question pops up. Can you get the documentation done in...I mutter yes to a suddenly shortened deadline window. I mutter good-bye as the sun sinks beyond the ridge.

Ratz.

Problem solved, but now can't miss Jeopardy—my one TV vice.

Okay, it is only a few minutes after eight; it is just under thirty degrees and falling as I follow the green LEDs up the driveway. At the top of the hill I look around, trying to see which way the weather is coming or going, and things turn for the better—our meteorological convergence zone is a few miles south—there is an almost clear sky above me.

The Pleiades, Maia and her sisters, call from high up in the late-fall sky. I search for Orion, but he is too low to find. The moon won't rise for several hours. I go up to do laps in the cemetery. The roads lie east, north, west, then south and give an open view to the night sky. The wind brings tears to my eyes, so I turn around and go the other way. There is no speed involved; it is just time on my feet, passed by looking for the strangers in the sky above latitude 48.213 north, longitude 122.708 west.

It isn't cold yet. The clouds that kept the little bit of warmth in are now across the strait and gathering moisture over the peninsula. I can feel the moisture in the sky but can see beneath the clouds all the way south to the lights of Seattle. There is snow in the forecast. If I stay out here, I will be able to watch the overhead lights disappear as the ceiling drops. Our air is too thick to see as many stars as when we go to the mountains, but we have more darkness here than most places. Another lap or two and I'll go. The cold is coming back, spitting and sputtering the first signs of an early winter storm. The lights of Seattle are gone now; sixty miles of visibility have shrunk to ten. I'll turn down the hill on the next lap.

Owls, great horned, I think, are hunting in the field just behind the cemetery. I wonder how old you need to be to not feel a certain chill when you have headstones all around, owls calling, and the barest whisper of wind. I know I haven't gotten there yet; goose bumps just drove a shiver through me. I know the technicality of why the owls are so quiet. That does not remove the eeriness.

One last look to the east and I find Orion way low in the sky, his belt forming an east-west line. Some day we will follow his line again. For now, I turn to the house.

Wind, Birds, and a Fallen Tree

I look up to the top of the trees on the hill above the house to see how much wind is hiding, waiting to laugh and perhaps tell me I need one more layer on my afternoon run. The madrones are swaying but not bent over. The Douglas firs are dancing, too, but to a waltz, not the tango of a wilder wind. Two layers will be enough. I close the door and turn toward the driveway.

A small bird, no, a tiny bird, with a bright yellow cap, flits down onto the driveway as I start up to cross the road to the prairie. It is mostly olive-gray but with a bright yellow crown and a curiosity that has it bouncing around only a couple of feet from me. She (the yellow crown gives it away) is a golden-crowned kinglet, chirping and tilting her head to look at me—a sudden giant in her world. A sign of an early spring? No, they just don't go very far south. I can feel the first tendrils of the wind passing as they go down the hill to the briar patches.

It is February, and various birds that can't read are starting to show up on the prairie, pausing before continuing northward. Their movement is governed by laws we do not know of and our precious calendars are of no use to them. The nuisance value of running with glasses on is outweighed by the chance of seeing some of these travelers. Some are on their way back to Arctic regions; one year we saw a shorebird that was a Siberian native. We tried to explain about our ultramarathon T-shirts, but it didn't work with this world traveler—not when it had thousands of miles done and thousands more to do just to get home. It just went back to finding food along the shore—an aid station in an ultra.

Working my way up the cemetery hill, I notice a silhouette on a partly bald lower limb of an old fir. I turn up and into the cemetery to pass closer. A kestrel, barely bigger than a jay; inquisitive eyes in a stripped face look at me. Raptors stare fearlessly. Even this one, the smallest of our hawks, looks and then dismisses me, goes back to scanning the grasses for food. At the end of the cemetery I go down the switchbacks to start across the upper edge of the prairie— whitecaps, visible on the water a half mile away, foretellers of the strengthening wind.

The whitecaps on the water are mirrored by the snowcaps of the mountains. Numbers come to mind—from here I can see crowns of snow that are measured in hundreds of inches—they measured 1140 inches of snow up on Mount Baker one year. It sits sixty or so miles behind me, not visible very often on these clouded-over wintry days. I quarter into the wind, pull up the zippers, and notice several big birds riding the wind curl on the bluff a half mile away. Eagles? Distraction comes as I drop into a dip in the trail. A northern harrier, female, rises on her slim and graceful long wings, starts to skim the tips of prairie grasses—the wind that I wish was at my back does the work for her.

The trail across the prairie ends at the tee-junction with the bluff trail. At the tee I am a hundred or so feet above the water. The beach is sandy today. The winds and currents play with the sand at Ebey's Landing, sculpting and molding redone almost daily. Today the sand is exposed by the low tide. Three harlequin ducks, clownish in their multihued faces and plaid sides, ride the surface, diving in the cold water to find lunch, unaware and unconcerned about how much I have to wear to be comfortable running out here. As I climb the trail up to follow the bluff, I can see three eagles playing on the wind curl. A raven greets me at the top; only a few feathers move as he sits almost motionless—nature's weather vane—a glider riding into the wind. A pointed tail flicks, and the gleaming blackness is gone. I am the only one hindered by the wind, the only one going against the wind; how far into it do I go today?

The fallen tree seems like a good turning point. Two or three hundred or so years ago, one Douglas fir won the battle with the wind and took root at bluff's edge. For many tens of years it stood out there alone. Far back, away from the edge, its brothers and sisters stood, safely sheltered from the almost constant wind, protecting each other, watching and waiting. Fifty or sixty years ago it fell. Even in falling it won its battle to live on the edge of the bluff. It fell parallel to the edge, digging its broken limbs deep into the soil, and stayed up here, two hundred and fifty feet above the waters. Its bark is mostly gone now; the exposed wood, wind-polished and smooth, offers shelter from today's wind. It will not become a nurse tree in this wind-torn site, but there are tiny seedlings here and there, seedlings that will challenge the wind and rain to live out here at bluff's edge. I will be long gone and buried before their victory or defeat is decided.

Today I pause to sit with my back against the now-horizontal trunk of the fallen tree and watch the three bald eagles playing in the sky. Three juveniles ride up there, with their mottled coats and dark beaks but fully developed wings. I can hear their whistling trills, see their loops and dives with talons touching—seven or eight feet of majestically strong wings with feathers that flick at the air just so. They are just kids playing up there in their world, a hundred or so feet above mine. As I get up to return to my running, the raven returns and alights nearby. Sometimes he starts telling who is doing what and why and which tree was first and how the glacier came and went and where the whales go, but today he just sits out of the wind for a while, turning his head to me, questioningly?

At Play in the Mud

Rain. Several times during the night it woke me. I lay there listening to its passing—soft, then wind-pushed and gone. After the wind, the rain is one of my favorite things to listen to, and in the convoluted caverns of my mind, that got me to thinking, not only about rain but what rain brings to running...rain brings mud.

Mud can be defined in enough ways to satisfy even the most discerning runner's seasonal encounters: baygall, bog, bottom, bottomland, bottoms, buffalo wallow, clay, dirt, dust, everglade, fen, fenland, glade, grime, gumbo, hog wallow, holm, marais, marish, marsh, marshland, meadow, mere, mire, moor, moorland, morass, moss, muck, mudflat, muddle, muddy, ooze, peat bog, quagmire, quicksand, rile, salt marsh, slime, slip, slob, slob land, slop, slosh, slough, sludge, slush, soot, sough, squash, sump, swale, swamp, swampland, swill, taiga, wallow, wash. I've deleted the expletives which we runners add dependent on the miles traveled or yet to go.

Mud was something my mother used to tell us to stay out of or to quit playing in. But on some days, when her memories nudged her just right, mud was something for making mud pies, and she showed us how. Mom never thought that her favorite *child*, having reached adulthood, having thrown good money after bad, and being all decked out in professional-level running gear, would be standing on a not-quite-on-a-map trail somewhere, getting ready to play in the mud, again.

I seldom run in the mud nowadays. I live on an island fashioned by the Vashon glacier, which, intentionally or not, provided me with an area of well-drained soil. There are only two short spots that get muddy in the twenty-eight miles of trails I call home, but as I run I sometimes think of some of the mud I have passed through.

The Mudderfell Six-Hour was the Finke's wonderful gift to the Pacific Northwest ultrarunning family. Six hours of back and forth on the Wildwood Trail in Portland, Oregon, in late January. It was a little over eight miles to the turnaround, then back to the start, mud getting churned worser and worser by the passing feet—each pass increasing the likelihood of another fall—sooner or later everyone fell. Saplings at the switchbacks were used as pivot posts, something grabbed by a runner to avoid sliding off into the brush, never to be heard from again, just an anonymous DNF sometimes mentioned around a campfire.

My second year at Mudderfell was, in some ways, more fun than the first. I was recovering from surgery. Kathy was running, so I volunteered to be an aid station worker. The aid stations were about two miles apart. I was at the 3rd (5th, 11th, and 13th) aid station just before (or after, depending on if you were outbound or inbound) the big gully. On the first pass the clean, enthusiastic, and cheerful runners had only gone about six miles on a fresh trail, and all their questions were about what we had to eat and drink.

On their return trip, the second pass, the not-quite-clean, almost-smiling, struggling-up-the-hill group weren't quite as choosy. The third pass, about twenty-one miles of mud clinging to the "everyone's wearing brown today," mud-spattered, faceless, non-gender-specific passersby nearly knocked the table down as they grabbed a cup of something to drink or a handful of soggy pretzels before disappearing into the abyss. On their fourth rush through the wilderness, I was unable to recognize anyone as they passed our aid station—including my wife. There was one woman (I think) who held up two mud-covered hands and asked if I would be so kind as to put a few potato chips in her mouth. As I was doing so I kept thinking about the idea that we pay to do this.

Capitol Forest, just west of Olympia, Washington, was a place where heavy rains would cause trails that were shared with motorcycles and horses during good days to become quagmires or sluiceways crossed in solitude on muddy days. Socks were ruined forever with only one trip to Wedekind or Capitol Peak, turned reddish brown as a badge of winter running. Many a time I stopped at the top of the power line service road, looked down at the quarter mile of rain-slickened darkness, and wondered if I could make it down without falling, always answering no and turning to the more conservative route. Then one day, when memories of youthful agility came calling (and there was enough rain that no one else would be within miles to bear witness), I turned down. I finally understood the phrase "It's all downhill from here."

On another rainy day, Kathy and I rounded a bend in the trail only to see our trail disappear into a beaver pond. Horse hoof prints in the muddy trail led in—not quite beckoning but showing the only route. We were finishing a six-hourish loop; maybe twenty minutes from the car. Turning back was no option in that January cold. And so we went into the frost-rimmed pond, ankle deep, then knees numbing as we crossed. The clearing through the trees was the only guide as we wandered on. Kathy's grip on my fanny pack tightened as the water deepened. I thought about how she disappears in what I think of as shallow puddles. Two hundred yards turned to three, and we both exhaled as we felt the "trail" turn upward. As we finally walked out, we looked back at our footprints in the black mud, water already swirling in to wash away our passage.

Our stay in Arkansas introduced us to the red clay of the Ozarks, gooey messes of gumbo that claimed a shoe every now and then. Downhills on a wet Ozark Highlands Trail were accentuated with resounding splats as balance points disappeared, grips on bushes were lost, and buttprints were left, possibly to be fossilized for the enrichment of future sociological research. A three-mile loop where I had done thirty-minute laps on a dry summer day became a challenging forty-five-minute lap and then an I-am-sure-I-can-improve sixty-minute lap after a spring rain.

Thunderstorms at Palo Duro in North Texas in '91 left us watching the rainbows and trying to discern the it's-only-wet sand from the ankle-deep mud in the bottom of the canyons as we ran along. The walls of the canyons were layered with orange, yellow, gray, maroon, red, and even white rocks—all contributing to the streaks of color in the mud we were slogging through. A sign at the top of one climb told us we had just run through four different geologic periods, covering some 240 million years as we climbed up out of the canyon. It was easily the longest time we had ever been on our feet.

I thought about the boulevard at Leadville, the sandy trails of Hog's Hunt down in Texas, and the McDonald Forest trails in Oregon and the totally different faces they put on with just a little bit of rain, just a little bit of mud.

Lambs, Llamas, Trilliums...
(The Passing of Spring in a Land Far Away)

How many words for gray? Ashen, sooty, pearly, silvery, dove gray, tattletale gray, darkening, foreboding, silver haired, even fuliginous or grizzled. The waters of Puget Sound were having troubles deciding what shade to be today. I was on pavement, trying to get from one wooded park to another and then onto the trail to the house.

Blues were trying to break through the upper layer of clouds, or were the clouds trying to close ranks to hide the blue sky? I zipped the front of my tattered Windbreaker as I passed the pasture with the llamas. Some time back there were llamas on Hope Pass 'neath a sky more blue than gray. I needed to top the hill so I could pretend to pick up the pace and warm my legs again. Cold has colors, too, mostly behind darkened doors. Grays and pale blues don't warm legs. Gloves had been put back on as salt spray touched me.

Anything would have brightened the run. One of those runs that is just a mile or two too long. Lambs? I didn't want lambs playing next to the fence as I trudged past. I wanted...What? Sympathy?

Yes, a display of commiseration would work.

I got lambs. Silly leaping lambs. Now they were playing with the baby llama. Lambs standing on their mother's back. Oh great, then the wind died and it was warm. A hundred yards to the trailhead; wild roses spread pinkish polka dots to tell me where to turn. Car noises died as I escaped into the woods again.

There was no gray in my woods, and I saw only patches of blue as I looked up through the cedars and madrones. We saw trilliums and dogwoods two weeks ago, gone now as the leaves had thickened. Summer was coming. Canada geese were in large number on Wednesday, singing their way north. Cormorants were returning, and the harlequins were gone to their mountain homes.

The unwanted two miles were lengthened as I turned to the Old Men, and footsteps fell away as the dirt of the trail became the needles of a thousand years. Through the darkness of the cedars' thickly-needled branches came slashes of light. Turning at the fork, I retraced the steps just made. Steps not mine anymore were set quicker now, legs of my youth, many years gone away, stretched out, and I smiled briefly as trudge became run, shoulders relaxed, and ground was covered; once more I felt I could run forever. If I had time, but I don't know what color time is.

CHAPTER NINE

Happiness is not a state to arrive at, but a manner of traveling.

—Margaret Lee Runbeck

No matter how old I get, the race remains one of life's most rewarding experiences. My times become slower and slower, but the experience of the race is unchanged: each race a drama, each race a challenge, each race stretching me in one way or another, and each race telling me more about myself and others.

—Dr. George Sheehan

The most important message I stress to beginners is to learn to love the sport. Like other endeavors, if running is not undertaken properly, it can be difficult and discouraging.

—Cliff Held

This is not about instant gratification. You have to work hard for it, sweat for it, give up sleeping in on Sunday mornings.

—Lauren Fessenden

"Why Run on Trails Versus Running on Roads?" A Collection of Responses

Meeting people from lots of other places with the same interest in running.

Seeing the stars from 11,000 feet at one o'clock in the morning from the Colorado Trail.

Creating memories on a day just south of Glacier National Park running Le Grizz.

Looking across Puget Sound with Kathy and pointing at the notches on the skyline of the Olympic Mountains that indicate the ends of two valleys so far apart it took us all day to run from one to the other. We both smile and remember running from the Staircase to Dosewallips and the scowl on the ranger's face when he found out what we had done.

Watching a frosty meadow become a field of diamonds and rainbows as the sun comes up on a meadow on a winter's predawn outing on the trails.

Meeting, meeting again, and then meeting yet again the friends and strangers of many courses, many states, other countries, other times.

Helping others learn about this world of running we occupy inside an otherwise wildly-tormented world.

Seeing an *Alice in Wonderland* sort of caterpillar while out on the trails.

So I could watch my wife, patience personified, 10 years and four months after her hip-replacement surgery, finish a 50k trail run.

The full moon, solstice, and a night run without flashlights.

The moose swimming across the lake during the awards ceremony at Le Grizz, a fitting way to end a day of running in the Northern Rockies.

A son pedaling alongside me as I run myself into the ground again. He has seen me miserable, and he has seen me win. We have memories to share.

The heat and hills of Strolling Jim in '87.

Suddenly looking down on the Golden Gate Bridge and the bay as you round the bend 50 miles into the 49er Double Marathon.

Working a finish line and watching the tired legs become overshadowed by smiles of triumph in those last few yards.

Ice forming on my beard on a frosty morning run.

Curiosity that causes you to stop the car and get out just to discover what running in 114 degrees Fahrenheit in this place called Badwater feels like.

Seeing a familiar face come out of the fog and drizzle on a trail that had become strangely lonely—even though only a smile and a wave are exchanged, the trail is no longer empty.

Days of running, days of racing.

Being delayed by a porcupine as it makes its way across "my" trail.

That rare day of light-footedness and speed recalled from years long gone as the trail flies by and you can run forever.

An early spring run when you reach a meadow in time to see the flowers waking up and turning to the sun.

Running through the redwoods, neck sore from looking up, wondering how long they have been waiting for me to run in their shadows.

Watching people come in and then leave our aid station, "thank yous" so sincere and heartfelt for the little we have done for them.

A sky full of geese an hour before dawn, hearing what Aldo Leopold meant when he wrote of "Goose Music."

A tiredness that will go away, memories that will last for a lifetime.

A herd of elk that let us pass within 50 feet—barely giving us a glance (except one, whose head slowly turns as we pass).

The look on the ranger's face when we answered the question, "Where did you folks run from?"

Finding the car again.

The quiet companionship of my wife those many long miles.

Ravens and their many voices.

Deer that don't run when you start talking to them (they just keep those big radar-dish ears turning).

Beaver ponds we had to cross because they don't show on maps and we couldn't turn back.

Dawn through tall frosty grass on a hillside.

Baby porcupines, unafraid of you in their world.

Things we heard but escaped from in the dark.

Mountain bikers I have passed on long uphill sections.

Greetings exchanged, smiles shared, many miles in and miles to go.

Fog so thick your familiar course becomes a stranger.

Saying hi to all on the back of an out and back.

Watching big horn sheep show me the "proper" way to ascend the hill.

The smell of redwoods, cedars, dogwoods...

The crunch of ice crystals in frozen mud.

Running down a hill with no time for any thought but where to put your feet.

Stopping to talk to animals and noticing they listen curiously.

Eating berries along the trail.

Soaking tired feet in an ice-cold stream.

The quiet silence of hearing only my footsteps and breathing in the darkness.

Roads:

I'll have to get back to you.

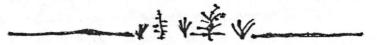

Travel and the Trails We Love

Robert Heinlein wrote of a stranger in a strange land and also of having time enough to love. Almost every trip out of town leads many of us to being a stranger in a strange land, and, except for the random calling of a DNF, almost every trip leads to a short love affair with a trail, a stream, or a mountain we have not seen before.

The island where we usually live, and where the daytime high seldom gets above seventy degrees, was quite a ways behind us now. Sea level was also something of a distant memory as we traveled a different journey for a year. We ran in the Blue Mountains of Oregon along a forestry road that wound through the first aspen groves of this trip. We were up in some high country meadows that were also home to cows that seemed undecided about us trespassing through their territory. Were we something they should charge, or was grazing not to be interrupted? A riffling wind sent the aspens in motion again, and all attention shifted to the gold and green shimmering of the trees as we ran.

Two days later on a trail barely on the Pacific side of the Sierra Nevada near the San Joaquin River, granite, mica schist, and basalt columns formed the trail. Our eyes saw fool's gold and the hexagonal columns of rock bent by Earth's heat, now cooled into a miniature giant's causeway. Our feet were drawn to the hexagons and their broken hopscotch patterns rather than to some metronomic pace. After our run, we discovered the real treat of this campground where the John Muir and Pacific Crest Trails run together—a mysterious building that attracts many a dusty traveler. A sign on the end wall reads: "The water for these showers is from a natural hot spring..." No cold creek-water bath tonight.

Two mornings later, our travel day became a rest day by default. We would travel, but we would not run. It was 34 degrees on the thermometer as we folded the tent; by the time we got to the bristlecone pines just north of Westgard Pass, we were breathing hot, dry air that was approaching the century mark. That evening, as we pulled into Valley of Fire State Park just north of Las Vegas, our Whidbey-Island-based moderate-temperature minds were trying to put the 108-degree stillness of the eroded redness of the desert into perspective. We managed a short walk on a trail surrounded by brilliantly red sandstone that reshapes as the wind and rain sculpt wrinkles and hoodoos, arches and waterholes—all done so slowly our eyes see only the permanence of the desert.

Heat lightning or a thunderstorm? We both looked at the darkening skies a couple of afternoons later just southwest of the Lower Scorpion campground at Gila Cliff Dwellings. At home we knew which way the clouds would go. Here the wind carried no telltale saltwater smell. Here we were strangers thinking about getting the compass out to sit on the table and pretend we could gain knowledge from knowing which way was north. Our lack of knowledge led us up a rocky trail along the valley's wall—wondering if rain would turn the trail in the floor of the valley to mud. The universal signs of nature were reassuring. The birds were still out. Some were chasing bugs, others were picking at the fruits or berries of the trees. A lone squirrel made its way through the limbs of an Arizona white oak looking for acorns. If a storm were near, neither the birds nor the squirrel would be out. They would be well into the brush waiting things out. With faith in their innate weather knowledge, we worked our way toward the ruins of an ancient civilization.

The next day found us in an accordion landscape with twenty-mile-long ripples of straight stretches leading to the towering face of El Capitan, the historical navigational guidepost in Guadalupe Mountains National Park out in west Texas. At about 2:35 in the afternoon some 260 million years ago, this great reef was formed just so we could have mountain trails to run on. The footing is made up of the fossilized remains of calcareous sponges, algae, and other lime-secreting marine organisms from a time so long ago our lives are only brief seconds in comparison. We noticed different kinds of what we think of as cactus as we ran—someone familiar with the area would have seen agave, prickly pear cacti, chollas, yuccas, and stool—some are cactus, some are not. The rocks and roots meant we paid attention to footing, but the constant attention also let us see a fossil or two. We managed to memorize one fossil and later identify that rockbound stranger as a brachiopod.

The next morning we found an escape from the heat that was slowly dragging us down—Carlsbad Caverns. Its constant fifty-six degrees was a welcome relief to us as we walked down down down into the world of 'mites and 'tites. Swallows gave way to bats, and finally the light of the mouth of the cave was gone. For almost three hours we walked and looked at the art of dripping water; the pervasive parallel of ultras came to mind—all we need is time and a trail.

In the following days, Texas took forever to come and go, then Oklahoma, and then a sign said we had crossed into Arkansas, my birth state. A short trail at a roadside park somewhere on the westerly edge of the Ouachita Mountains took us into a forest of oaks. There was a time when I could have just glanced and said white oak or red oak or black oak without so much as a second thought. But our years in the conifer forests of the Pacific Northwest have dimmed that memory. Now, as I tried to recall the coarseness or patterns of bark, shapes of leaves, or sizes of acorns, one tree stood out. "A sweet gum tree." I proclaimed loudly. Kathy looked at me. Something special about it? As the picture from long ago formed, I found my pocket knife and cut a branch of a certain size—about as thick as your little finger, my mother had said. Now trim the end of the bark, she said. Now cut into it several times. See how the fibers become a brush. A brush? Yes, my mother explained those years ago—this was what we used for a toothbrush when I was a child. The memory of a walk long gone removed all the strangeness and unfamiliarity of the day's trail. These may have been the trails we loved the most.

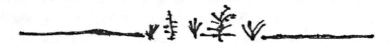

The Gift of Time

Time. Funny, all we ever need is time. If I could save time in a...Is there enough time to do this? Do I have time to get ready for...

Time. I am fixing banana bread and trying to coax this column from my head to, well, at least to the keyboard. I got up a few minutes early (stole some time) because I put off (didn't take the time) baking last night. Time. Running takes time, or is it running requires time? What if a runner takes a wrong turn, gets lost, stops early? I don't feel I have lost time because I turned left and added another thirty minutes to a run. Or because I got lost and saw something I might not have seen. Or even if I go home early. The time on the trails adds to—never lessens—my day.

The other day I was coming down a forestry road half thinking about the one hill left to climb before turning toward the house when I saw Eric, who also spends time on trails, climbing up toward me. Morning, Eric. He smiled, almost laughingly, and replied, what time did you come out today? About six thirty, why? John, it's two o'clock and you're still saying good morning. Oh. I hadn't seen anyone all day. I had just kept turning away from a homeward direction because I needed eight or so hours on the trails on that particular Saturday. Time flies when you're...

Time. Distance. Time gives us distance. When walking across Spain on *el Camino de Santiago,* Kathy and I could see mountain passes that were four days behind us. If we had known where to look, we probably could have seen those same four days ahead. One morning as we sat on a rock wall somewhere in Spain, we found ourselves talking about how long an ultra seems when you try to relate it to the time it takes to drive that distance. We looked out across the valley spreading westward and had no concern with distance, only time. We would walk about five more hours that day. Maybe. Tomorrow we'd walk again for however far we wanted to walk. We had this gift of time—given to us each day.

Distance. Time. Distance takes time. How long until sunset? It isn't what time the sun sets that is critical to us when out on a trail. The critical piece of information is how much longer can we see— how much more time do we have before we cannot see to follow the trail? Trail tip #4,837: With an arm fully extended toward the sun, wrist bent with fingers horizontal on the horizon, straightened and not spread, the amount of time to sunset is about fifteen minutes for each finger between the bottom of the sun and the horizon.

One afternoon in early spring in Devil's Den State Park in Arkansas, we had run out of time. Partway through a thought-to-be three-hour run, we realized the distance to the car required more time (daylight time) than the horizon was going to give us. Distance we had aplenty, but light was growing scarce. We finally separated. A knight with a damsel awaiting, I ran at breakneck speed, careening off trees, leaping across creeks, hurdling rocks (and one raccoon)—onward to the car to get flashlights. Kathy would follow until it was too dark to see, then she would sit down in the middle of the trail and wait for my return. *Most* people will need this to happen to them only once and a small light is forevermore in the fanny pack.

Time and distance become toys to play with in our minds as we run. Routes visualized as so many minutes because a map showing distances never seemed to be found were time runs, not mile runs. I knew I could get from Hayes campground to Fall Creek in about ninety minutes of easy running, eighty minutes if I paid attention.

A hundred minutes was a day of dreams and distractions. And that one day of seventy-six minutes was like an unwitnessed hole-in-one. When I had finished on that day, I stood there, actually leaned there against an old cedar, gasping for air, slowly settling down enough to work the pump handle at the horse trough. I drank my fill, rubbed a bit of cold water on my aching hamstrings, and turned back to the trail and the more leisurely return route. I never timed that run again.

Time? How long does it take to run fifty miles? One day? People who simply cannot understand how far we can run become strangely disappointed with our "slowness" when we talk about miles per hour. Or are they secretly pleased at our sudden humanness? They cannot comprehend how far we can travel on foot, but suddenly they *know* we aren't *really* running, just sort of jogging along. We know, though, that it is the number of hours that we can just sort of jog on down the trail that lets us get to the next ridgeline, across the canyon (and back), or on through the night and into the waiting dawn of pushed-back time.

"Time is Tight"—okay when played by Booker T. & the M.G.'s, but not so good when the tightness is the closing window of cutoff for the next aid station and your heart, mind, and muscles have gone off in different directions. People hurry as the sun descends ever lower. Time shrinks when the sun goes down and roots and rocks emerge to make a flat and fast trail a stumbling nightmare, when the rustlings in the brush slowly creep toward the trail, when the moon just won't come out to help, when the weakening battery draws more of your attention than the trail. Dawn will be a long time coming.

Time might not forgive, nor necessarily lead to better things. Nature is not concerned with your plans, nor mine. Just because you take the time to totally change your training method, your diet, and your dedication, there is no mutually-agreed-upon pact with nature. The minor goddesses of trails (if paying attention at all) might be mischievous, might not be aware of our frailties and doubts, might at some late hour of the day come calling with the bad news. The new training plan is not meant for you—later you will be heard talking to someone no one else can see or hear, but some of those who overhear will understand. They, too, have had their time with the misadventures of training.

Time can expand and reward if you believe in yourself. Silly grins and giddiness will appear as you realize you are doing so much more than you ever have before, more distance in less time or even more time on less effort. As our runs become untiring, the constraints of time vanish. The strength of relaxed muscles and mind comes calling. This time you run faster. This time you run with new nimbleness and lightness. This time is yours, because you believe in all you have done and time has proven you right. This time you get to the finish line before the banana bread is gone—and that's the gift of time.

Old Trails, New Trails

Scattered thoughts on leaving a forest behind.

It is four-tenths of a mile to the bottom; eight hundred paces going up, seven fifty or so coming down. It will take a hard-earned five minutes going up and some days a giggling, terrifying, fell-running three-minute descent coming down. There was no crowd, no finish line that anyone could see, and no T-shirt waited for me. Just a series of switchbacks, steep at first then flattening out to trail's end. For seven years this trail, this seven hundred and four yards, had been the main entrance to the trails of home.

Tomorrow we would leave these trails in Corvallis, Oregon. We had left trails in Fayetteville, Arkansas, just as we had left them in Ellensburg, Washington. We felt saddened, as we always did, at leaving familiar stretches of dirt, forests, rocks, and roots. We had come to know every crook and turn by heart, to know where the toe-grabbers were, and to know where the friendly stretches waited. I knew which trails I ran on rainy days when I did not want the wet grass soaking my legs. I knew where the red-tail hawk lurked in ambush on those early morning runs, waiting to screech at me but never when I expected it.

The four miles up to McCulloch had four "breath-catchers," stretches of trail just long enough at a flatter grade that you could almost catch your breath and almost be ready for the next slightly steeper section. I knew when I got to the two huge alders that the first flat stretch of the trail was only a few steps more. The second flat stretch, not as long but still a place to pull your tongue up from the trail (or is it trial?), was just past the spring that never went dry and always had newts to watch, if one wanted to stop and watch. The third sign was the hardest to pass: a huge Douglas fir in a glen of ferns. One day I counted and ended up with forty-'leben shades of green—all counted as I continued on around the edge of the mountain. The last pause came near a raven's nest. Their songs changed over the years as they cheered or laughed at my efforts. On wind-laden days that last climb was heavy with a scent and sense of salt from the Pacific Ocean somewhere unseen off to the west. It would be hard to leave this forest.

Sixteen hundred miles from our beloved ocean and years earlier, on our first trip to the Butterfield Trail, we looked at the bulletin board, duly memorized the fifteen-mile route, and set off into the woods of Devil's Den State Park in Arkansas. It wasn't that it was rooty. I'd seen worse. It wasn't that it was rocky. I'd seen worse than that, too. It twisted a lot, but so did other trails. It just never seemed level, and looking up longer than an instant brought a runner tumbling down, again. We followed the trail right up to the bottom of a waterfall. We looked right, left, up, and, finally behind. We took our unexpected shower and looked at our watches more often.

Fifteen miles can't take this long. Can it? We paid dearly on that first trip as daylight disappeared. I ran for the lights as Kathy sat in the dark. Over the next three years that trail only gave up about twenty minutes from that first four-hour excursion. Clockwise, counter-clockwise, fall, or summer, nothing seemed to help. We just knew there was a secret to be unlocked, something we could correct, something we could fix. When last we crossed from Arkansas into Tennessee, those secrets were still safe from our prying ways. We still miss that forest.

Full moons and the seasonal changes have caused us to choose routes with more care than usual. We could go up on the Manastash in central Washington and find a deserted forestry road where the moon would be enough to guide us. When the moon and the clouds cooperate in the North Cascades, the peaks are closer, the ridges draw in to arm's length, and Mount Rainier's broad shoulders seem to be around every bend. We would pause to argue about which peak we were looking at; no compass to tell us the direction, no crow to tell us how far to travel, just this name or that and an argument that would continue the next time we ran 'neath a full moon in that sparse forest

Almost every full-moon run brought back the memory of that one run through White Sands National Monument. The park service recognized the special beauty of the white gypsum dunes in the Tularosa Basin by extending closing time so you could remain in the dunes under a full moon. The run became a walk as the show of shadows and sandscapes made us stop to look here, then there, then slowly turn all the way around. The starkness of moon shadows was unexpected. Our pace slowed so the noise of our footsteps would not intrude. All conversations were in conspiratorial whispers. No colors were ever as enhancing as that night's blacks and whites.

Back in Corvallis, even when wet, Dan's Trail wasn't bad. Waddayaknow was slippery, and Stick-in-the-Eye was like an otter chute. Baker Creek was a half mile of hanging onto the trees because the mud was slicker than I had guessed, but after that it was a gravel road or two, ears always alert for downhill mountain bikers avoiding the muddy messes I had just crossed. And then I was in the meadows. My five miles to the meadows would turn into about eight going home, not wanting to fight the mud in both directions. I drew some small comfort in knowing which trails had gravel, which had clay, which had trees to grab, which had blackberry thickets that cling. I passed the game trail that curiosity had sent me up one spring. How do game trails look so runnable one minute and disappear so completely, so quickly, the next? I turned left onto Contour, an almost flat stretch of logging road from years ago. Yellows and whites, purples and blues and reds and oranges of spring—the meadows were in bloom.

On that last day's last four-tenths of a mile, I consciously did not look back up the hill as I crossed the street to the apartment near which sat a U-Haul truck. We tried not to look in the morning as we drove away.

When we got to Whidbey Island, I mentioned trails to the owner of the house we were thinking about renting for a while. He pointed across the highway to a paved bike path. I started to say that's not a trail, but he continued, pointing and saying that if I followed the bike path about a mile north I would be in the "kettles," miles and miles and miles of trails. The next day we made our way to those "kettles" he mentioned.

We found four trailheads at what most knew to be hilltop, south, middle, and north gates. We would come to know them as the entrances to four different forests—the rhododendron forest, the yew forest, the cedar forest, and the fir forest; the entrances to our new *home*.

Running in the Dark, Never Seeing the Light...

We were driving to Spokane to visit one of our daughters. As we got to Wenatchee, I decided to turn left and go on across on U.S. Highway 2 instead of dropping down south to I-90. A vague memory of a hill just a few miles up the road had slipped into my head. It was a hill I had run up on the first day of November some years ago at about three o'clock in the morning. I was running a 100k that had started at midnight on Halloween in East Wenatchee. I had never seen that hill by the light of day.

November 1, 1986; it was an hour or two past the middle of the night, and the roads and highways were almost deserted. This was apple orchard country, not a partying and up-all-night neighborhood. The driveways were a mile apart or so; occasionally a dog would give a yip or woof from a distant farmhouse. The big trucks of the night seemed to be our only company on the road as we ran. I wondered at the drivers' head-scratching that went on up there in the cab—it's almost three in the morning and there's folks jogging out here—maybe a hand went to the microphone to tell the empty night sky and anyone within radio range to watch the shoulder on the southbound side, a word of warning we never heard but were thankful for as oncoming headlights would dim and the southbound 18-wheelers would move across the centerline to give us a small buffer from the windstorm they carried with them. Several times a soft bleat from an air horn was heard. Another memory, much older, stirred.

I had talked with a driver once about running. We were sharing the counter at a truck stop somewhere near Yreka. He had asked about my T-shirt and had I really run fifty miles to get it? Yes, I had. He replied with a story about how he had trained for, and completed, a marathon while driving. While driving? Yep. Wow. I had been behind the wheel a lifetime or so ago and could not quite see how you could combine those days of fourteen, and often many more, hours behind the wheel with running—how'd you do that?

Well, he went on, I had a regular route then, Coachella Valley in California to a produce warehouse in Atlanta, Georgia. On the eastbound leg, I was in a hurry to get the lettuce or carrots or whatever to market, but I could still squeeze in a few miles out behind a truck stop each day. The long runs were the hard part. On the westbound trips, I had a little bit of choice in where I went as long as I was back in the valley for another load of produce fairly soon. I would find a load for the return trip that wasn't ready to be picked up for a few hours, maybe not until the next morning; next I'd find a place to park, jump in the sleeper to change clothes, and be out the door—thankful for all the industrial areas I knew about. There was one warehouse in Texas I could park inside the fence and the manager would let me run on their fitness trail. They even let me use the shower room. I couldn't do it unless I was on the way home and the trailer refrigerator didn't need to be running.

It took me almost eight months of training here and there in scattered back lots and loading areas, but I did it. I did the training and then completed a marathon. The hard part was finding a marathon close to where I could park the truck. He pointed out at the parking lot, where his truck and trailer and all those other great big boxes sat waiting for their drivers. You can't park a 50-foot trailer just anywhere, but I finally found one in Albuquerque. I sent in my entry fee and hoped for a schedule that worked. Someone smiled on me, and everything came together. I ran my official, paid-a-fee, got-a-T-shirt marathon. It took me dang near four hours, but I got done, got my T-shirt, climbed back in my truck, and then smiled all the way back to the valley. I asked him if he had ever wanted to do another one. Oh yeah, I think about it, but I also think it was a one-time thing. I was just plain lucky to find parking places and never have the truck stolen or vandalized.

Another soft moan from an air horn and I came back to those early morning post-Halloween hours as we worked our way up the stretch where U.S. 2 and U.S. 97 share the roadbed alongside the Columbia River. The shoulder was wide enough that the five of us were running three abreast with Lary Webster, Ike Hessler, and Bob Thomas making up the front row, while a newcomer ran alongside me a few steps behind them. Eventually, we would leave Highway 97 at Orondo and follow Highway 2 easterly up onto the surrounding high prairie, the Palouse of eastern Washington. The conversation shifted from runs here and there to wondering how far out in front Brian Kessler was and whether he had put a shirt on yet. It had been 21ºF at the midnight starting time, probably a little colder now, but there was Brian at the starting line with no shirt on. He was somewhere out in front of us, running alone in the lead. I wondered at his running alone, no company but the white line at pavement's edge and the starkness of a cold winter's sky. Another shooting star caught my eye, pushing Brian out of my thoughts. The clearness of the cold, crisp air seemed to magnify the brilliance of the stars. I drifted in and out of the conversation as the miles passed beneath our footsteps.

It was the natural distraction of the Leonids meteor shower that had helped, too. As we climbed, it was natural to look at the sky. Where there had been the walls of the Columbia River's gorge to limit our skyward view, now the walls were gone. My eyes picked up one streak and then another, a short burst of light, then one that burned long enough to shout, "Look over there." The muted crunching of gravel from the padding of five pairs of shoes, the flashes of meteor trails, and the eerily synchronized breathing sounds took over as conversation ceased and we continued up the last of the climb out of the gorge. Now our horizon was almost horizontal—not a one of us knew the darkness to our right was Badger Mountain and another climb for us a couple of hours later—for now we could see the full of the Milky Way, and we could feel the first bit of flatness beneath our feet. Are we on top? I think so. Yeah, I can see stars all the way to the ground. We're up. One voice said we'd climbed for an hour.

Now here I was driving along the same route but for the first time in the light of day. Just like on that November night when we turned to the right in Orondo to climb up out of the Columbia's home, this time, too, we turned to the right. Only this time I could look out in front of us at the road and the side of the river's gorge. This time I could see the hill. That is a long hill, I said to Kathy. Yup. We ran that? Yes, you went right up it, slowed from nines to nine thirties, but yes, you ran right up it. Good thing it was night, I said. I could never have run that in the daytime, what with being able to see it like this.

So, if you can see the hills, then you can't run up them? No, that isn't quite what I mean, although there is some support for that idea. Well, we couldn't see it, and I had no idea how long it went on. I just ran on up it because everyone else was running up it—no one took a walk break. We rounded another curve, and the highway continued to climb up this side canyon, up and out of the riverbed. I tried to read the downhill sign that warned of a steep grade for the next however many miles, but since I was driving I couldn't. It did make me wonder, though, about an aggressive tactic safely hidden in the darkness. If we cannot see the climb in front of us, can we run it more aggressively than our self-belief would normally allow?

I was thinking back to when I paced Linda Samet at the Western States Endurance Run. Linda and I had pushed on into the darkening evening, trying to get as many miles in as we could before needing to turn our lights on. The world of running turns ever slower as the flashlights are turned on. It would be dark long before we got to Rucky Chucky and its surreal river crossing—at least a million miles from any known civilization. Rucky Chucky and its cable to guide us across the American River to freedom, or at least to Green Gate—how many have seen it in the darkness? The real point of curiosity for me is how many people have seen it in the daylight? Most of the folks running that course never see those trails in the light of day.

At Leadville the out-and-back nature of the course assures everyone at least a few miles of daylight over the entire course. Cascade Crest and its ten-o'clock-in-the-morning start gives everyone some fun in the dark—if Cascade Crest would alternate directions *à la* Hardrock, the views, and the run, would be totally different. At the other end of the spectrum are courses such as Barkley, which are only to be run under astrological guidance and tossed-bone readings with no concern for light or dark anyway.

Kathy's voice jerked me back to the present. "You stopped here." What? Here? I pointed upward to where the road curved out of sight. Why would I stop before being on top?

This is where you changed shirts. Huh? I thought we were on top and you would like a dry shirt, so I stopped. It turned out there were about two more miles before it flattened out. It didn't get flat, but now you were on the Palouse, and it just rolled gently up and down forever. I thought about how darkness is good to us. Okay, maybe not good, but there is certainly kindness in hiding the work of a long climb from the mind's eye.

We had never been back, Kathy and I. From here, the 100k course took us to the airport north of Waterville, then back through town, and south, up and over Badger Mountain, where we would fall off the mountain, dropping almost 4,000 feet in the sevenish miles back down into the valley floor where we had started. There was no reason to ever come this way again. It wasn't conveniently on the way to anywhere of interest, until now.

How much farther? A mile or so, and then it just sort of does the up-and-down-forever thing. Quite different in the light of day, isn't it? Yes. Yes it is. My, oh my—I don't know that I could have held on to that pace if I had been able to see it. I looked southerly at Badger Mountain. The darkness had hidden that climb, too. We could not have seen it even if we had known to look over there. Darkness, for some people, is sometimes associated with emotional distress, the forces of evil, things that go bonk in the night, or other things not generally having positive vibrations. This was not so on our long climb up this hill in the dark. The darkness kept us from seeing how difficult our task was, and so we just went ahead and ran.

I recalled numerous times on one trail or another that I had looked to the east, wanting some sign of light, that age-old purveyor of good tidings, to tell me I had made it through another night and the strength of dawn was within my grasp. I pulled over at the officially proclaimed scenic overlook. The winding snake of a highway slithered down to Orondo, visible just enough times to be able to follow it all the way down. I realized I would not like to run down it either, not in the light of day anyway—but maybe on a dark and cloudless night with a full moon and good company matching me stride for stride—maybe then.

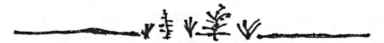

Leadville from the *Camino* and from the Island

One Saturday morning a few years ago, we had been walking for almost five hours when I made the comment, "They have just started at Leadville." We were walking across northern Spain—way far removed from ultras, six time zones to the east of Leadville, Colorado, USA. As the day wore on we made comments back and forth about where the runners were, how they might be, and so on. That evening as we stopped for the day, I mentioned how they would still be out there when we pulled the backpacks on the next morning.

Now I am one time zone to the west of Leadville. The moon's last shadows let me just make out the outline of the trees with the waters of Penn Cove in the background. It is just about three o'clock in the morning. I quietly make coffee, get dressed to go out, and then play at writing as the light of the moon leaves. I am waiting for the first, but false, presence of dawn.

At about the same time as Merilee and Ken send their last mass of footfalls down the street, I head out. It is purely pragmatic of me, not any sort of spiritual link. The weather is forecast to be beautiful today. The campground is full. The bluff trail and the kettles will be infested with kidlets, big and small, with people who will leave pop cans and candy wrappers behind, with the GPSers bushwhacking because they have no understanding of the lay of the land. None of them get up early.

The grasses of the prairie wet my knees and the backs of my hands as I cross toward the bluff. The last two owls hoot either hello or good-bye as I leave the cemetery. A dog that long ago gave up barking at my passage makes one small yip and rolls over—quiet returns. The almost visible line of the North Cascades sixty or so miles east hides a direct-line-of-sight view of the folks in the Rockies (1200ish miles too far). The humongous throng is on the boulevard by now. I am alone and climbing to the trees along the bluff.

Not quite alone—a couple sits in one hillside meadow; coffee cups raise in hello, no words; I smile, nod, and head on to the End of Trail sign, touch it (why? always crosses my mind, but I do it none-theless; who knows, but someone might be counting the number of times I touch that sign), and head down the zigzags.

"Rock rattlers"—the rattling sound of the rocks being rearranged by the waves of the tide has never been thought of as noise, not by me. It is just one of nature's sounds, something that greets me as I get to water's edge. I wish I had one of the cups of coffee with me—sitting on an old driftwood log counting waves and watching the wa-ter rearrange the gravel while the first runners might be at Tabor. If I go along the beach for a while before I recross the prairie, I'll get to the cemetery about the same time they will get to May Queen.

As the sun breaks the distant mountain line, the thought that I am but one of many tenuous strands that connect one running trail to another as someone else's footsteps touch the ground we all touched before crosses my mind. It is too silly to be put on paper, so I leave it next to a headstone as the lead runners clear May Queen.

A North Dakota Sunrise

Just another lapse in concentration—endurance running, like any other sport, requires concentration. A lapse of attention and months of training and planning can go awry. In some ways, though, endurance running—our adventures that take us somewhere beyond the standard marathon distance—is more forgiving of our mental meanderings. An instance of distraction can be forgiven because there is often enough time, or distance, to recover. As time passes, some distractions shift, no longer intruding but gently becoming part of our reasons for running. The occasional distraction can actually reward, even invigorate. I was struggling through the snow and ice of another morning of doing what I was calling running in a subzero winter morning in North Dakota when the turn toward the hill brought me face to face with sunrise. It was a pause-for-a-while distraction of another sunrise.

The psychological warmth of sunrise, whether when I am just out for a few miles or when, like others, I have been waiting for it those last long hours of an all-night run, has an almost sensual quality. The promise of another day intertwines with the completion of another run. The senses become aware of the barely perceptible change from darkness. A few steps without the light are tried—still too dark, but now the sense of anticipation of running out of the dark awakens mind and body. The pace, while not necessarily quickened, becomes lighter feeling. That world of darkness, so fuzzily described by my beams of light, is now expanding, seemingly taking shape with each passing step.

When Kathy and I walked *el Camino de Santiago,* our first steps up and into the Pyrenees Mountains in southwestern France were taken in the predawn darkness similar to many other starting lines. A need to be out and moving and sleep interrupted by nervous anticipation drove us out into the deserted streets. Our conversations were whispered. The rubber tips left on the trekking poles kept our departure silent. Kathy whispered, "Dawn's coming," as we left town behind, walking and climbing westerly. We found ourselves glancing back at ever-shorter intervals. We were both aware of the coming dawn—our first on the *camino.* The colors on dawn's easel were changing from grays and blue blacks to the pastels of the coming light, and then finally to fire. We turned to watch that first sunrise with no thought of the distraction from our walking. We could feel the flood of warmth and the comfort of daylight. The gift of that new day caused us to decide to always be on the way a few minutes before sunrise.

Each sunrise, while running, can bring as many messages or fleeting thoughts as the colors in the sky. Dawn means a highway crossing and a last few miles on tired legs. Sunrise takes forever and a day to paint Turquoise Lake. The coming of dawn and a cut-off time brings a weary mind back to full attention on the trail and the need to be at a certain aid station before the sun is full up. Dawn at Capitol Reef was so quiet you could hear the colors climbing each canyon wall. As fall shortens daylight hours, the start of many events is in the dark—the gloom of apprehension hangs over those runners who hadn't thought to prepare for a few miles without light. Sunrise brings frost diamonds and quick glances at the prisms of nature. Dawn at Smuggler's Notch in Vermont was New England's fall colors coming to life. Sunrise means it is time to turn back toward the house to put breakfast on the stove. Dawn means the first one out of the tent starts the fire and puts the pan of water on the stove. Dawn is a contest to see who can be stillest in the sleeping bag, who can pretend to be asleep, in case the morning air has the first trace of winter cold.

A passing car honked, jerking me back to the present. How long had I paused? The undersides of the clouds were being repainted while I stood on the hilltop. I never have any problem giving names to the many shades of yellows, oranges, and reds. We have flowers, birds, and even ice creams to help us with the vibrant colors—that vibrancy fills the new life each dawn brings to us. It is the grays and those last streaks of midnight blue that I cannot attach names to as they fade before being fully seen, vanishing as I pass the cemetery, gone by the corner, replaced by the vastness of blue that now stretched across the flatness of the North Dakota landscape. The sun was not up yet. It was just below the horizon, not high enough to color anything but the sky. A few more minutes were all I would need to see the whole show.

How long until sunrise? Just a few minutes more. Okay. The internal conversation had been going on forever. I needed daylight. The light of day brings the truth, no matter how faintly seen. I was sure I had been running uphill for most of the night. I was just as sure that the trail had to be going downhill, since it was taking me to the river. Dawn brings back the truth of our surroundings.

Dawn released the shadows that dusk had taken from me somewhere back along the trail. As the roundness of the sun broke the horizon, I was no longer alone, so I turned to chase my shadow back to the corner. Dawn in Palo Duro Canyon let our shadows run on their own trails hundreds of feet away from where we ran along the rim, slowly returning to us as the sun climbed into the Texas sky. Sunrise on a peak in the Rockies just above Pagosa Springs transposed the mountain peaks into islands in a sea of clouds; our shadows vanished into a sea we could never reach.

My westward leg let me see how near our morning fog was. Dawn in the winter of North Dakota often brings a fog that freezes on contact—almost instantly. The distractions of those many dawns were replaced with a need to be up the hill to St. Ann's before the fog caught up with me.

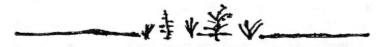

Ptarmigans, Long Riders, and Cinnamon Rolls

We drove easterly along SR 20, more commonly known as the "North Cascades Highway" here in Washington, pausing to do the "ooh" and "ahh" at our mountains and valleys. There was food and firewood, trekking poles and trail shoes, binoculars and other stuff almost orderly packed in behind us—all indicative of us being undecided about the day and not being sure of where the mountains would let us go this early in the spring.

We pulled off at one roadside stop to eat a bite, look at the melting snow and waterfalls, and just generally enjoy being out of the car for a few minutes. The day held no purpose; no schedule had been made. One huge snowfield (later we would learn it was Colonial Glacier) sent its many watery fingers down the two miles of mountainside, gathering into streams twinkling their way down, dropping as waterfalls, always gathering size, diamonds now, clouds of mist a hundred feet long for one, a hundred feet wide for another; we watched and watched. A bicyclist we had passed a few miles earlier pulled off the road to join us—an old guy on a long ride, judging from the packs and bags and flags on his bike.

"Good morning," I offered as he unbent from his bike.

"Good morning," he returned with a smile.

I looked at the panniers, the flags. "And where are you bound for?"

"Maine." (About 3,000 miles east of where we stood.)

"Hmmmm. Would you like a PB&J?" Through-walkers and long-riders don't get to carry heavy things like peanut butter and jelly...a smile and a nod. We learned he was from New Zealand—he was a long way from home, but, as he pointed out, not as long a way from Maine. We fixed a second sandwich and told him of Going-to-the-Sun Road waiting for him in Glacier National Park way far away in Montana and the eternity of North Dakota. We talked of the wonderful gift of time and glanced at the diamonds on the mountainside. A few, or many, minutes of conversation passed, and then he moved toward the patiently waiting bicycle. He smiled, thanked us for the sandwiches, pointed toward the pass, and said, "Time to go."

"*Buen viaje*" came forth unconsciously—the "Good journey" said to so many parting travelers in Spain.

"*Buen viaje*" came back with a newly broadened smile as he pointed at the Spanish flag on one pannier.

We turned up the road to Sauk Mountain, set the odometer to zero, noted the altimeter, cut off another piece of cinnamon roll, and worked our way up the switchbacks. In and out of clear-cuts—graveyards filled with stumps two and three ax handles wide—the reds and oranges and yellows of Indian paintbrushes covered the hillsides; phlox and columbine patches lined the road as we climbed back into the second-growth forests.

A lone ptarmigan stood ground not quite on the side of the road. No need. We would have stopped to watch anyway. It was brown and black and tan and speckled and almost invisible...as if waiting for something on the side of the mountain. Aha, a rustling in the leaves told us it was a she. She was waiting for us to go by so she could tell her newly hatched, "All is clear, come out." We strained to see, to hear—finding one brave one, barely sparrow-sized, still fluffy with down, come out of the leaves to find Mom. We left them, broke off another piece of cinnamon roll, and entered the meadow.

Mount Baker, still mostly covered with ice and snow, twenty miles away yet in the same instance sitting at arm's reach watched our progress. One patch of snow, barely a hundred feet wide now, seemed to shrink as we drove by. It would not see August. We looked at our hundred miles and more of volcanoes and ridges; of Puget

Sound and glaciers; of blue sky and the oranges, reds, yellows, blues, and whites of the alpine meadows—these days of indecision have ways to satisfy.

At which point, for whatever reason, Kathy said, "We are 8.1 miles in, 4380 feet up—why don't you run back down? You could use some 'speed' work."

I muttered, "Stop at two miles so I can check on things." She left as I was lacing the last shoe, knowing I would quickly realize the foolhardiness of this challenge. One tall-as-I-am tiger lily waved its blossoms at me—*buen viaje*?

Phlox and paintbrushes passed by; quilted hillsides of reds, blues, purples, and whites—lupine and columbine, asters, too; the greens of salal and Oregon grape took over as I dropped down into the forests. Loose gravel and aching ankles—no long hills had I seen in many months. Memories of runs many miles long brought back the checklist...relax, get off the washboard...two young black-tailed deer crossed the road, paused to watch the intruder, and then showed me how to run downhill.

Knowing how wasn't the issue. I knew how. I remembered it quite well. There just seemed to be a communication problem betwixt the brain and the legs. Foolishness, or knowing I could not stop if I wanted to, rushed in as I passed where Kathy had parked. "Check me at four."

Open space at a switchback as I entered a clear-cut—how could a hillside be so purple—how far away was Mount Rainier—which peak was tha...and I was back in the trees—the darkness of shadows cooled the dust-laden air as I sought to find the relaxing stride of memory—a creek crossing burbled, and a pocket of cool air refreshed. The car again. Warmth. The 72 degrees at the upper meadow was climbing back to the 88 degrees of the valley floor. Dust as Kathy passed. A welcome flatness to this section. The Skagit River, home to so many eagles when winter comes, glinted in the valley as its blues merged with the muddied waters of the Sauk. I could run to there. I knew I could.

Relax arms...check. Relax chest...check. Pull air in deep...check. Switch to faster cadence? No way, Charlie. No way at all. One last open space where the lavenders of thistles had taken over. The dust of the dirt road choked back the colors as I dropped through the active logging area. Pieces of bark and strips of cedar, fallen from the trees taken from their hillsides, are all that is left of a forest passed.

The car and a dry shirt. Back behind the wheel. Turned into the lowering sun and drove toward it and the island. A herd of elk was in a meadow to the left of the highway. We made one last pause to play sightseer. The last of the cinnamon buns used up the last of the chocolate milk.

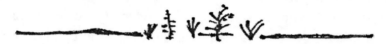

Why I Am Here

These last few weeks of fall find us in between Thanksgiving and Christmas, a time for being thankful for what we have and a time that is perhaps our most sharing time of the year. My immediate thanks, because I am at the keyboard again, is for my column—this gift of getting to write about running gives back to me in so many ways. I don't know which of you I would have met anyway, but I am sure there are several I never would have met had it not been for these words I place here and there in the middle of each month. Actually, it is not important that I place them appropriately, it is that you read them. That is the important part. It is for your continued reading that I am thankful.

As important as running is in this household, it all but disappeared during the early part of this year. Our winter in North Dakota (everyone should have one) gradually brought our running to a halt. When we finally packed to return home to the Pacific Northwest, one thought easily outshined the running we had missed. We had been able to help others—not in some earthshaking, headline-grabbing way but in small ways that led us to many houses, many families, and many faces and new friends. We helped in a way that made us thankful for being there, doing what little we could.

We managed to get to Spokane for a daughter's commencement. Her many years of classes while homeschooling her four children were concluded. As she walked across the stage, we thought of, and were thankful for, the strength, courage, and determination she had demonstrated—certainly as much as any of us during our runs—her finish line was not a trailhead but a stage. She did not get a T-shirt but a diploma. Later that day I was thankful for the company of a grandchild on a trail alongside the Spokane River—running's tapestry continues to bring simple pleasures and rewards.

We were barely settled in, back on this island northwest of Seattle, when we had company in July; three visitors, one from Maryland, one from Minnesota, and one from Wisconsin. None of them had ever spent time in this northwest corner of the United States. We took them for walks on our trails, and suddenly they were not our trails. They became their trails, then they became our trails again, but our number was now five instead of two. The three new sets of eyes gave us new views of trails we had covered so many times. The five of us tried to join hands to reach around a tree and failed. A bug with a billion legs was found—giggles of glee and childlike curiosity seemed to be at every turn. A pause for a sandwich near the misty rapids of a creek with no name passed almost without a word—each of us quiet, looks covering thoughts that had turned inward. As the hours and miles passed, the spirituality of the old-growth trees and the quiet of the forest caused us to pause, thankful for the day, the place, and our presence.

We are back in a place where some form of running has returned to our daily routine. I am thankful for both its presence and for my continued love of what it gives me. This gift of health; the physical and occasionally mental well-being we have been given is often overlooked at this time of the year. We look in this store's window or that shop's doorway as the season's shopping takes us to the crowds of a mall or to a Web site where a few clicks can send a gift to loved ones near or far. Gadgets and gimmicks in many shapes and sizes arrive, securely wrapped to prevent shaking, peeking, poking, or prodding from disclosing the contents. The number of days until the small package wrapped in blue paper with striped ribbons that you know contains the new 19-function altimeter, heart-rate monitor, Blu-ray player, pace, stride, and calorie analyzer, GPS, and DNA sampler is counted each morning. The plea that knowing what it is should make it okay to open it a few days early (17 to be exact) falls on deaf ears. Grumbling not quite under my breath, I head for the door for a few more miles of antidepressants on the trails under the trees—and the gifts begin.

My fingers hang at an inconvenient height on some days. In Oregon they were at just the right height to brush the tops of the poison oak leaves that were so plentiful. In the desert trails of the Southwest, I could be assured of at least one encounter with cactus needles. This morning it is the frost that touches my fingers as the trail drops into a low spot on the way to the bluffs. I turn and look back. The northeasterly run of the trail shows glints and glitters of nature's diamonds as the early morning sun catches the frost on the tops of the remains of the recently mown barley—not enough to make any crunching sound as I run—not yet—just enough for a brief crop of diamonds and rainbows, just enough to get my fingers wet because they are at an inconvenient height.

On this late-fall morning, the crispness of air that doesn't recognize a calendar gives a winter's starkness to the mountains, changes their faraway distance to arm's length—I should be able to touch the snowlines, rearranging them as I go, but I can't. I give up and move on to the next challenge, thinking I should be able to find the sea lion I hear so clearly. I am sure the speed with which I am covering ground prevents me from succeeding in my search, so I pause at the next high point. I check the Admiralty Head buoy but see nothing clinging to it. A water slap and the splash give away the location of the three travelers. I am wearing layers of Brooks, REI, and some other long-faded brand of cold-weather running stuff and am comfortably warm *as long as I run*—they are unaware of any need for special clothing. The next splash is followed by silence, and the riddle of how long can they stay down comes to mind. A long time is all we ever end up with—I search, eyes going here and there, but they are gone, and the wind prods me to return to running. That is what I am here for, the running, isn't it?

CHAPTER TEN

As a runner I wasn't so much a has-been as I was a never-will-be.

—Me

Jogging is very beneficial. It's good for your legs and your feet. It's also good for the ground. It makes it feel needed.

—Charles Schulz

May your trails be crooked, winding, steep, lonesome, dangerous, and leading to the most amazing views. May your mountains rise into and above the clouds.

—Edward Abbey

Life is a challenge, meet it!
Life is a dream, realize it!
Life is a game, play it!
Life is love, enjoy it!

—Sri Sathya Sai Baba

No Footsteps but Mine...

Echoes of Kathy Mattea, Joni Mitchell, Robert Goulet, Etta James, and Willie, and Ella rattled around my head as I locked the car. The variety of names and music was indicative of a restless mind that drove me away from the desk to the shelter of the trails, again. The noises of passing cars and the highway faded in the growing darkness behind me. My quiet passing put one more set of footprints on a trail I could almost run blindfolded. A new rain and wind, but the same branches of trees touched me as I passed by once more. I was still a half mile from the water, but I could already taste the salt on the wind. I had wanted sunset, but I was slow leaving the house.

I wanted company but not of people. Cedars and firs, rocks and roots, black squirrels and a rabbit or two were seen in passing. A noisy something crashing in the brush told me there were deer nearby—safe from the hunters for one more year. *A noisy something*—that was how the words had flowed today—even using "flow" was wrong. They did not flow today. They tripped and stumbled with none seeming to find their right position on the page. You can only stare at the white spaces for so long when they refuse your every attempt at arrangement to match a thought.

Owls were calling as I winded my way around and down into Cedar Hollow kettle. I paused as I passed the game trail that had taken me to the "lost kettle" just a few days ago. For an hour and more that hole fashioned by the long-gone Vashon glacier combined with a morning of dense fog had kept me confused and disoriented. It was a day of being thwarted by the fog, rain, and wind that ended with the conclusion that game trails always end in a small meadow on the backside of nowhere in particular. Game trails are games played on us by the game in the woods. I could feel them laughing as I climbed up and down and over and slipped and slid and looked up for a landmark. Tonight the whispered softness of muffled wings told me an owl was nearby. For just a moment I wondered if my green light bothered them. There were no hoots as I passed.

The wind on the bluff was dominating all sound now. The highway sounds, just a few miles away, were gone now—banished by the simple movement of air. Gaia smiled, sprinkling more salt from the airborne spray in each breath I took. Whitecaps danced, and greenish-gray swells rolled toward me. I paused to direct them this way and that as the trail took me to water's edge, then away, then near again. Two logs did their clumsy, slow-motion Dance of the Hippos as they came to shore. One must have been four or five feet in diameter, thirty feet long, moved only by wind and water. I stood watching and wondering where it had been and where I should tell the wind to leave it. My day was ending with more questions than answers, and that seemed to match my run, a run filled with starts and stops that matched the rising and falling and shifting winds.

Vivaldi...not Wagner...these were Vivaldi winds. No thunderous clashes, just rising and falling, gulls and terns traveling the currents with hardly a wing beat. An eagle, perhaps tired from fighting the wind for its right to perch in a bare fir alongside the trail, did not fly as I passed only twenty feet away. The urge to stop to see it clearly was strong, but the strings changed pitch as if to push me past; with barely a glance upward I followed the zigzag of the trail on down the bluff. The flashlight was finally needed as the gray of evening became the black of night. The time taken to climb up the Pacific Northwest Trail had let the darkness come in, making the light beam more distinct. The darkened trails leading back to the car would be caves cut only by green and white beams as I turned toward the trailhead and the noise of the highway.

The hooting of owls, rustlings in the bushes, and whispers of wind soon to be replaced by Willie and Ella and company seemed more orderly now.

Wakopa and the Elusive North Dakota Moose

First, please accept my wish for a Happy just-past New Year (Gregorian calendar) and almost-here New Year (Julian calendar) to each and all of you. This New Year finds us in North Dakota. More specifically, we are in Belcourt, North Dakota, on the Turtle Mountain Band of the Chippewa's Turtle Mountain Indian Reservation for a year of volunteer work. Kathy, my wife, has taken me on another challenging and rewarding adventure to this part of the U.S., a part that is so different from our recent home on Whidbey Island in Washington State.

The Turtle Mountains are, to us, a series of rolling hills that rise only a few hundred feet above the flatness of the northern North Dakota plains. Oak, elm, and cottonwood have replaced our towering firs and cedars. The constant green of the Pacific Northwest has been replaced by the skeletal, brown bareness of winter trees, all shorn of their leaves. The gray and white bark of birch, ash, and aspen line the trails and dirt roads. The trees will be empty of leaves now and for the next several months. The first benefit of all these fallen leaves is to recall a certain childhood joy—and so we run through knee-deep piles of leaves as the trail dips and winds its way among the many lakes.

We don't know these woods or trails. So we park and run, only to find another short dead-end trail. So far the day's excitement has been watching the muskrats walking around on the surface of the frozen lakes. For a mile or so the trill of an occasional raven is the only sound beyond our breathing and the rustlings of leaves; then a series of chirps, whistles, and yunks announces the passing of some boreal chickadees and maybe a nuthatch or two—small, acrobatic birds that are seldom still long enough for us to see the eye-ring or wing-banding that identifies them. They are gone before we are fully stopped to look at them.

We keep an eye open for wildlife as we run, eager to see the wonders that our Pacific Northwest doesn't have. So when we get back to the car and someone says, "Did you see the moose?" we answer hopefully, "Moose?" At the car, two hunters stand, rifles in hand. They ask us again if we saw the moose. Moose? "Yeah, there was a bull moose just back"—points the way we came from—"there." Hmmm, is it moose-shooting season? No. We don't think they should be out here looking for moose. The hunters ask a question or two about our "stuff", and a few minutes pass as we compare some of their traditional hunting garb with our lightweight, high-tech running clothing. Finally, they drive away, and we refill our bottles and start on search number 381 for a moose—a North Dakota moose.

We are in the Wakopa Wildlife Management Area, just about as far north as you can get and still be in the U.S. without going to Alaska. We had sighted several moose on the way up from Belcourt—two were Herefords, one a Charolais, and the last a Jersey—not a good start. Someone had told us the moose like to cross from Lake Upsilon to Dion Lake and then go north through the thickets toward the border. With only the knowledge gained from two earlier trips to Wakopa, we had started talking earlier that morning about which trailhead to park at for the day's pursuit. We don't have a detailed map of the area, just several trips to Google and some bonding sessions with the monitor on the desktop. Some of the trailheads have signs. None have any information about it being a loop, a dead end, or maybe going all the way to Canada—just a sign saying Trail—No Motorized Vehicles.

This kind of running is close to not even being running. The least little noise and we stop to see what caused it. One pile of rustling leaves takes us back to Arkansas and the memory of armadillos wandering around almost hidden within the many years' layers of leaves. We watch for a moment, finally spot the movement, and in a few seconds a raccoon emerges. Kathy says, "That's progress, it has four legs and fur and isn't on the ice." Encouraged, we do our run, jog, pause, listen, look, jog, shuffle, and pause for another thirty minutes or so, finally deciding to sit on a log at the edge of a large clearing. I get out two PB&Js—grape jelly—would a moose like a PB&J with grape jelly?

I should point out that we are not hunters nor wild-animal be-havior experts by any stretch of the imagination. We have quite a few bird books but no animal books. We seldom get close to large wild animals. We did pass through a herd of elk on the Olympic Peninsula on one run, but there was no pausing to take a picture of me standing next to one of them. We have this idea about the size structure of deer-type animals. There are the smallish deer of the southeastern U.S., and then come antelopes out in the foothills of many of our northwestern states. Mule deer are the next size up in our deerlike family, and then come the elk. There is nothing scientific in this imaginary imagery chart. There are no weights in our schema, only the idea that these are bigger than those and in turn some other these are bigger than some other those...wish I had some milk to go with the PB&J...hmmm, a horse...with horns.

A horse with horns? At another time, a conversation about the difference between horns and antlers might have taken place, but not now. It appears our relative sizing of deer-like animals needs a bit of tweaking to allow for the moose just over to our right; a bull moose to be exact (has antlers). A moose, when seen up close (about 40 feet, which seems real close) is about the same size as a horse. We do not discuss what kind of horse—quarter, draft, or pinto—we just sit there listening to our hearts, sure that he can hear them and wondering when he will turn to see what is causing the loud thumping sounds. Apparently we are far enough down on the scale of importance to not be worth investigation. If he notices us at all, it does not show.

Motionless, we sit there, PB&Js in hand, not pointing, just watching as he crosses the meadow, goes into an aspen thicket, and then, in the magical way that animals in the wild can do things, disappears. One North Dakota moose complete with antlers—check. A few administrative details are taken care of, and now we can get back to running.

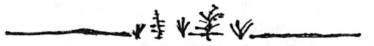

Friends, Strangers, Running on Memory

Little things will keep you inside. "Injured" has so many names: damaged, impaired, hurt, harmed, wounded, ruined, and none are conducive to getting you out the door. I'm not injured. I keep telling myself it is just one of those nagging little aches that intrude into my consciousness just enough to worry and distract.

That settled, I head down the trail—walking and waiting for the first twinge. A quarter mile passes, walk turns to shuffle, and off I go onto Humpty Dumpty, down into the kettles again. Friends and strangers are always in the kettles, and the gradual drop to the old cedar is an easy warm-up. Two spotted towhees burst out of the undergrowth, looking like robins in plaid coats, still partly covered with the down that marks them as babies; they spot me and disappear back into their leaf-strewn world.

Just as I make the turn to the big cedar, Woody Woodpecker laughter fills the woods. It only takes a few seconds to spot the two pileated woodpeckers, crow-sized, easily the largest of the woodpeckers, their red, white, and black heads bobbing back and forth as they chisel a hole into an aging cedar. The pause for review completed, my feet take me on around and down into the hole left by the big ice cube some ten or twelve thousand years ago.

Sometimes speed calls for agility, sometimes a hundred yards of six-foot-tall nettles calls for agility...or do I yield to the occasional sadistic pleasure of brushing nettles to wake up tired legs? I look at the old cedar, hidden down here in the bottom. We have guessed it to be six hundred years old. It is the only old tree down here; alders and ocean spray off to one side, a field of thimbleberries on another, a scattering of wings as this year's generation of bushtits learn their acrobatics—the ever-still, never-still forest draws me in again.

The distraction of the birds and the rolling zigzags of High Traverse are interrupted by the awakening thought—no pain, no discomfort, no twitchies—of relaxed running. Suddenly aware of everything seeming to function as intended, I change directions and head away from the trailhead, going, instead, to Lake Pondilla. There were two ospreys there last week, not full-time residents but frequent visitors. And the trail goes through the biggest wild black-berry thicket of the area.

The whole run falls apart as I pull-test a blackberry. If they come off easily, they are (usually) ripe. It practically falls into my hand. The newest aid station of the forest is open. I sacrifice speed for cal-ories—gotta be able to get back to the car, dontcha know. A handful or two later and I continue on to Lake Pondilla, where I find school is in session for a family of belted kingfishers. I sit on a stump in the shade and watch as Mom, then Dad, hovers, dives, gets a fish, goes to perch—then drops the fish back in the lake as if to say, "Now you try it." The two newest strangers to the lake leave the branch, and the Kingfisher Comedy Hour begins. They hover okay. They dive fairly well. They fail to get a fish and appear panic stricken about getting out of the water. The rattling *click-click-click* from Mom and Dad scolds and instructs. Eventually a lesson is learned, and one of the kids returns to the branch with a meal.

I walk for a few hundred yards up from the lake; the warmth of the afternoon sun feels good as I go from walk to shuffle to run to...well, almost to this-feels-good-and-I-could-run-forever. The waters of Admiralty Inlet are touched with whites and blues as the wind from the Strait of Juan de Fuca plays with the tidal currents. A freighter with a gazillion tons of resource depletion is outbound. Two kayaks hug the shore, riding the tide back into Puget Sound. The bluff trail is wide and smooth enough to run without worrying about footing—water and mountains pull at the mind as legs and shoulders relax.

The switchbacks and shadows of Cedar Grove wake me up. Roots and turns, vines pulling at sleeves, the climb to the old men is a transition into quiet. The floor is covered with who knows how many hundreds of years of cedar needles. There are a dozen or so trees showing their age, deeply drooping branches, burls and woodpecker holes, trunks twisted and turned from centuries of seeking the sun, and always a raven to scold me for intruding, again. I mutter, "Sorry," and turn to leave.

The trail finally straightens, then widens. Two hikers at a junction are looking at a map, each pointing in different directions. I pause. Where? Here. Where to? There. Down there, right at the first fork, left at the...at least they have a map. Gravel crunching now—the narrow gravel road has no quiet spots, but it is free of roots, and I want to open the stride again, just to check—just to push a bit. It is effort, not pace, that I want to be comfortable with when on trails. Birds and berries, waves and wind have been acknowledged; now I want to put my mind to running. It is a mile to the car. Old friends and strangers are left behind again as breathing becomes rhythmical and the running on memory returns.

Wingbeats and Foghorns

Runs with time constraints are annoying. That's what we kept saying yesterday. We had to hurry to be back at the house—not good when you have noticed the rhodies are blooming. Emilie's Ridge has the most rhodies. We wanted to run Emilie's, but it was time to turn toward the car.

We left earlier this morning. Fog awaited. Thick fog, not quite thick enough to need a knife but thick enough to change the familiar, shroud it in mystery, and quiet our passing as we wound our way down Cedar Hollow and up to the bluff.

We could hear the waves rattling the beach gravel and sea lions barking below; then a foghorn reverberated through the damp morning air, and silence followed. I wondered if the newly born sea lion pups were suddenly looking at Mom and asking what was that? We passed on, two hundred feet above them, unseen, probably not unheard.

Almost unheard were the wingbeats. Kathy paused, finger to lips, and pointed up just as I heard it—air being gently pushed in passing. Breaths were held. Where? Oh. Oh, wow (quiet "wow")! An adult bald eagle, female judging from its size and beak, came out of the fog, eye level to us and barely twenty feet away. Its head turned toward us, cast judgment, and was gone. We swore we could feel the air moving.

Seconds passed; our frozen poses slowly thawed. We turned down Kettles and started toward the car; cedar needles quieted our passing. The sounds of the unseen animals and ships faded as we went farther into the woods. The whispered wingbeats echoed through our minds all the way home.

Failing Lights and Noises That Aren't

I came out on the gun battery meadow from Water Tower Trail just starting to feel a sense of urgency. Four deer, three does and one buck, antlers wrapped in the velvet of early summer, raised their heads briefly to acknowledge my presence. I refilled my bottle and decided to catch the last of sunset before looking at my watch. Just having the watch on meant I was flirting with darkness on a run when I had no flashlight. Watches intrude during the day, but late in the evening the intrusion, though still there, might make the last mile under darkening skies a little easier (if a person had forgotten a light).

Vancouver Island accepted the sun from our sky. Canada owns the light for a few more weeks. Soon it will sink into the waters of the Strait of Juan de Fuca; then slowly on some days, quickly on others, it will start setting behind the Olympic Mountains. As it moves southerly the days will turn gray and sunsets might go unseen for weeks at a time, but not today. I got to bluff's edge and paused—orange? Yellow, gold, red, white, and then blue with only the barest orange at the top of the arc of the sun's globe showing above where the lights of Victoria, British Columbia, would soon reflect at water's edge. I thought sunset was at 9:13, but that is a number for paper, not for trails. Sunset had just happened was all I knew. Okay, not all; I knew I was 2.7 miles from the car by the direct route, 3.4 miles by the second route, and 4.2 miles on the bluff route. I glanced at the clearness of the sky and the sliver of a new moon, not even a quarter of a disk yet, but it was enough for the bluff trail, if I hurried.

It wouldn't work. There were two adult bald eagles sitting in a tree just below the washout. Eagles turn their heads toward each other as they talk. I have never got tired of watching them. They sit still, then one head turns toward the other, then the other looks back, sometimes moves a tiny bit closer as if to whisper, then they are still again. They were far enough below and the wind was loud enough to hide the noise of my passing, but time had been used, not wasted but used. The roots and turns of Cedar Hollow waited for me. A ballet of toe-prancing steps for the first three switchbacks was needed as I felt my way through the roots of the kettle's side. The forest was at its thickest there. I just needed to get through another tenth or two and the root-enhanced stretch would be behind me. I could almost, no, I could feel my shoulders relax as I got to the end of Cedar Hollow. As I came out from under the cedars, I could see someone at the kiosk. She was straddling her bicycle and trying to read the map. The maps, hard to read in the daylight, are impossible to read in the failing light.

"Hi."

"Hi."

"Are you okay? Do you know where you are?"

"No. No, not really." Laugh. "I am somewhere with a new light that doesn't work."

"Oh." I didn't want to guide her back to the campground. That was about a mile in the wrong direction.

"Are you camped here in the park?"

"No. I parked out by the highway."

"Oh. That's where I am going. We can go up to Grancy's. It will add two or three minutes, but you will have a wider trail and can see better."

"Okay."

"Ride here often?"

"No. This was the first time. I just bought the bike today. I was having so much fun, and then it was dark and I couldn't read the map."

"Ah...you'll need to learn about sunset times and how much time it takes to get back to your car—and other professional-grade stuff."

As I was showing her the one-finger sunset-timing trick, on cue, just like in a movie...

Woo hoahoo wooo, woo hoohoa woooo

"What is that!"

"An owl, a great horned. It's time for it to start looking for dinner."

"An owl? You can tell?"

The remaining fifteen minutes were filled with lies and tales and comments about the trails in the park. A pileated woodpecker contributed to the sounds as we passed Limbo. She called them noises. I said no, not noises, just the sounds of the forest as light changes to dark. If you sit for a few minutes, you will start to hear all sorts of things. The next hour or so is one of the most active times of the forest.

We passed the last junction, and the dark of the trail changed to the white gravel of the service road. The sounds of cars on the highway could be heard, then headlights were seen. I thanked whoever watches over me for letting me miss all the roots on the way out of the forest. The reward was not her thanks but her comment as she pointed at the highway, "Now I see what you mean by sounds that are noise."

I got a flashlight out of the car and helped her put her one-ride-old bicycle on the one-day-old rack, reminding her to check on the light and learn about sunset times and things that go bonk in the night.

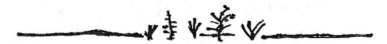

Owls in the Darkness

Laboring up a hill in the dark
of this morning's run,
few stars showing through the clouds,
motion more sensed than seen.

Owls don't make any noise,
these welcome ghosts of my predawn world,
winging silently away,
making my labor up the hill
in the darkness
easier.

An Eighty-Seven Percenter

That's what it says on the tide-table printout in the percent-of-moon-visible column. I had put off this, slid that back, missed picking up another surplus computer, and the Linux project was on hold again—hmm, why not a night run? Sure, why not, the progress seems to have ground to a halt anyway.

Clouds? There are shadows on the porch. The moon is already outlining the house—no clouds in this night's sky. From way up above, the two Dippers beckon to us again. Batteries? Nah, just grab a couple of extra lights. I'll slip 'em in the pouch. Out the door, green LEDs outline the driveway. Almost. Moon shadows are plainly visible on the ground. Light switches are twisted to "off." An eighty-seven percenter the printout read. We won't need the lights for a while, maybe not at all.

We walk up the hill and across to the paved path to the trails. Orion points at the Pleiades. Even the missing sister welcomes us as a lone owl asks who we are and where we are going. "To the kettles," we reply, "with our lights turned off so we won't disturb you." "Wo wo whooo," comes softly back in approval.

Rabbits on late-night snack patrol pause at our approach. We are too noisy to be stalking, to be dangerous. One small one, perhaps just out of the warren, waits...waits...ears extended...waits...and gone! Mom called?

Lights go on as we go down Humpty Dump. Alders, madrone, and rhodies close in on us. Headlights join the handheld lights to let me see the roots I am tripping on, again. We zig and zag onto Fern Ridge and up to High Traverse. Turning toward the bluffs we run straight toward Maia and her sisters that form the Pleiades as she shines through the trees for us—no one but us—the trails are ours. Almost. Two eyes reflect in the flashlight beams and then scurry away.

Now they look back from the forest. I point a flashlight in that direction and see a raccoon's bandit mask staring at our intrusion. The watchful eyes follow us as we get to the picnic table overlooking the bluff. Two hundred or so feet below us the tide is playing quietly, moving the scoters and buffleheads up and down as it works its way up the beach. Many of the visitors here are only pausing before flying to the Arctic regions for springtime breeding. The sense of urgency has started. Survival depends on getting there within such a small window. Where our cutoff times only mean we need to make better plans, their cutoff times mean death of a family. No T-shirts, no next time—our efforts compared to their journey are so pale. They face the ultimate DNF—no ancestors.

We look at the white patches sleeping, scattered along the water's surface, the many heads tucked into the warmth of downy wings, and turn inland. I suppose we only saw eighty-seven percent of the travelers, or did we see all of them but with only eighty-seven percent clarity? No eyes greet us as we pass the meadow on the way out. The raccoon seen on the way in is long gone on its nocturnal meandering. We head up Cedar Hollow toward the house and freshly baked banana bread at eleven o'dark in the thirteen percent darkness.

One owl whispers as we turn to the driveway, "Wo wo whooo..." Good night to you, too.

Graveyard Jazz

"Jazz from the Graveyard," the voice from KPLU informs me almost as if hearing me wonder what I am listening to at two in the morning. I am trying to decide between Herbie Hancock's *Possibilities* or Eartha Kitt's *Back in Business* when he says something about an uninterrupted hour of women singing the blues. I leave the radio on—one less decision on the list of distractions.

Lately the running has been categorized as weird running, sort of running, almost running, or just out and about on the island stuff. Yesterday afternoon after three days of thick fog, a breeze was clearing the air. I decided to run Cedar Grove, trying to get to the bluff for sunset, meditate a while on this, that, and t'other, and, finally, follow my brand-new, hasn't-been-taken-outside-yet, six-LED light 'em upper back to the car.

I sometimes wonder what sort of fool drivers think they are seeing in the trailhead parking lot, if they see me at all. I pull on the last layer—rain shell, gloves, cap—pat pockets for lights, and head off into the wind and drizzle. It is not the weather to be going away from the car in—a sensible person would be in a comfortable chair with a book. I am following the *crunch, crunch, crunch* of my footsteps down the gravel; winding away from the sound of cars hurrying home, I round the curve and their lights go away. The dusk of evening thickens as memory takes me down Humpty Dump to Alder Grove and up to Escape. Cold water droplets form into cascades from the brushed limbs. The gravel road is left behind, and the leaves of a thousand trees hide all sound—footsteps' echoes are gone, breathing and heartbeats become the only noise. Their rhythm joins my legs as I turn up onto Cedar Grove.

In *Last Child in the Woods* we are told the current generation is not going out in the woods enough, is not leaving the protective supervision of playgrounds in subdivisions, is losing the imagination nature wants us to develop. I am from two generations back. There are days when I feel I do not go out enough, days when I should stay out longer, but I seldom miss a day. These are my woods most of the time, the place my imagination plays. I am but an old child wandering along, unsupervised.

I pass the Old Men of Cedar Grove; fog shrouded, cedar boughs bent and dripping brush my shoulder as I start the drop into the kettle and the darkening trail. There have been no shadows. It is too cloudy for sunset, and dropping down the side of the kettle the challenge that has been whispering comes forth loudly: You can get to the bluff without turning on your light if you hurry.

Hurry? Well, at least shuffle faster. Okay. An old thought comes back as I go up the switchbacks. On how many trails do I know the exact number of switchbacks they each have—Dimple, Mount Erie, Stick in the Eye, Butterfield, this one, and that one across the water—water? The clouds have lifted enough to see the Olympic Mountains over on the peninsula. One last ray of setting sun fights for its glory, failing and becoming a waning sunbeam it becomes a waning sunbeam as I come up out of the kettle above the Strait of Juan de Fuca.

I sit on a knotted root of a many-years-old Alaskan Cedar scanning the waters, looking at mountains silhouetted across the sound. As I glance down toward the water, a patch of white moves, then another—two adult bald eagles are perched on the remnants of a tree, enjoying sunset from just above the beach. Maybe the huge nest up on Cedar Grove that was empty last year will have a family this year. I leave in the gathering darkness, right, left, past the fallen one, right, and around to the top. No lights yet.

The games we play when out here. Can I make it to Grancy's Run without turning on my brand-new flashlight? The bluff is left behind, the sun's last ray snuffed as I cheat and turn downward to the quarter mile of pavement on the park road, thereby avoiding the roots and turns on the trail to the same junction, then left toward the gate that marks the start of Grancy's Run. Another owl's *hoo hoo huaoo* greets me as I quicken the stride. I can see the gate that marks the beginning of Grancy's Run. It is one of many gates and benches made by my hands scattered throughout this park. They are not fancy, in fact, they are basic products of labor; they gave so much more satisfaction in their construction than ever did the programs written on computer screens at other times. I slip by the gate and start up the alley of darkness. It is a mile and a tenth to the car. My mind enjoys a seldom-felt challenge. My eyes see rather than search for the trail. It's only dark for another quarter mile, and then the whiteness of the old gravel road will be visible. I slip the unused light back into its scabbard.

The dirt trail of Grancy's Run is behind me. Now I am listening to gravel crunching beneath my feet as I follow the almost ghostly ribbon of white through the alleys of ocean spray, cedars, and alders. At the crest of the last hill, the lights of cars on the highway tell me another night run is over. The sounds of my last few steps are drowned by the hiss and whine of tires on wet asphalt. I pause at the last turn to look back—some nights I feel like I have left something out there, never quite feeling what it is or if leaving it was intentional. Tomorrow is another day, and I will go back to make sure it is still there.

CHAPTER ELEVEN

Patience? Patience be damned, I'm going out fast.

Strange, it didn't look this steep on the Web profile.

Have you run this before?
Yes.
Where are we headed?
See that fifth ridge out there?
Yes.
Through that gun sight and look for a tent in the valley.
Okay. Can we make it by dark?
I don't think so.

Pain: *n.* hurt, ache, distress, torment, agony, tribu-
lation, discomposure, thorn in one's side, childbirth,
travail, bale, unhappiness, nuisance, pique, vexation,
gall, cross, desolation, twinge, discomfort...

If I Can Just Get Out the Door
(Postinterview Meanderings)

Time-lines and Gantt charts, functional, needs, and gap analysis with a little bit of strategic goal setting thrown in; harried looks on tense faces and cell phones in every driver's ear and three hours on a rain-swept highway to the ferry where the mind's slowing down could finally start. The fragmented day was ending by finding time to reassemble itself in the thinning traffic as I get farther onto the island.

Trails—the weather was clear enough this morning that I could see Mount Rainier's snowy shoulders through the windows as I did this chart and that and ("trails" something whispered from the window) mentioned process, root-cause analysis, and functional analysis, and... yes, thank you, and good-bye and... which route home? Up Hood Canal on the slow, winding road or up I-5 in a hurry to the house and to the trails... I-5 and cell phones and...

An anonymous author somewhere gave credit to the "miracle of e-mail." I decided if e-mail is a miracle, then so are the 1.3 billion coffee stands alongside our roads in the Pacific Northwest—one 16-ounce double-shot, a ferry ride, and a short drive, and I am home.

Out the door? No! Discipline, what little there is left of it, says unpack, put things away almost orderly, check this and check that, close enough...just four miles, just a little loop in the dark and the wind of Ebey's Prairie. A surprised bike rider and I both think we are alone, so we have our lights turned off, and laughingly say "Sorry" as we sense something and hit the switches in time to swerve, miss each other, and then vanish back inside the cocoon of the dark.

My old yellow Windbreaker is way past old, but it fits so well and the "wind to your back" corner is coming up. The corner is turned—ahhh, suddenly it feels 23.7 degrees warmer, shoulders un-scrunch, neck relaxes, rhythm of stride is regained.

Fortissimo! Fortissimo! A hundred miles of Puget Sound wind play bass on the bare limbs of a gnarled and previously useless apple tree. Frozen at the suddenness of the string group's appearance, I stand there. The wind dances, and the mid wires become cellos and viols, the high wires are the violins, and no one hears but me, and I have no cell phone to hold up so someone else can hear.

I bow to tonight's conductors, the waters and the wind, and head up the hill to the cemetery. I pass the tombstone: 1832–1896 he lived, in the Ohio Infantry Volunteers and Illinois Infantry Volunteers he served. I sometimes wonder if, in that war that so wracked our nation, he ever stood on his line and looked across and saw the eyes of some of my kin. He never tells.

The flag at the top of the hill is straight out, obeying the wind, and bathed in light. Its red, white, and blue rippling and snapping in the wind. Memories from the headstones dance and flicker on every run as I pass by. Ghosts come calling, but still not answering for one more night as I turn and run on back into the darkness.

Down the switchbacks, wondering if the eagle that watched me on Monday is up there. The trail is just white enough I don't need the light, but if I turn on the light I can look up in the tree. I run on down the white-graveled trail and turn by the Doug fir someone broke the top off of many years ago. Scarred now, broken, it still hurls cones at me when I don't watch, but not tonight.

The trails are done and pavement returns. Cars pass in another world only a few feet away on the other side of the fog line. People with cell phones, ever disconnected from their travel, search for another acorn. I turn to go down the dark driveway to the house—empty and dark earlier—much lighter now.

I got out.

The Interview That Wasn't
(No One Can Run That Far)

Running ultramarathons is not generally done for fame, fortune, or wealth. The monetary rewards I have accrued during my racing events have consisted of a $25 gift certificate to an ice cream parlor in Placerville, California; a free latté and sandwich in Coos Bay, Oregon; a $5 gift certificate to a local yoghurt spot in some soon-forgotten coastal town; a $50 gift certificate to an outdoor outfitters store in Bremerton, Washington, that was won so long ago that the $50 fully paid for a pair of shoes; and a pair of shoes long gone the way of all running shoes. As my evolution from racing to running continued, I slowly faced the sad realization that running ultramarathons would not make me financially independent.

The fickleness of fame seemed to overshadow my efforts at national headlines, regional telecasts, and even a chance inclusion in the local newspaper. Several top-ten finishes went unheralded in the local media. An age-group (43–45 right-handed with brown hair) record was unnoticed outside the city limits of Siletz, Oregon (population 997). An apparent world record was invalidated by an uncaring and insensitive bureaucracy when the documentation packet, which included the verification, certification, substantiation, and a filled-in rebate coupon, was lost, stolen, or slain. I was just about to give up on ever gaining my proper recognition. Automatic door openers no longer recognized me—the greeter at WalMarché barely nodded—was it all for naught?

The last chance at fame *and* fortune started with the dramatic, though not witnessed, act of my taking the lead in a 100k run on the eastern slopes of the Cascade Mountains in Washington State. Running side-by-side, Lary Webster and Ike Hessler had led through the early miles. I was trying to stay inside my head and not pay any attention to them. I rounded a curve, and the long descent into the valley started. I could just see Lary and Ike disappearing at the end of the straightaway way down the hill out in front of me. They were there only long enough for me to know they were still out there, and then they would round a curve and be out of my sight. I would be alone again.

The advantage of mass slowly crept into the equation. I am big. Lary is not. Ike is not. Gathering no moss but lots of momentum, I gently shoved Ike off into the sagebrush as I passed him at around 85k, and on down the hills into the valley I went. I caught Lary as we entered the edge of town, two miles to go. Victory was mine, but the postrace giddiness was interrupted by an interview for the local television station. Fame was assured. Surely fortune would not be far behind. At the awards ceremony the race director asked for someone to come up and draw from the bowl. The 100k was not the only event. There was also a 50k, a 25k, and a 10k. The drawing was to decide which event would be used to determine the cash awards (in addition to trophies). Aha! Fate would come calling in the form of a 12-year-old girl who would reach into the jar. Dame Fortune was about to answer my call, or so I thought. Sure enough, she pulled out the scrap of paper with "100k" written thereon. First a television interview, then a trunk filled with worldly goods awaited.

What was this? The race director now asked the young lady to do the same sort of drawing from a newly produced jar—an ugly jar ripe with foreboding, evil misfortune emanating from its translucent sides. The jar contained the names of all the 100k runners. The runner whose name was drawn would receive a one hundred dollar bill. *Ulp.* It wasn't even restricted to the top three finishers. It could go to anyone. No, noooo. My whole life flashed before my eyes as the maiden reached into the abyss—okay, maybe it was just a passing thought of an afternoon from June of 1966, but it was an ill wind that stirred the numbers in the cauldron. She withdrew her hand, which was no longer covered in soft white skin, but now was darkened with age, wrinkled from succumbing to the evils of the glass container. She handed the slip of charred parchment to the race director. Even as he handled it ever so carefully there were blackened fragments falling from the edges, carried away by some misplaced mistral; would he be able to read the name before all was borne away—carried on the cackle of laughter that only I seemed to hear? He looked down at the paper and whispered,

"Lary Webster."

The fortune mythically amassed through the realness of night was gone. Ah well, there's always the television interview—fame will outlast fortune, eh? We slept through the afternoon news. Sunday morning found us on the road back to Olympia with nary a glance at the television as we checked the room before leaving. The stop at the Cle Elum Bakery for torcettis, an Italian pastry that would stave off hunger most of the way home, brightened the day.

As always we unpacked the car in a ritual of putting things where they go, spreading out tent and sleeping bags so they could air out, then changing to running clothes and heading for a loosen-up-from-the-trip five-miler around the lake. We said hi to this person and that person as we shuffled around the lake. It was November, and the lake had many duck-like birds to distract us—that and the fact that I ran a 100k the day before made for a many-stop run-shuffle-jog around the loop. About halfway, as we were watching more travelers land on the lake, someone said hi. We looked around, and it was some woman Kathy knows and a man neither of us knew. Introductions were made all around, and Dave said he had wanted to meet me. Oh? Yes. He had heard of these ultramarathon things and wanted to talk to me about them. Oh. Have you run any lately? Yes—and the story of winning the 100k evolved. He had lots of questions, finally explaining he worked on the sports desk of the local newspaper, and asked if I could call for an interview for an article. Aha! Fame reentered the picture. We agreed to talk in the morning so he could make the deadline for a local-athletes-of-interest sort of thing in each Friday edition. The fleeting, flickering flame of fame was rekindled. I slept with visions of full-page photo spreads, shoe-string endorsement contracts, and free bananas for life and dreamed of finding the correct shoes to wear for the interview.

The interview went well. Dave asked questions, so I got to talk about the world of ultramarathons without being labeled crazy, extreme, or overly weird. How long, how far, when, how often, what do we eat...an actual I-am-curious sort of interview. We parted with an assurance the interview would appear in Friday's paper.

The week dragged on and on. Friday, being totally unaware of my impatience, finally arrived. I checked the newsstand at 11:30, 12:15, 1:00, 1:20, 1:29, and, finally, at 1:33 the paper arrived. I pulled out the sports section and scanned the pages looking for... hmmm, nothing here. I went back to the front of the sports section and went through it slowly, looking at each page carefully...it was not there. I started at the front page of the newspaper. My eyes went up and down and back and forth and across and diagonally and... nothing. What had happened? I looked at the pile of quarters I had brought so I could buy copies of the newspaper to send to my adoring, even if as yet unformed, public.

I called the newspaper and asked for Dave.

"Dave, I can't find the interview. Didn't you say today, this Friday?"

"Well, yes, but..."

"But...er, but what?"

"John, my editor looked at the interview. He said no one can run that far and cut the article. Sorry."

"Oh."

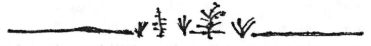

Relaxation While Running, Relaxing and Running

Wow! How did I get here? That question directed inward—I hoped it had not been uttered aloud—was both scary and rewarding. I was standing at a crosswalk. I had stopped because the light was red. That was good. My last clear thought of where I was put me about four miles back toward town along a busy, curvy road. It is a road with narrow shoulders. I had to have crossed several intersections, too. I moved back from the edge of the intersection and thought about what had just happened—something bad, not evil but bad in the sense that I had endangered both myself and my running, had taken place. I was running while angry. I still was, but now it was changing from the wrought-up mess of the workday to inner discontent with my letting the carryover take place.

I have injured myself a time or two by leaving the house for a run while some form of anger was still on the surface. The footsteps pound into the pavement as if to take retribution from the earth's surface. The real retribution comes in the form of strained or pulled muscles from going too fast when not warmed up for the run. Retribution comes in stepping on a rock and rolling an ankle—said rock being overlooked because my mind was still on a thing from several hours ago, something that should not be here with me on my run. The running should be mine. The running is for me.

I thought for a minute. Where was the nearest place I could go and not worry about traffic? Aha! Priest Point Park was about a mile back and has wide trails with remarkably few exposed roots—nice friendly trails. I crossed to the other side of the street and started running back to where I could run relaxed and under my terms.

Don't go out angry. Keep the running yours.

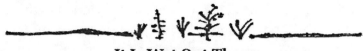

It Is Wet Out There

But, mousie, thou art not alone,
In proving foresight may be in vain,
The best laid schemes of mice and men,
Go oft astray,
And leave us nought but grief and pain,
To rend our day.

—Robert Burns, *To a Mouse*

8:02 a.m.–12:43 p.m. PST, January 10, 2009

I wasn't plowing. I was running. Three hours was planned for a sixteen-mile figure eight. I said to myself, "The rain isn't that hard," as I left the car. Three miles in was the first fallen tree; a mere side trip of forty or fifty yards through the bushes and briars and brambles and I was zooming down the trail again. No mud was seen as I rounded Little Cranberry Lake, but on the 128 I found the second fallen tree and friends. Three of them, each about two feet in diameter, lay across the trail. Their falling had left a huge hole in the trail. A hole now filled with water.

I picked up a limb and poked at the water in the hole, knee deep and soft. Salal and rhodies formed a solid wall on both sides of the trail—I pushed off, grabbed a nearby branch, pulled, leaped, slipped, and fell into the ooze. I not-so-quickly returned to the trail, clearly an early entrant and odds-on favorite in the "mud ball of the month" contest.

I ran up 109, past a pond with no name, and around and down 129 to the bridge at the upper end of Little Beaver Pond (maybe the pond with no name is Red Ryder Pond?). Strange, I know there was a bridge here last summer. I know there was because I met Kathy coming from the other way. Some of the posts were still there. Okay, I was at a decision point, about halfway around, twenty feet of still water in front of me, fallen trees not too far behind—I stepped into the water. It did not resist...in fact it welcomed me by letting me sink almost waist deep. Oops.

I grabbed an old bridge post, one, then another, found a root to stand on, reached another post, thought about how good the cold water felt on an aching knee...oh God, please don't let the shoe-sucking monster show up. One more post and the water was only a little over ankle deep. I was out, damp, kinda muddy, and looking at the water bottle out there by the third post. I felt for the other one...Aha! The one that fell out was the empty one. Two chocolate chip cookies, one gulp of water, and off I went, empty water bottle abandoned. I was halfway around.

The mile-and-a-half-long trail to the unnamed viewpoint has a creek running down the middle of it. I told myself to send an e-mail to the trail designer to emphasize that dual use of trails as drainage structures is not appreciated. Once on top I could see several hundred feet in all directions as the rain was getting heavier and the clouds were dropping lower with the weight of the water they carried. I left the unnamed—and not-really-a-viewpoint—viewpoint and started down the mile or so of switchbacks to Mitten Pond where I...hmmm, more trees stacked in a somewhat disorganized manner across the trail. This might take a while. Nope. About seven steps into a cautious bushwhack, *arrggghhhh* preceded a butt slide, and I covered the 35 or 40 feet to the trail below with both speed and surprisingly creative style, and I was right side up.

Forestry Road 10 and the gradual downhill to the trailhead were a welcome sight. However, it being the kind of day it had been meant the two people I saw coming toward me a few hundred yards later would greet me with "The low-water bridge is gone." I turned and headed back around to the 124 and the 113 and some other trail number that I no longer recall. All I recall is that it meant my three-hour run slowly became an almost five-hour, but I got 17 miles instead of 16, I think.

It's January and it is wet up here in the Pacific Northwest.

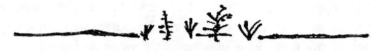

Brown Shoes, Black Shoes

There are these two old men that I see wandering here and there, never quite entering my running environment for some reason. I have seen them when I am pedaling to the store, driving to the post office, or from a bus but have never encountered them while on foot. When I first saw them their number was three. Time being what it is, their age being what it appeared to be, a reduction in numbers was not unexpected, but I watched more closely during their next few appearances—yes, three have become two.

Of the two that are left, having no names to put with them, I know one always has on black shoes, brown corduroy pants, green flannel shirt, khaki jacket, and a herringbone hat with a blue ribbon that almost matches blue eyes that are undimmed by the passing years. The other wears brown shoes, khaki pants, and shirt—creased from the years of wear and many years of ironing.

On one bike trip to the store I was close enough to see the word "Normandy" on brown shoes' baseball cap. I was flying on the downhill—too fast to stop, even though I was becoming aware of an emerging need. That word on his cap, two smiles, and a chuckle as I zoomed on by were all that managed to be recorded in the abstractions of my mental scratchboard that morning.

Yesterday as I turned up the last quarter mile of trail, I could see Kathy talking to, hmm, two old men. As I got close I could hear words, then a laugh, then black shoes pointed at me and said, "Better give the lad some room," and motioned for them to move over. Kathy laughed, and I stopped. She explained they (brown shoes and black shoes) were picking mushrooms for soup—and they were showing her which ones **not** to pick. Minutes passed, old fingers, bent from age, pointed at white mushrooms, red mushrooms—tan and black were disapproved—a good "crop" this year, black shoes said; brown shoes agreed and sliced off a piece of a red cap for Kathy.

A part of my mind was playing with faces and numbers—1944 minus 16 (some 18-year-olds had lied about those last two years just to be in uniform) would be 1928, which would make them 82 years or so old. Okay, seemed to fit.

Mutterings continued back and forth. My curiosity killing me, I finally asked brown shoes about the cap. "Were you at Normandy?" "Yes." "What outfit?" A pause, they looked at each other, then, "The 82nd." Oh. There was an aura of quiet. Me and my stupid curiosity and question asking—ratz—then Kathy said, "Sainte Mère Église?" Brown shoes looked at her, then looked at black shoes; both smiled. "Have you been there?" Kathy replied, "Yes, 2004." Black shoes looked at her, then at me. "2004, sixty years gone by. Quieter now, I suppose?" Kathy nodded. "Yes."

Four generations have come and gone since brown shoes and black shoes were born. Kathy and I have seen two more generations. Just long enough to listen to someone pass on the knowledge of which mushrooms to pick for dinner—and other things along the way.

A Day Full of Ones...

I have shelves full of books mathematical; the calculus, trigonometry, geometry, both plane and solid, number theory, and statistics books all help with the never-ending sagging-shelf study. I was thinking of them, and all their numbers, today while noting that all I could relate my run to was the recurring intrusion of "one."

I went down one trail at a time. I was of one mind to run with no particular pace or effort beneath the one sky we have. There was not even a single cloud today—one blue vastness. Starting with the always-snow-capped Mount Baker in the north, I could turn slowly to look into Glacier Peak Wilderness almost due east and then on around to the broad shoulders of the one mountain the Pacific Northwest is known for, Mount Rainier. One mountain range on the Ring of Fire here on the easterly rim of the Pacific Ocean. One peninsula, the Olympic, showed off some of its many snowy-shouldered peaks from the southwest of me.

One tree, its upper limbs bare from the years of standing in the face of onshore winds, came into view. I had seen it before, but today there was something on it, a big something. An eagle? No white feathers. Aha, one immature bald eagle. It was big. As I inched closer I silently asked for one minute more. One minute of stealth so as not to disturb...oh. It was not an immature bald eagle. It was an adult golden eagle, shoulders shining, glinting in the sun—probably flew over from Vancouver Island. One step closer. Pause. It turned its head toward me. The bird book uses "majestic" as the word to describe the golden eagle. Yes, majestic—the one word that works.

One could see royalty in those eyes.

I ran on, slowly. One glance back. One curve rounded.

One more moment on the bluffs frozen in my mind's eye.

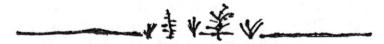

The First Tuesday of the Week
(With Apologies to Songwriters Everywhere)

It isn't even dark yet. It will be soon. Evening comes earlier as we get deeper into fall. I had stopped writing, meaning to be out the door and gone to the trails for an hour or two. But I was sidetracked, again, busy going through CDs, cassettes, and even albums, trying to find out how many versions of "Time After Time" are around the house—how many artists have covered it? If you hear it by Willie Nelson about twenty minutes after hearing it by Etta James, things like that bother you—well, okay, not you, just me.

Willie, Tony Bennett, Etta, Ella, even Cyndi Lauper...was this what Mssrs. Cahn and Styne intended?

It is still not dark yet. It is 4:41 in the evening as I turn into the wind and down the hill toward the prairie. I promised to get the running back to where it resembled running. But that was last year. Time after time I, oops...probably just violated a copyright somewhere, headed out the door full of disciplined thoughts and visions of this workout or that, but there were distractions. The lack of discipline opens doors for distractions or wandering or memories of a request for help one weekend a few months back.

Saturday as we came off the trail, Aaron the park ranger was driving by. He pulled over to ask if we had been on the bluff down by the big kettle. No, we had been over in Kyle's Kettles—a series of smaller glacier dripping stops. Oh. There's a big fir tree down, completely blocking the trail. Can you help tomorrow morning? Sure.

The next morning we arrived with chainsaw and axe. Oh. It was one of my "old men." It was over four feet in diameter, perhaps a hundred and fifty feet tall, a wind fighter of how many years before the onslaught of those gusts of ninety miles an hour last week. Limbs over fifteen inches in diameter, now splintered, now cut and pulled aside. I leaned on the saw and cut from this side, climbed over and cut from that side. Finally the first segment, a bark-rimmed wheel, fell out. We rolled it aside and laid it over. Years and years of growth rings stared up at us. Aaron started counting rings from the middle as my finger marked and counted from the bark. Wars and celebrations go by; victories and defeats, kings are crowned, overthrown, and nations are born; our fingers moved toward each other—touched—how many?

"168."

"134."

Three hundred and two years.

We cut the thigh-sized limbs, pulled them aside, cut more wheels, looked at the rings; thin ones, thick ones, volcanic eruptions, earthquakes, and fires, all hidden from our ears. After almost three hours of falsely quieted, almost morose cutting and dragging, the trail was clear. We looked at the hole in the canopy where the "old man" had stood; the wind had given back to the sky what the tree had worked those hundreds of years to claim—a false ownership. A golden eagle perched way high in its limbs had tolerated my passing and pausing one day.

We gathered tools to leave. Neither of us thought, "There are plenty of trees in the park," not the old ones anyway. We can't plant three-hundred-year-old trees. I thought about how many hikers would pass, and maybe pause to look at the rings, see the years gone by, and marvel at this fallen giant that now straddles the trail it once cast shadows on.

That was the last Saturday of last year. This is the first Tuesday of this week. I'll run the prairie, where no trees can fall to distract me. There is still the echo from years ago when someone told me I needed to take running more seriously to enjoy it. I'll run the prairie. There's nothing there but some power lines hanging from some poles. I have never wondered how old a power pole is.

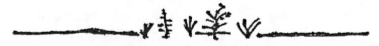

Fog Running and the Bluff

The daylight equivalent of running in the small circle of light from a flashlight beam on a trail at night would be the running in the fog I did this morning. I had looked out at Penn Cove as I gave my usual vague thought to which direction to go. The water of the cove was almost glassy from the calm air and slack tide, but the sound of traffic almost always sends me up the driveway to cross the prairie and head for the beach, bluff, or forest full of kettles. The anorak, grabbed from the nail on the garage wall at the last minute, was tied around my waist. One layer warm was always better than wishing for one more layer when a chill came calling.

At the top of the driveway, looking easterly I could see the outline of the Glacier Peak Wilderness area sixty miles away, deep in the North Cascades. This is the first visibility checkpoint—always falsely encouraging, since looking at it means I am looking away from where most of our weather comes from, but the last glow from sunrise pulled the eyes there first, and, besides, I could barely see the tops of the mountains through the trees to the southwest. The clearness of the air teased me with the thought I would be able to see from Mount Baker up near the US-Canada border down to Mount Rainier—150 miles of mountain peaks—so I turned down toward the prairie to find out. A run across the prairie, along the bluff, down the zigzags to the beach, then northwesterly along Admiralty Inlet to the next decision point entered my mind.

The hardest part of a sunrise run is to wait to look until the right time. I had already seen the hint of fire on the eastern horizon. I kept my eyes on the ground, somewhat, to the right, somewhat, and carefully avoided looking to the north for the first few minutes until I could turn up the hill into Sunnyside Cemetery. The line of pines along the cemetery's edge hides the view to the north. I could look around now. The view up the hill in the cemetery seldom changes. There are three headstones that always cause me to turn my head as I pass through. Two of them drew a quiet "good morning" and one only a glance because there was no newly disturbed soil. The recently mown grass glistened, waiting.

The end of the cemetery road and the start of the trail alongside the barley and alfalfa fields of the prairie marked the end of the don't-look-up game. To the north, about 60 miles away, was Mount

Baker, straight east into the sun was the Glacier Peak Wilderness, and southeast of me lay Mount Rainier and its snows that never go away. I suppose a person should get used to the view, get to where they can pass this way on a clear dawn morning and not need to stop, but I also suppose I will win the lottery. I put off going to buy a ticket by turning to go down the trail. To the southwest there was a strange landscape unfolding. A string of islands stood where none should be. They weren't real islands. Without breaking stride I noted that it was the mountains of the Olympic Peninsula sticking up above the fog. I had been paying attention to the sunrise view and had not noticed the fog. When we first moved here the tides and fogs sent me to books and Web sites. The tides were simple enough, put the moon here, the sun there, and the water goes somewhere else then comes back; sometimes a lot, sometimes not so much. I can go to any of several Web sites and get charts that tell me just what time and by how much the water will change—not so with the fog.

Fog, like the wind, comes in a variety of, of...hmmm, shapes? Thicknesses? It even comes in colors, sort of. We get radiation, advection, and upslope fogs, sometimes all three within just a few hours as the sun, cold water of the sound, and even the variations of temperature of the prairie (different crops and planted or not) play their little games with the air. Thin wisps of whiteness filled the lower part of Ebey's Landing; some were placed like swirls of icing on the chocolate of the prairie's topsoil. The water was hidden, veiled in a fog that muffles and hides. The mountain islands across the strait had disappeared, but I could see the Cascades sixty miles away. The fence alongside the trail vanished beyond the eighth post. At the bluff I turned up and listened to sand beneath my shoes. Was that sound always there? Okay, I am old, ugly, and out of shape, but surely that gasping sound was not me, was it? Up top, recovered and running along the bluff, for the first time I thought of night running with no flashlight. It wasn't darkness, just the restriction from a sense of a decreased environment. I could see about thirty feet.

I could feel the tension in my shoulders and the heightened sensitivity of each foot plant—should be fun going down the zigzags to water's edge.

Now what? The fog was all gone. Weird? There is a couple hundred feet of the bluff trail that is forty to fifty feet higher than the rest of the trail, and it was above the fog. The fog behind me was white, in front of me was gray—warmer air over colder water? The trail descended into the fog, and I headed down the zigzags to the beach. I might as well have been running in the shower—I was soaked by the fog and tense from being back inside this small circle of sight. I finally remembered I had a jacket tied around my waist and stopped at the bottom to slip it on and then turned to follow the curve of the shore around to Admiralty Point. I suppose that, like whoever is in charge of sunsets and thunderstorms, whoever is in charge of fog has a sense of irony and humor, because just after putting on the jacket and getting warm, I ran out of the fog. I ran out of it so abruptly that I stopped and turned. Yes. It was still there. A wave sent rocks rattling along as if the fog's laughter was rasping out a good-bye.

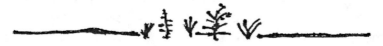

Patience Through Geography

The house of mirrors in my memory is playfully distorting the blackboard in my mind. The long and easy stride that was used to eat up hours and miles for so many years now seems strangely awkward. Each step has that clumsiness you feel when your foot touches the ground about an inch higher than the mind told you it would. You don't fall, but the next step is already off balance. The rhythmical breathing once used to bring the body into a synchronized movement is a loud series of grunts, gasps, and groans that brings confusion, embarrassment, and even pauses to try to start over. "Get it started right this time," an inner voice says. "I just can't have forgotten it all," echoes another.

I tried to run on a recently thawed trail only to discover my weakened ankles made running in the stiff prairie grass a foolish endeavor. Face-plants into the snow are refreshing but hardly my intention. Could these be the ankles that had kept me upright and balanced as I made my way up and down trails in the many mountains along the years? I turned back and ran along the forest road, soon discovering that although I could still judge the distance to some distant tree, rock, or slow-moving cow, I could no longer instinctively follow the running line, the imaginary dotted line our mind creates that guides us to sure footing. Running was a series of mixed strides, jogs, shuffles, stutter steps, even hops and skips—with nothing to cast the blame on. No crutches seemed ready to hold me while I worked my way through my befuddlement as I walked back to the car. What next?

A few days later I pedaled out to the trails behind the Turtle Mountain Community College campus. The twenty minutes on the bike would loosen up the legs, warm up the muscles and have them ready for running—not a cold start like getting out of the car and starting down some overgrown, grassy prairie mooseway. Yeah. Right. Sure. The two hills on the way to campus became mountains that found me in the lowest gear, barely making way fast enough to keep my balance—steerage is what boat people call it. I was barely going fast enough to steer on a hill that would not be called a hill if I took it back to Washington with me. Okay, I'm over the hill and at the trailhead. I'm here. I'm...uh, I'm sitting here recovering from pedaling out here so I can run? This return to fitness is going to take a while. I will need a plan.

And so goes this return to running fitness. As with all grand schemes, allowances for life's little intrusions (can't run that many minutes yet—20 didn't seem like all that big a number when I wrote it down for Tuesday) are made and adjustments for current conditions (doing intervals using fence posts instead of power poles) carefully allowed. Hills that were laughed at last fall are now used as baselines for repeats—triumph coming last week when the fifth repeat did not require external exhortations of gods not called upon for years. The clash between memory and mind still comes forth quickly. In the olden days a few deep breaths ("Try belly breathing," says the memory monster) and the stride would lengthen, muscles would relax while in full flight, shoulders would pull back, and newly found strength would come forth. Now, a few weeks into this house of mirrors (or house of cards, never quite sure what I am playing with here) and I find an annoyingly high amount of attention must be paid just to get the breathing working in a pattern that doesn't distract from the other thing I am doing, running.

The memory of what I could once do intrudes on the restraint I must show if I am going to progress without injury to do it again. Progress is not going to come in leaps and bounds, maybe not even in hops and steps. Progress will only come with patience; reclaiming patience will be just as crucial to my relearning speed as it is to regaining endurance. Patience is a learned virtue (if a virtue at all) that will keep my memory from gaining control and vainly trying to leap from week five to week nine. I have time. I have time to slowly assemble all the bits and pieces that winter tore apart. Spring has started the rebuilding that some yet-to-be-chosen run this summer will need. Time will be the bridge between was and is, then melds them into "will be."

The hardest decision was stepping off the porch a few weeks back when I had penciled in "3 hours." The first three-hour of this year—I could do that. The route was simple enough. I would use one of the 4-mile blocks that are the rule around here, big blocks that surround wheat fields. I can do this, I repeated. The trepidation was the same I had felt that long-ago first time I had written "3 hours" as a goal. At my speed I'd be out there long enough to either learn one type of wheat from another as it matured during my passing or, the worst-case scenario, I'd still be there when harvest time arrived—surely on the second lap by then. I could do this, but alone?

Company arrived in the form of two kids on bicycles that recognized me from St. Ann's School. Hi, Mr. Morelock, where ya goin'? Around the block. Can we go with you? Go ask your mom. In just a few minutes they were back. Mom said to ask you if you can help us with our geography test, and if you said yes, we can go with you. Oh. Sure. In the same way we sometimes try to find a song that will play over and over as the steps cover first one trail and then another, I had found the mind game I needed. Geography? I could do that. Lap one was about finding the Americas (always a good topic with Native American children), then trying to explain why Constantinople isn't—surprisingly, singing my rendition of The Four Lads song didn't seem to help—but we rounded the corner, and suddenly we were into a discussion of the lunch meat one. Huh? The lunch meat town, Timmy said and laughed. Lunch meat town. Geography. Travis said, yeah, haven't you ever had a bologna sandwich? There's a town in Italy named after a sandwich. Oh. And some sort of relaxation took over. It wasn't about speed or intervals. It was about two young Turtle Mountain Chippewa boys studying geography in the wheat fields as the afternoon passed.

While Waiting to Heal

It has now been six weeks since I last tried to run down a trail or up a trail. I did run, sort of, across a trail. I even paused in the middle and looked at it in both directions just to be sure I could still recognize a trail when I returned to run one again. One more week, I said. I'll give it one more week of rest and then try to escape the smoothness of asphalt, concrete, and rubberized track surfaces again.

The process of leaving trails behind was a two-step sequence. Step one was on a day when we were about four hours into a six-hour driving day. As we were passing through a small town somewhere in southern Iowa, I noticed the local high school track next to the road. Let's get out and do a few laps just to stretch our legs. Sure. Why not? Other times and other places I would have walked a lap, maybe two, before starting to run. That was not to be today. It was hot, well above ninety degrees—why waste time warming up?

Halfway through the third lap a twinge started in my right leg. Fortunately, I am incredibly tough and continued to run. In the middle of the sixth lap, the left leg decided to commiserate with the right leg. The good thing about this was that I was upright, fully vertical again, no longer needing to lean to one side to compensate for an uncooperative leg. A secondary internal conversation continued regarding how well I was running for having been sitting for so long. With about two hundred yards to go for the completion of the intended two miles, I apparently kicked an unseen ice pick, which, upon being kicked, promptly embedded itself in my left calf (see note about lap six). I slowed, walked a cool-down lap or two, and we returned to the highway. Two hours later in the campground for the night, memory being what it is, I could not understand why it was so difficult to get out of the car. So, I stood in the creek, enjoying the cold-water massage for a while.

A few days later, step two was set in motion by a small snake happily living in Bemidji, Minnesota, probably with no harmful intentions in its heart. It put in its appearance just before my right foot left the ground, just at that moment when you can still change from run to jump, leap, or fly—in this case it was mostly a jump because a snake had just slithered out of the grass onto the trail and neither of us wanted anything to do with the other. The jump, which I thought quite creative, only earned a 7.36 for the landing because either the snake had sunk its fangs into my calf or I had stumbled on another ice pick. Seeing the snake's tail disappear into the trailside grasses,

I looked to see where the ice pick was protruding. Hours later, when I had hobbled back into camp, Kathy was impressed at both my description of the snake, apparently the largest of its species ever seen in Minnesota, and my ability to remain calm enough to jump over it. She listened while fixing an ice pack.

Having successfully completed the two-step sequence needed to injure myself, I entered that wonderful realm we all hold so near and dear to our hearts: needing to stay off trails and, oh, by the way, no running for a—hmmm, just how long is one of these 'whiles' people talk about?

After inguinal hernia repair a few years ago, it took almost three months to feel like I was at full strength again. After an appendectomy, it was only a few days before all seemed right with the world again. But these pesky muscle and joint things tend to drive us crazy. The twists and sprains and strains and pulls never seem to get the attention they deserve until we stab ourselves with an ice pick. To ultramarathon runners, the DNF (did not finish) remains overwhelmingly preferable to the DNS (did not start).

The healing powers of a starting line, whether in Havre de Grace, Pinckney, or Okeechobee, are well known. Folks at Burrells Ford have been known to forsake elastic bandages they have worn, maybe even slept in, for weeks. One runner in Pittsfield was said to have—well, let's just say that legends are born as the dead and dying approach the starting line—limps and lumps fully masked for the day. The flesh wounds of the Black Knight are mere scratches for the entrant from Saskatoon. When a question about "do I need to rest, or can I run through a..." is raised, it is quickly dispatched with the barest of shrugs. Nothing can stop our ascent to superpersondom. Can it?

Resting is hard. Resting and recuperating are very hard. Resting, recuperating, and rehabilitating approach "cleaning the stables" hard. Just about the time you accept that rest is needed, that maybe you have worn yourself out and all those little aches and pains are real injuries, not just points of discomfort but injuries on the verge of those ice picks in muscles you hadn't felt in years, you find an article about active rest. Aha!

If I stay on the gentle trails, I'll be okay. If I walk for a ways and then ease into a shuffle for just a few steps, I'll be okay. If I wasn't aware that this is the weekend that I am supposed to be miles away, eating breakfast with old friends, maybe making a new friend or two, maybe rest and recuperation would be easier. The various e-portals to all sorts of running don't help. I can go in the next room, open the browser, and see what weather I would have been in, watch the progression of drops and finishers from almost any place in the world, and wonder where I might be on that trail had I been uninjured. I can look at the finishing times of a race I should have been running in and just know that I would have been ahead of him, maybe even her—carefully ignoring the mud and cold Mother Nature might be tossing their way.

Twice, once six weeks ago and once eight weeks ago, I turned from the paved bike path to the trail through the aspens. Twice, I was stopped before the ice pick returned. Once by a young porcupine whose only concern was eating—perhaps it did wonder what I was doing on its trail or why I was just standing there watching. The other time I stopped for a gathering of wood ducks in a lake alongside the trail—beautiful patterns of green, black, red, yellow, copper, and brown. I had never before seen more than three at one time. That day there were more than a dozen. I slowed to a walk, running forgotten for a while, nature's beauty to be watched for a while.

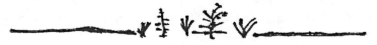

You Got Lost Again, Didn't You?

No. I wasn't lost. I just didn't come out where I thought I would.

Sometimes our best intentions go astray. Not-quite-idle curiosity can alter the day's plans, especially if you are on "home turf"—that area that you know like the back of your hand, that area where you don't carry maps because you know every trail out there. Well, almost every trail.

We were running the Mima-Porter Trail from Fall Creek Campground down to Porter Creek Campground, and then we were going to run back up on Mount Molly-Porter Trail and finish on the Green Line back down to Fall Creek. We knew these trails: old friends. As we passed one junction, I remembered I was going to try a new route. "I'm sure I can go up this road and then connect across to you. Leave some sort of marker if you get to Mount Molly Trail first," I muttered to Kathy, and off I went. I recalled that on the map, indelibly laid out on a page in my brain, there was about 175 feet of climb across the hillside and about a half mile on what I thought would be a deserted logging-railroad bed.

My visualized long-abandoned railroad bed soon became a single-track trail with not much sign of use. The single-track trail quickly became a game trail, still with not much sign of use. Then it became a place to bushwhack from, through, to—did not matter to me anymore. Bushwhacking is bushwhacking. That point where it will take just as long to go back as to continue forward had been reached, and decisions after that seem moot.

There appeared to be at least one missing contour line on the map in my head, because I had dropped to a creek (also not shown) and now was going up the other side, having for some reason decided to cross it. I paused. The underbrush was thick, and my legs (summer and just wearing shorts) were already a mess of welts and scratches. I began to eye the flora-less water, looking at how clear of brush it was if I stayed in the creek. I was already wet. Why not? It went in the right direction, sort of, didn't it?

A *short* time later I came out on a road. Progress, right? But what road? If it's the C4100, I turn left. If it's the B1000, I turn right.

But it couldn't be the B1000, because I hadn't crossed a trail yet, and the trail Kathy was running was between me and the B1000. I turned left. At least I could make better time on the road. Thoughts started forming in my mind as I ran. We drive out here so we can run. We park in only three or four places, and then we run. Maybe we don't know the area as well as we think. We know the trails but not the roads. Maybe it isn't impossible to get lost. Several times I went over to look down the hillside for a trail. I thought, surely I'll see a familiar single-track winding through the trees. Right after looking again, I rounded a curve and the road ended. Oops. Should I admit that I'm lost yet, I wondered? Nope, because now I could see a familiar power line...which I wished was not in front of me. Well darn, I'd turned left when I should have turned right. I turned around and started running again, a slight sense of urgency in my legs. I passed where I had come out of the brush (the small cairn I built was still there).

Aha! A trail-crossing sign was just ahead. I was good. Things were under control now. I was at, uh...Green Line #6? Hmm, not as good as I had hoped. I took what comfort there was in knowing I was about two miles from where I thought I was an hour or so ago and kept running. I could use the forestry road to make up time, because this road paralleled the trail (no, I don't recall saying something like that earlier).

About four miles later, I paused as I got to where I could turn onto Green Line and head down to Fall Creek, where we had started. I now knew where I was but had no idea where she was. We had been separated a little over two hours. I was about six hours into our four-hour run. Where was she? I finally noticed the neat little arrow made of rocks on the ground, with another one made of sticks about ten feet down the trail. I assured myself it only took a few seconds for me to notice the arrows. Off I went down Green Line. It was all downhill to Fall Creek. I thought I should be able to catch her. Various stories to explain my delay were taking shape in the misty regions of my mind—alien abduction attempts, kidnappings thwarted, discovering Amelia Earhart's plane—each sounding surprisingly plausible.

Just as I was negotiating the last of the upper switchbacks, I met three mountain bikers coming up. I stopped to let them by, but they paused. The front one said, you must be John. I nodded yes. We met your wife just crossing C-Line. She mentioned you were probably up here—something about trying to find a way across South Porter Creek. (South Porter Creek? Is that where I was?) Yes. That's what I did, not a good trail though, not for bikes anyway. Thanks. She was at C-Line? Almost, maybe a hundred yards uphill. A small inner voice said, you can still catch her. Okay, bye, thanks.

There are times when our feet take wing, trails are dry, and footing is sure; the eye-foot coordination is so smooth you are sure a legend is being born as the trees become blurs on either side of the trail. On other days there are people on horses, people with dogs on leashes, people with little people on leashes—doesn't anyone stay home and watch television anymore? Okay, I was really glad they were out there, but I was rapidly running out of time and trail in my mad pursuit. Each time someone asked me how far it was to such and such, to the top, to "a good turnaround place," I paused to reply. After all, these people, these total strangers, had immediately recognized in me a person obviously knowledgeable of the area. The least I could do was help—and three of them had said the woman in the yellow shirt and blue shorts was just a little ways on down the trail.

I crossed the D3340 road. My dead quads welcomed the wide dirt trail and the gentle slope down to the campground. I was running out of bends in the trail. I made the last turn, expecting to see Kathy at the car, but she wasn't. Aha? Yes! I did it. I slowed to a walk, feeling the energy drain away, but I had done it. I'll just...

Hi, you want a sandwich? What? Where? Oh nooo. Kathy has the picnic stuff all spread out over there on a table, even has a sandwich made. How long have you been here? I don't know, seems like quite a while. Those people said you were just in front of me. Oh. I asked them to do that, but I wasn't sure they would. They did.

You got lost again, didn't you?

CHAPTER TWELVE

On a wall of the *albergue* in Fisterra, Galicia, Spain,
October 2nd, 2004.

Wanderer, your footsteps are the road,
and nothing more;
Wanderer, there is no road,
the road is made by wandering.

By walking one makes the road,
and upon glancing behind
one sees the path
that will never be trod again.

Wanderer, there is no road—
Only wakes upon the sea.

—Antonio Machado,
"Proverbios y Cantares – XXIX"

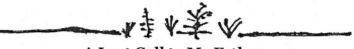

A Last Call to My Father

I almost shouted into the telephone, "Hi, Dad! I won! I won!"

My father replied, "Does that mean you were second again?"

What? Oh. No. I was first overall. I won.

Three weeks ago I had called to tell him of the course record I had set at Le Grizz. Then I had to explain how I could set a course record without winning (I was second overall but won the masters division). Rick Spady, the overall winner, was so far out in front that he probably had no idea a race was going on somewhere behind him. I, in turn, had no idea of the assault I was mounting on the masters record for Pat Caffrey's 50-mile course alongside Hungry Horse Reservoir just south of Glacier National Park in Montana. Larry Carroll and I had played cat and mouse for many miles. When I finally passed him that last time, I started running against the most challenging competitors I knew—the watch on my wrist and the unsympathetic demons in my head. It would be fun to pretend it was something romantic like the age-old "You do your best and the rest of the day will take care of itself," but it wasn't. I had simply raced my watch with little thought about how that would do in the overall standings.

I thought of that conversation and told him no. This time there was no one in front of me. I was the overall winner.

I was calling from a motel room in East Wenatchee, Washington, late Saturday afternoon. I usually waited until the trip was over and we were back home to call and tell him of the latest running trip. His interest was never at the level of excitement from years ago when I ran one lap or less—distances and events he could understand. He had never approved of this endurance stuff, these hours-and-hours-at-a-time runs—not good for your joints, he would say. Still I would call, perhaps still seeking his approval as any other aging child seeks a parent's affirming nod. These last few years we had slowly bridged the gulf created those many years ago. It might be we had both learned along the way—surely he learned more than I—how was I to know of the abilities he had seen in me, tried to coax out of me during those years when I already knew everything? Surely his inability to talk was more the problem than my inability to listen.

This time, for whatever reason, I called before we started home. The 100k had started at midnight on Halloween, October 31, 1986. There were no aid stations. Kathy was up all night, stopping every three miles to feed and water me and whoever else was near. She was mysteriously correct at judging when I would want a dry shirt, a nibble of this, a drink of that, and all the while punching all the right buttons to keep the frayed ends of my mind together through that night.

Her mastery of my mind reached the peak as I took the lead at just past sixty miles and then labored through the paranoia- and anxiety-laden last few blocks as the course returned us to town and then the final turn up the two blocks to the finish line. I had won an ultra. We sat around waiting for the other events to complete. There was a 50k, 25k, and 15k being run on the same course. The staggered starting times made for quite a mix of finishers at the end. Finally everyone was in or accounted for, then various rounds of applause for awards, "oohs" and "ahhs" and cheers and laughter, rose and fell with each announcement, then finally died as the last runner was hailed. Those of us from the 100k said good-bye or see you in a few weeks. Kathy and I headed to the motel, too worn out to consider the 150 miles back to Olympia.

The motel had an outdoor Jacuzzi—a Jacuzzi being a major selling point if we are not camping. After a shower and the requisite 47 minutes in the warm, whirling waters I decided I should call my father now instead of waiting. He should know of this one.

Hi, Dad! I won! I won!

Does that mean you were second again?

No. This time I was the overall winner.

Was this another 50-miler?

No, it was a 100 kilometers.

A 100k, how far is that?

Uh, just over 62 miles.

And you won?

Yes.

That's a long ways to run.

Yes, my longest so far.

How long did that take?

About nine hours and fifteen minutes.

For the first time there was a conversation with all the old interest from the years of track and field—sprints, hurdles, and jumps. The years where my performances, though erratic on a grand scale and full of high potential, were more showcases of my bullheaded refusal to be coached than anything else seemed to be set aside. We talked for a few minutes, questions about the course, about the field, and so on; finally I said I needed to get some sleep before I fell asleep with the phone in my hand. His last words still echo so wonderfully clear:

Sixty-two miles; John, that's a long ways to run.

Yes, it was a long night on the mountains.

And you won.

Yes. Yes, Dad, I did.

Good, that's real good.

I didn't have to pretend I could hear the soft chuckle of approval.

Bye, talk to you next time, Dad.

Good-bye.

Ten days later when I answered the telephone it was my mother calling to tell me my father had died that evening and I needed to come home.

Over the years I have been thankful many times for that last phone call with my father. We were left with many things still needing to be said, but we had said many other things. I am more thankful for what was said than I am remorseful for not getting to what we still had left to say.

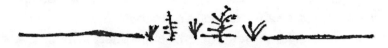

el Camino de Santiago
A Different Kind of Ultra

In 2004 we walked from Saint-Jean-Pied-de-Port, France, to Santiago de Compostela, Spain, and then on to Cabo Fisterra, meaning Land's End, as it is at the westerly tip of the Iberian Peninsula. On the afternoon of our arrival in Saint-Jean-Pied-de-Port, the starting point of our pilgrimage, I wrote a brief (for me) bit about my thoughts of getting to St. Jean. Later, after several weeks and a few hundred miles of walking, Kathy and I managed a few more thoughts about the pilgrimage. They will be the basis for a book about our wandering across northern Spain. I hope you enjoy the preview.

Getting to the Starting Line—August 15, 2004, 6:24 a.m.

60 hours ago we had departed Phoenix, Arizona. I was reading *The Basque History of the World* as we flew across the Atlantic Ocean toward Paris, France.

42 hours ago we landed at Charles de Gaulle Airport, deciphered our first French train schedules, and spent the afternoon walking around Paris.

18 hours ago we left Paris on one of the wonderful TGV trains, bound for southwest France—I was still reading my history book, Kathy, her art and religious history information book.

12 hours ago we arrived in Saint-Jean-Pied-de-Port, France, a village in the Basque region and situated at the foot of a route over the Pyrenees Mountains from France into Spain. When we arrived the traditional red bandanas and white shirts of the Basque were everywhere, brass bands played, and people danced, or those not dancing shouted encouragement and applauded in approval of the swirling, twisting dancers. We had arrived in the midst of a village holiday—obviously a holiday enjoyed by all. My history book had come to life—our reading was over.

6 hours ago the last band played one last song of farewell and the village assumed a shadowy darkness and a quietness that left us staring at the ceiling of our *refugio* awaiting sleep. Yet sleep refused to come because our thoughts were on our departure.

1 hour ago we awoke in the darkness of our room and started getting ready for the first day of our pilgrimage—our walk out of France into and across northern Spain. We were going to walk *el Camino de Santiago* (The Way of Saint James).

1 minute ago we left our brief night of comfort and looked at the first of many old Roman arch bridges we were to cross. We hugged, sighed, smiled, and crossed the river Nive and headed up and out of Saint-Jean-Pied-de-Port toward Santiago de Compostela, Galicia, Spain—over 500 some-odd miles away—on foot.

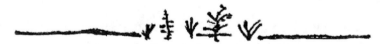

Basque Fiestas to Galician Rituals: Walking Across Northern Spain
(Kathy & John Morelock, coauthors)

We weren't the first pilgrims to walk across northern Spain on the *Camino de Santiago*, now a UNESCO World Heritage site. Ever since the bones of Christ's apostle James (in Spanish Santiago) were discovered in the Galician foothills in the 9th century, poor peasants and affluent queens, conquerors and politicians, medieval heroes and twentieth-century movie stars, CPAs and teachers and popes have journeyed to the beautiful city of Santiago de Compostela. Reasons are as varied as the individuals traveling: to honor a promise, to find an answer, to pray for forgiveness, to experience an adventure, to meet interesting people, to rest and relax away from the challenges of "ordinary" life. Our reasons encompassed all of these and one more, to create a transition from our working years to our retirement years.

When we finally arrived in the beautiful medieval city of Santiago de Compostela in late September, the stone towers of the cathedral rising in the morning sun to greet us as we wound our way through the cobblestone streets, past souvenir shops and bakeries and outdoor cafes and fish markets and vendors selling sweet pretzels, and into the Plaza de la Quintana on the east side of the cathedral, we laughed and cried and hugged each other, hardly able to comprehend the journey we had just made through time and space.

Forty-seven days ago we had departed Phoenix, Arizona. John was reading Mark Kurlansky's *The Basque History of the World* as we flew across the Atlantic Ocean toward Paris, France. We landed at Charles de Gaulle Airport, deciphered our first French train schedules, and spent the afternoon by walking around Paris. The following morning we left Paris on one of the high-speed TGV trains bound for Saint-Jean-Pied-de-Port in southwest France, a village in the Basque region situated at the foot of a route over the Pyrenees Mountains which would take us into Spain. Two hundred years earlier, Napoleon had followed this same route in his mad dash to conquer the world. Although pilgrims begin their walks on the *camino* from many locations, Saint-Jean-Pied-de-Port remains one of the most popular starting points. We wanted to walk into Spain, and this little village lies near the Spanish border, which, alas, runs along the top of the Pyrenees.

Our arrival in Saint-Jean-Pied-de-Port coincided with a local Basque fiesta celebrating the founding of the village. The traditional red bandanas and white shirts of the Basques whirled through the streets as the people danced and the brass bands played. Restaurants and cafes surrounding the central plaza overflowed with applauding and cheering patrons. Children ran among the dancers' legs, wineglasses were filled and emptied, the aromas of fish and ham and onions enticed newcomers, and dogs yapped joyously while their owners sang. John's history book had come to life.

Forty-four days ago we had awakened to one last band playing one last song in the shadowy darkness just before dawn, sleep turned away, our thoughts upon our departure. We rose in the dark, as we would every day on the *camino*, packed our gear (hers in the small pack to accommodate an artificial hip, his [and some of hers] in the big pack to assure comfort along the way), and left our brief night of unquiet. We searched for and found the way markers, the yellow arrows and scallop signs indicating the *camino*, crossed the first of many old Roman arch bridges, this one over the river Nive, and headed up and out of Saint-Jean-Pied-de-Port toward Santiago de Compostela, Galicia, Spain—some five hundred-odd miles away— on foot. Two "sixty something" Americans in a strange land.

Given the choice, the *camino* always seemed to go up (often simply a false perception of weary walkers); originally, this was because higher ground discouraged bands of robbers that medieval pilgrims wanted to avoid. Modern-day pilgrims often have a choice between the river valleys and the mountaintops, the paved roads and the trodden trails. When the occasion presented itself, we took the higher route as being the road less traveled and more scenic. Crossing the Pyrenees proved difficult (the most difficult day of the *camino* as it would turn out), but walking through the high green pastures among the Percherons and herds of sheep and French-speaking Holsteins, the tinkling of their bells, or "Basque wind chimes" as John referred to them, echoing across the ridges, rewarded our effort. At our feet, purple crocuses stuck their heads between the rocks of the trail. Above us, we glimpsed rare Spanish imperial eagles riding updrafts and lammergeyers circling in the hot blue sky. And at the Fountain of Roland, near where Roland blew his horn to warn Charlemagne of impending doom more than 1200 years earlier, we rested, refilled our water bottles, and listened to the wind in the trees.

Our destination that first day was Roncesvalles, where our first *albergue* (place of refuge) awaited our weary bodies. As we descended the mountains, we could see through the trees the rebuilt Augustinian monastery and pilgrim hospital, originally built in the early 12th century, which now offered a night's lodging to *peregrinos* (Spanish for pilgrims). Meeting us at the door, the Dutch *hospitaleros* (Spanish for hosts) helped us off with our packs and arranged for our beds (two lower bunks side by side). Throughout our journey, we came to appreciate the system of *albergues* along the *camino*. We ended our days in 14th-century stone churches, Benedictine monasteries, old schoolhouses, 18th-century farmhouses, 10th-century pilgrim hospitals, and 21st-century bunkhouses, each run by a unique group of volunteer Dutchmen, Spaniards, Brazilians, Flemings, Germans, Canadians, Brits, Australians, or Americans. We paid little, sometimes nothing, for these wonderful accommodations: a bunk or a mat on which to lay our sleeping bags, a shower, sometimes hot, sometimes not so hot, to wash off the sweat of the day, a sink to wash clothes in, sometimes a kitchen, and views out the windows that were unsurpassed. We watched the sun go down over churches and vineyards and bridges and rivers and plazas and mountains and valleys and chestnut groves and stands of eucalyptus trees covering the hillsides.

Forty-one days ago we had entered the first of the big cities that the *camino* runs through—Pamplona (with its history of bulls and Hemingway). Later, we would spend time traipsing around Burgos (home of El Cid) and León (once a Roman garrison town) before stopping at the last city, Santiago de Compostela. While we liked the big cities, watching people, visiting museums, window-shopping, sampling pastries and chocolates and breads, exploring parks and river walks, and visiting the cathedrals, we felt most immersed in the experience of the *camino* in the smaller towns and even smaller villages. Spanish dogs greeted us as we entered these centuries-old villages, shopkeepers wished us a *buen camino* (good journey for pilgrims), children practiced their English, widows walking together asked us where we were from, farmers asked us where we had started our *camino*, and other pilgrims asked us why we were walking 500-plus miles across Spain. In our halting Spanish, we asked them where the *albergue* was and where we could buy food. We stocked up for the evening meal by buying soup stock or salad ingredients or pasta and tomatoes if we knew the *albergue* had a kitchen, bread and cheese and *salchichón* (sausage) and fruit if there was no kitchen.

Thirty-two days ago we had awakened as usual before dawn in order to be on the *camino* for sunrise, as Spain seemed to do sunrises quite well. We had set as our goal an *albergue* in the little village of Grañón, recommended by an Irish pilgrim returning home. Eating nectarines as we walked (why, oh why, were the nectarines in Spain so delicious?), we watched for the church towers or steeples, always the first indication that a village lay just over the hill. Once in Grañón, the yellow arrows of the *camino* led us to the old church; Middle 12th Century, a placard said; *Albergue*, another sign indicated. An old wooden door at the foot of a stone tower creaked eerily as we pushed on it, but we went up anyway, up a dark and musty spiral stone staircase (fully expecting to meet Lon Chaney or Bela Lugosi coming down) to a lively room with a small kitchen, a tiny library beside a fireplace, and a dining room with a table to seat maybe twelve people. Another ten steps took us up to a sleeping platform and another five or six to the washroom. We hung our clothes to dry in a tiny stone alcove above the altar of this Norman church.

As had become routine after stopping for the day, John went out to buy food at the *mercado* (grocery) before the two o'clock *siesta* (naptime) started. He returned with a bag of pasta, garlic, tomatoes, bread, and a huge red watermelon (almost as tasty as the nectarines). For the first time on the *camino*, however, the *hospitalera* would not let us in the kitchen. In this *albergue* the hosts cooked, she said...for everyone. At 7:45, a stack of folding tables and a stack of folding chairs were uncovered; in minutes, a dining room for forty-eight *peregrinos* was created. And from the tiny kitchen came bowls of green salad with tuna and trays of fresh bread. And *paella*, a traditional Spanish rice dish that varied in seasoning and contents from region to region. In Grañón, garlic, saffron, onions, and chicken enhanced the rice. As did the conversation around the tables, some in English, some in Spanish, some in Italian, some in Danish, some in Portuguese, some in Japanese, some in German— the language of the *camino*. These communal meals every so often along the way became a treasured memory, all of us at home so far from home.

Twenty-eight days ago with Burgos behind us and the *meseta* (high desert or plateau), which one travel book noted was a hot and sweltering dustbowl in summer (and we were in high summer), before us, we had trudged into what we expected would be unbearable heat, unrelenting wind, undulating expanses reaching into infinity, and a descent into delirium with the effort. As happened so often on the *camino*, however, we were denied all our imagined hardships by the kindness of strangers. Passing through the small village of Rabé de las Calzadas, an aged nun, her face the color of dried parchment, her thin body shrinking into her bent shoulders, her veined hands filled with tiny golden St. Mary medallions strung on pink yarn, lifted her warm brown eyes to us and asked if we were *peregrinos*. We nodded yes. Onto our packs she tied her gift, and we were suddenly protected from whatever the *meseta* would throw at us.

Our days on the *meseta* passed slowly as we crossed this countryside that reminded us of the Palouse in eastern Washington or the wheat fields of Kansas or the long, barren stretches of Nevada. We found a rhythm in those days of rising early, walking beneath the fading stars of the Milky Way, climbing and descending the arroyos, and pausing to rest on wayside benches beneath trees planted for shade. We were grateful for the cloud-covered sky and only a whisper of wind. We grew to love the brown and yellow harvested fields. And the *meseta* storms.

Many days we wondered if we would find our *albergue* before these storms found us; a line of distant clouds off to our left would draw glances and then longer looks all day. We walked listening to the far-off thunder, feeling cooler breaths of wind gaining strength, watching birds flying ever lower in the sky. Without fail, however, we watched the storms break over us from the refuge of our *albergue*. We watched a particularly violent storm come rushing toward us from the safety of our room in Castrojeriz, a hilltop *albergue* looking down upon the *meseta* plains. Huge slashing and crashing bolts of lightning lit up the black sky, its thunder shaking the windows and rattling the walls. Rain poured from the clouds, settling the dust of the *meseta*, deafening the silences between thunder. We watched for hours the spectacular beauty of this Spanish storm, finally crawling into our sleeping bags at midnight. In the morning, the rising sun lit up the cloudless sky and, once again, cast our two shadows westward.

Seventeen days ago leaving León, we had found ourselves lost for the first time. "How long do we go without seeing one of our *flechas amarillas* (yellow arrows)?" Kathy paused midstride. "How long since we passed one?" "I think about four blocks." "That's too long." We had become used to our constant companions—the little yellow arrows pointing us toward Santiago de Compostela. Painted on the twisted boles of chestnut trees, fading away on rock walls, high on the corners of buildings in towns and villages, on steles beneath the scallop-shell symbols or stylized *peregrino* figure also indicative of the *camino*, on the railings of bridges, at every crossroad, T-intersection, or fork in the trail, we had been following for three hundred miles these little yellow arrows.

As we stood at the side of a street, discussing our dilemma, a car pulled over and stopped. *"Peregrinos?"* a young woman asked. We nodded and followed her as she walked us back to the *camino*. Over and over again, we met such kindnesses, people taking time out of their lives to walk us out of town, to bring us cold water from village fountains, to offer us sandwiches from their own picnic baskets high on mountain trails, to hand us purple grapes from their vineyards, to bring us chamomile tea at the end of the day.

We found our next yellow arrow and headed out of the last large city to cross the *páramo* (almost barren plains—there were lots of oak trees) between us and the mountain passes leading out of Castilla y León into Galicia, our last region to cross. The last mountain range was only faintly visible in the morning sun.

Nine days ago we had been sitting in the fog at O Cebreiro—the highest point of the *camino* in Spain. In less than an hour, a day of almost unlimited visibility had disappeared. In less than an hour, our view back to the pass we had crossed four days earlier disappeared. In less than an hour, the hillside covered with chestnut groves and ravens begging for crumbs and green valleys filled with sheep and rock fences and hamlets of slate-roofed farmhouses had vanished. We could not see our yellow arrows or our scalloped-shell markers. But we knew where we were. We were in Galicia. Lush, green Galicia, with its fogs and mists and pastoral scenery. In a moment of self-deception, we noted that it was downhill from here to the cathedral in Santiago. We adjusted our packs and silently headed down the road.

Twenty-four hours ago we had walked our longest day (ten hours) and stopped for the night three miles from Santiago. In this last *albergue* before the end of our journey, we talked about what lay behind us as the sun sank in the west. We avoided talking about the next day. We remembered San Juan de Ortega and the old priest who made us garlic soup; and Rabanal del Camino with its four Benedictine monks singing vespers; and the *cigüeñas* (storks) staring down at us from their high perches; and the Gaudí palace in Astorga rising beside Norman, Romanesque, and Baroque buildings; and a hundred statues of *peregrinos* and St. James, and a hundred different crosses beside the trail, and a hundred altar *retablos* (devotional paintings) in amazing churches built in tiny villages; and a hundred *panaderías* (bakeries) our noses always found; and the Spanish landscape, its variety and depth of beauty; and the people, a thousand years and five hundred miles of people.

Two hours ago we had awakened again before dawn and shouldered our packs. We feared that our arrival in Santiago might be anticlimactic; we, almost reluctantly, started west. We stopped for *café con leche y tostadas* (coffee with cream and toast) in the modern outskirts of town. We watched other *peregrinos* pass along the *camino*; most were quiet and contemplative. We took thirty minutes to walk the last one hundred yards through shops selling cheese and rosaries and pastries and T-shirts. Finally, we turned the corner into the Plaza de la Quintana and stared up at the great gray cathedral, overcome by unexpected emotion. We laughed and cried and hugged each other.

Journey's end. There are rituals that *peregrinos* go through when they reach journey's end. We walked through the Holy Door, hugged the gilded statue of St. James, visited the crypt where his bones lie, attended mass, applauded the monks swinging the world's largest *botafumeiro* (incense burner), picked up our *compostela* (official certificate of completion), and understood, finally, why *peregrinos* return to walk again the *Camino de Santiago*.

We would actually walk a little over 600 miles because we would go on past Santiago to *Cabo Fisterra* (Galician) or *Finisterre* (Spanish), or Land's End (English), Galicia, Spain. We stopped walking westerly late in the afternoon on October 4, 2004, and spent an almost quiet several minutes looking down at the Atlantic Ocean two or three hundred feet below us.

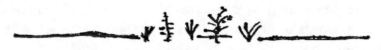

What Had We Done?

September 27, 2004, we were sitting on a stone bench in the plaza (praza da Quintana), looking across at the cathedral (Catedral de Santiago). Were we on the northerly side? I think so. What time did we get there? Over? Is it over? Jumbled thoughts...no, not even thoughts...flashes of images; weeks of mountains and sidewalks, *albergues* and highways, villages and empty plains...crashed to a stop just as we crashed to the bench, numbed.

We sat there wondering at what we had done. We had walked over 500 miles. The number of miles does not tell the story. We had spent 44 days walking. The days simply blended into our weeks on *el Camino de Santiago*. My wife was 59 years of age and I was 62—numbers we were asked for almost daily. Our age in years does not tell the story. Numbers are for spreadsheets, accountants, and administrators—our story is beyond the realm of any numbers.

Somewhere along the crossing of northern Spain lay the many events and incidents affecting our spirits, our health, our outlooks, and our diet. Each day took us to places of historical or religious interest. Each evening's conversation brought forth questions about origins and homelands, "wheres" and "whys," and requests for advice about practical actions needed to get through another day's walk. There were questions regarding the Spain we were traveling through as we followed the aged and fading footsteps of pilgrims before us: the early days of crossing the Pyrenees on the route of Charlemagne and Roland's disaster; through the Basque region with its sheep, cows, and horses, each with their own bells, which we called the Basque wind chimes); onto the plains and farms of the *meseta*; the *páramo* with hills in the distance drawing ever closer; and finally entering the lush greenness and mist of Galicia. Hidden within each day were people and places of particular interest, smiles of greeting, words of kindness—these events are where the story is, not in the numbers.

Time became our measuring stick. Early on we had left the *albergue* just before dawn with the intent of covering some fixed number of kilometers before stopping for the day. This fixed distance did not allow for the pauses to view the countryside laid out before us. Our daily walking became governed by simply being somewhere in Spain following an ancient way; somewhere in Spain, we ate cheese and nectarines sitting 'neath a tree; somewhere in Spain, we wandered in the coolness of a chestnut grove; somewhere in Spain, we crossed one more old Roman bridge. Our rigid plans were scrapped; the number of miles to walk each day faded to unimportance as time became meaningless. We had the gift of time. We accepted the days we would spend wandering westerly on *el Camino de Santiago*, somewhere in Spain.

Do I Have a Hero?

There is someone who has been a source of inspiration to me, an absolute bedrock of faith and quiet strength.

She has a first-place award for a 50k in Hawaii in 1981. She won that before I even knew what an ultramarathon was—I barely knew the word "marathon."

Arthritis was already advancing in her hip and knees when we met in 1985. She has the old-fashioned zippers in her knees. She won a 75k road run in Seattle while tolerating me as crew. Scars from cancer can be seen across her abdomen. I counted laps during her 12-hour trail run—one smile per lap and a wave as she went past the bench—208 laps and we were done and headed for the house.

Halloween and all through the night she crewed—second-guessing what I needed to race a 100k. The right bite of something was held out for me. A dry shirt was waiting. She knew how fragile I was when racing. She offered words that calmed and ran a couple of miles with me to rewrap a loosened mind. We won that. I could not have done that alone. She knew which buttons to push to quiet fears, to inspire, to revive.

At night I could hear the bones grinding, but I never heard the complaints. No one did. December 1991 and the left hip was replaced. Six weeks later she was teaching English to unknowing college freshmen. She would smile as I pushed her on her bicycle on our roads northwest of Fayetteville—left foot tied to the pedal—always smiling because she was outside again. Spring came, and we alternated biking and running—bigger smiles, silly grins, and laughter. We were outside again.

Sixteen months later came a half marathon. Who would have thought that someone who ran Strolling Jim's forty miles of Tennessee hills followed by fifty miles of hard trails a week later in Oregon could be so broken down with emotion and pride by a measly 13.1 miles? We found trails to run in the Ozarks.

She had caught me once in a 50k, didn't even look back as she passed. There was a time at the end of a 28ish-mile training run when I turned my head and said, "It's about a mile to the car, I'm going to kick it on in." As I slowed at the car I noticed the shadow just behind me—and a truly annoyingly smug grin. She cannot do that anymore, but we left the roads behind anyway.

We went to the trails. It was being out there that mattered. Trophies were for tripping over, memories to share. Still she wanted one more ultra. She would come in from the hills—teary eyed and defeated by the mud. The artificial hip hated mud. The fatigue on the body came long before her mind gave up. I would wander here and there on the trails as she went in the same general direction on the forestry roads. She got stronger.

Along the way she pointed out plants and birds. I knew they were there. She knew their names. I knew where the pictures were—she wanted me to see the words. I explained geology and climatology. She countered with biology and botany. We ran through the seasons, the blackboards in our minds being changed by the winds.

The Leadville Trail 100 called in 2000. She had gotten me through it in 1999. The grand scheme of getting to Winfield together then deciding what to do was agreed upon. Forty-mile weekends came and went. All through the spring and summer I would watch that slightly canted gait, see the bottom of the eight-inch scar that hid the metal joint, see the grimaces as we practiced those long downhill stretches. Faith and confidence are such fragile things, all so easily destroyed by a flash of lightning high in the Rockies. All the belief went away in the muddy reaches of "the Boulevard" at Leadville.

The tears of the trip home went away. Still she pushed me out the door. She talked of another ultra somewhere. Something we could control. It turned out to be in Spain in 2004—a thing called "*el Camino de Santiago*"—The Way of St. James. A route for pilgrims.

We walked from Saint-Jean-Pied-de-Port, France, up and over the Pyrenees and six hundred and some-odd miles across northern Spain to "land's end" of old. Every morning we would slip on the backpacks. I would look over and ask, "Ready?" She would smile and nod. We would walk west. Nine weeks on foot. Someone watches over pilgrims. Old, old nuns would find her. Old women so wrinkled with age that all that was left was the gentle air of care and concern that takes you in for comforting and a restoration of faith. Nine weeks of walking across whatever was out there. Nine weeks and she never, never, ever did anything but say yes each morning when I asked, "Ready?"

We came back to the states, not home. We have no permanent home. We found a place to stop. Beaches, bluffs, mountains, birds, water, and trails—and pain. We were back to running alone; walking was together but running was alone. She told me to learn the trees and tides while she learned our new birds.

She fell in July 2007. We needed one more trip to the trails up in the North Cascades, one more waterfall before the snows closed that part of our world for the winter. She fell. Our worst fear. The trekking poles saved her—the poles that had become second nature in Spain. It was two hours to cover a couple of miles back to the car.

She was housebound, could not walk. The wonders of health care slowly dragged on. She would smile and push me out the door. "I don't care if you walk, get out for a while. One of us has to be out there." She would eat books and wait, while I would go listen to the quietness of the trails.

January 23, 2008—the first artificial hip was replaced. The single telling comment from the surgeon came when he gave me the replaced parts (sort of like a car repair). "She just wore it out." She had checked her diaries—approximately 16,000 miles on that first hip. Now it is time to regroup. Six months of sitting on the floor must be undone.

Ten days ago we returned the walker. She wore out three sets of rubber feet on the walker from sliding it along the paved bike path. I know she would have gone off down the trail if I hadn't been there to stop her. She walked 45 minutes inside the house—twice a day. It is just like Fayetteville again. There is no one to guide her. She just does what can be done without pain. Last week she walked (with cane) two miles. She smiled. Yesterday she did 2.5 miles using the trekking poles. Twenty-eight-minute miles and spring is coming. She almost giggled with glee. Things will get better.

So, do I have a hero? I know someone who would never want that word associated with her. She is simply the most courageous person I have ever known—selfless and inspiring and tolerant—yes, I suppose I do.

[Update: May 2009, back in business, 32.25 miles of trails at Tom Ripley and Chris Ralph's Redmond Watershed 12 Hour, big smiles and giggles as we drove home that afternoon.]

About the Author

Widely unacclaimed as a writer, bearer of bad jokes, and possessing a poor memory for what went wrong last time, John Morelock is currently an almost retired whale spotter, mirage analyst, baker, wool gatherer, maintainer of trails, and nature lecturer. Morelock took up running on August 17, 1984 at 4:33 in the afternoon and completed his first ultramarathon in January of 1986. He has long since completed several more ultramarathons; most of them in the Pacific Northwest, but also in places as diverse as Texas, Colorado, Tennessee, and Arkansas.

He established his trail running credentials early by successfully returning to the trailhead where he had left the car on many training runs in the Olympic and Cascade Mountains. Although largely unfocused as a racer, he managed a victory in each of his first two decades of running, one at the 100-kilometer distance and one at the more standard 34.5-mile venue. In 2002 he noted that his total running miles had reached 50,027. Having accomplished this feat without once kicking or tripping over a porcupine, he reasoned that it was a good point at which to quit tracking such things and made no more log entries.

Now, with time slipping by, philosophical meandering and trailside distractions have led to less racing and more running with pauses. He lives on Whidbey Island in Washington State enjoying the trails with his wife, Kathy.

CPSIA information can be obtained at www.ICGtesting.com
Printed in the USA
LVOW08s1932121213

365049LV00002B/287/P